Growing up Rich, Though Dirt Poor

Also by Bruce Vaughan

Emma, We Love You

Shiloh Reflections

Surviving Technology

Growing up Rich,
Though Dirt Poor

∽

BRUCE VAUGHAN

Farmhouse Books
2010

Copyright © 2010 by Bruce Vaughan

All rights reserved
Manufactured in the United States of America

ISBN-13: 978-0-9829455-2-0

Designed by Liz Lester

Some of this material was previously published by Bruce Vaughan as *23 Skidoo.*

This book is respectfully dedicated to my grandfather,
Manfred E. 'Mack' Gibson, blacksmith
(1874–1974)

Change is inevitable. In a progressive country, change is constant.
—Benjamin Disraeli

∼

*To the Pioneers...
The cowards never started.
The weak died along the way.
Only the bravest and strongest survived.*

—from a plaque found in Harold Warp's "Pioneer Village" in Minden, Nebraska

∼

This book contains observations from one who has lived to see many changes, almost all of which he opposed.

—Bruce Vaughan

CONTENTS

	Introduction	ix
Chapter 1	The Vaughans	1
Chapter 2	The End of Innocence—The Beginning of Technology	13
Chapter 3	Mack and Alice	23
Chapter 4	The Century Begins	29
Chapter 5	Charlie Vaughan	49
Chapter 6	Habberton	53
Chapter 7	Medicine Shows, Tent Preachers, Con Men, Hucksters, and Other Entertainment	79
Chapter 8	A Far Better Place	99
Chapter 9	The Depression Years	115
Chapter 10	The Magnificent Model T	123
Chapter 11	The Discovery Years	131
Chapter 12	Clarence	151
Chapter 13	Pearl Harbor	163
Chapter 14	The Troop Carrier Command	187
Chapter 15	Merrie Olde England	207
Chapter 16	Heroes are Made, Not Born or How I Won the Air Medal	231
Chapter 17	The War Ends	235
	Epilogue	263
	Bibliography	265

INTRODUCTION

The man who writes about himself and his own time is the only man who writes about all people and all time.

—GEORGE BERNARD SHAW (1856–1950)
Anglo-Irish playwright and critic

FEBRUARY 6, 1922: The Roaring Twenties were little more than a soft moan escaping from the throat of a nation badly injured financially, politically, and morally from the effects of World War I. The stage was being set by our elected officials for what would forever be known as "the lawless decade."

In New York City, Will Rogers was receiving rave reviews for his Ziegfeld Follies act. Babe Ruth was crowned the King of Swat. Amelia Earhart was teaching school, earning enough money to keep taking flying lessons. At air shows across the country a skinny young man named Charles Lindbergh entertained crowds with his flying ability. The entire country was talking about a young man, Rudolph Valentino, Hollywood's newest movie star, and his performance in *The Sheik*. William S. Hart, Douglas Fairbanks, Mary Pickford, Theda Bara, Gloria Swanson, Charlie Chaplin, Buster Keaton, Harold Lloyd, and Norma Talmadge were familiar names to practically everyone in this country. It was the heyday of the silent screen. D.W. Griffith was producing pictures that would survive the technological onslaught now imminent. "Talking pictures," according to the press, were just around the corner—a corner not to be reached until the end of the Roaring Twenties.

Prohibition was the most popular subject of the press. A few unthinking individuals would soon sway enough votes to make millionaires of hundreds of small-time hoodlums. Organized crime was destined to prosper during the coming years as never before. Only when this ridiculous law was repealed would peace return to the streets of our cities. Gangs and organized crime would have to return to things like "numbers" and prostitution to bring in illegal dollars. Neither produced anything like the profits realized from bootleg liquor and bathtub gin. The great experiment had failed miserably. There is a close parallel—for those who dare to think—between prohibition and the narcotics laws of today.

George Gershwin was busy writing *Rhapsody in Blue,* his most unforgettable composition. It would be played for the first time in front of an audience at New York's Aeolian Theater some two years later. The leader of the orchestra was an unemployed car salesman turned bandleader named Paul Whiteman. Rudy Vallee was a collegiate freshman, and Ted Lewis ("Is everybody happy?") was playing the leading bistros in New York City. The age of hip flasks, jazz, flappers, raccoon coats, and the Charleston was upon the country. I remember reading a line written years ago by Frederick Lewis Allen:

> And so the saxophone wailed, and the hip flask went its rounds and the dancers made their treadmill circuit with half-closed eyes, and the outside world, so merciless and insane, was shut away for a restless night ... 23 Skidoo.

Henry Ford brought the questionable pleasures of motoring to the people of America. In 1922 he introduced the Ford Fordor—a fully enclosed four-door car. In this car you could keep dry in a rainstorm and thoroughly chilled to the bone in winter. A good car heater had yet to be developed to a practical standpoint. This all-enclosed car was powered by a twenty horsepower, four-cylinder engine and was capable of speeds in excess of 20 mph. It had a one hundred-inch wheelbase, and rode on three-by-thirty inch tires. Gasoline capacity was ten gallons. Ford also offered the Model T runabout, a coupe, and as a two-seated touring car. Prices started at $300 for the runabout.

My Ford

I love my Ford, it gave to me

the Mountains and the trees,
the flowers of the field,
the Wild Bird's song,
the Ocean's cooling breeze.

It burst the bars that formed my city cell,
and set me free to wander where I would,
it hurried and brought back my fleeting youth,
and made me feel that living still was good.

And Oh, I hope that should the time ere come,
When I must yield aught my modest hoard,
that it may be my house, my land, my clothes,
but not my precious Ford.

Buyers of motor cars were not limited to three manufacturers in 1922. I am unsure just how many makes they had to choose from, but here are a few makes I remember: Jewett, Doble, Packard, Stutz, Chalmers, Mercer, Rickenbacker, Saxon, Durant, Dort, Kissel, DuPont, Willis, Maxwell, J.I. Case, Cole, Moon, Hupmobile, Overland, Pierce Arrow, Dodge, Cadillac, Ford, Studebaker, Columbia, Chevrolet, Reo, Apperson, Hudson, Star, and Dorris. I am sure there were at least twenty to thirty more that I no longer remember. Customers had a wide price range to choose from. The cheapest was probably the Ford which was priced lower than $300. The Doble, Packard, and Stutz could run into big money very quickly with models priced in the $10,000 range. Models ranged from near racing machines like the Stutz Bearcat and Mercer Race About, to luxurious seven-passenger sedans.

In Little Rock, Arkansas, a fine automobile called the Climber was manufactured. Nicely finished and well constructed, the automobile never caught on with buyers. Therefore, the company was in trouble from its beginning until the last Climber was built in the late '20s. I believe the car was not different enough or attractive enough to have buyer appeal. It followed too closely the design of the day. I would describe the Climber as a Model T Ford on steroids.

Buyers in the early days could choose their source of power. Most cars were designed to run on gasoline, but there were several electrics to choose from, and of course, if you liked steam there was the expensive but highly desirable Doble. The last Doble was built in 1928.

In those early years every auto trip was an adventure. Tires were a constant problem. All better cars came with two spare tires, and if you drove very far you were sure to need them. Every car carried a jack, lug wrench, hand-operated tire pump, inner tube patching kit, spark plug wrench, pliers, screwdrivers, adjustable wrench, tire tape, and whatever tools the owner wanted to add to those that came with the car. Five thousand miles was considered good tire life. By the time World War II was over tires had improved. It was my practice in the late '40s to buy a new set of tires at 10,000 miles. Today, 40,000 miles is not considered unusual for a good grade auto tire.

This will be difficult for young people to believe but some roads, especially in less populated areas, ran through private land. You would be driving along and find a gate across the road. Someone had to get out, open the gate, wait until the auto pulled through, and then close and fasten the gate. If you left a gate open you might very well cause a lot of problems if the farmer's livestock got out and wandered off.

Spark plugs needed cleaning often. When Dad had the Habberton Store I can remember riding with him to Springdale—probably about eleven miles. Very often he would stop, remove and clean a spark plug and proceed on our way. It was only a ten-minute job. Trips were dirty and uncomfortable—you were either too hot or too cold. The roads were muddy when it rained, and so dusty in the summer that when you met a car you had to slow down because you could not see the road ahead for the dust. It was like a heavy fog.

America loved it—dust, mud, tire trouble, and all the other problems.

∼

Burma Shave, a shaving cream manufacturer, launched an advertising campaign in the Model T days that was among the most cost-effective advertising ideas ever conceived. It consisted of a series of five or six signs nailed to fence posts at an angle facing on-coming traffic. The little signs were spaced about one hundred feet apart. Each sign carried short line of a poem or jingle. The final sign simply said, "Burma Shave." At speeds of 25 to 35 mph, which was about the average then, even the driver had no problem reading the jingles.

Tourists, as they were known back then, looked forward to seeing a Burma Shave sign. It was always good for a laugh, and broke the monotony of a long drive. The signs became less effective when cars whizzed past at 70 mph. Here are some I still remember:

> He Missed the Curve,
> His Car Was Whizzin'
> The Fault Was Her'n
> The Funeral His'n
> **Burma Shave**
>
> At Intersections
> Look Each Way
> A Harp Sounds Nice
> But it's Hard to Play
> **Burma Shave**
>
> Broken Romance
> Stated Fully
> She Went Wild
> When He Went Wooly
> **Burma Shave**
>
> Car in Ditch
> Driver in Tree
> The Moon was Full
> So Was He
> **Burma Shave**

∼

Many homes had a hand-cranked telephone on the wall. Much of our country was serviced by small independent telephone companies. In rural areas individuals within a certain area often shared the cost of stringing telephone lines. In the early part of the last century it was a common sight to see a gleaming slender wire supported by small, fragile poles which were not set deep enough in the ground. Such telephone wires joined two or more rural houses together, forming a "party line." If there were more than two houses together, then each house had its own ring. For example, one house might be called by two short rings. A second house might have one long ring; a third house, a long and a short; a fourth home, two longs and a short, etc. Each rural telephone had a hand cranked generator. If you wished to call the Jones family, and their ring was a long and a short, you cranked the generator three or four seconds, paused, and then gave the crank a couple of turns.

All this sounds like it might work. There were two major problems with the party line system. Some rude people would refuse to relinquish the phone to let a neighbor call the doctor or volunteer fire department. This may sound like an amusing story but more than once a selfish person stayed on the telephone and let a neighbor's house burn.

The second problem was the village gossips. They lifted their receiver every time the phone rang and remained still as a mouse while listening to their neighbor's telephone call. Those party lines were a lot like e-mail today—you never said anything that you did not want the entire neighborhood to know about.

Now to the upside. The heyday of party lines was from 1900 to about 1925. There were very few radios in use for entertainment until about the time party lines disappeared. While the quality was poor, it was not uncommon for the party lines to be used as an entertainment medium. Uncle Zed might play a fiddle tune, someone else sing a song, and one of the younger children might recite a poem on the party line while everyone listened.

~

A hand-cranked phonograph—Edison and Victor were the most popular—could be found in almost every home. The novelty of recorded music was in the past; phonographs, when played, were for musical enjoyment, dancing, or entertaining visitors. The majority of those buying phonographs bought very few records. Even then, a single record represented thirty to fifty percent of a day's pay—big money. I don't think I ever saw more than thirty records in any household. Thirty records would furnish between two and three hours of recorded entertainment.

The phonograph, or Victrola as it was commonly called, would slowly be replaced by the radio as a means of entertainment in homes across America. The change, which at the time seemed a sure death knell for recorded music, increased record sales to a level those in the industry thought impossible. Record sales continued to increase to levels exceeding the dreams of record company executives.

When the Westinghouse Electric and Manufacturing Company broadcast the first election returns from a specially built penthouse atop the highest building in Pittsburgh, Pennsylvania, very few people heard the broadcast. Most of America found out that Warren Harding had beaten James D. Cox, the Democratic candidate for president, when they read the election returns the following day in their newspapers. Nevertheless, this broadcast from KDKA was a momentous event, marking the birth of radio broadcasting in America.

Actually, Dr. Frank Conrad should receive all the credit for introducing commercial radio broadcasting to America. As chief engineer with Westinghouse, he started sending out two-hour broadcasts every Wednesday and Saturday during the summer of 1920. These broadcasts were aimed at the nation's 12,000 radio amateurs, or "hams," and originated from his garage in East Pittsburgh, Pennsylvania. He broadcast such things as baseball scores and music from phonograph records.

The music store lending him records for the broadcast found that when he played a certain record on the air, that record sold out within hours. This meant that, even without advertising, radio could be used to sell products. In the fall of 1920, a music store advertised a low-priced crystal detector radio. They sold out the following day—thus commercial radio broadcasting began in America.

The growth of radio was slowed by the absence of electricity in many homes. The phonograph could be hand cranked, but radio demanded a constant supply of electricity, whether it was supplied by batteries or power mains in the home. Early crystal radio receivers demanded no power other than that transmitted by the broadcast station and picked up by the antenna at the receiving end. This sounds like an ideal situation but due to the minute amount of power to the receiver, stations were weak and furnished only enough energy to drive a headset. Any sort of speaker for comfortable listening was not possible.

With the advent of the vacuum tube, long distance communication loud enough to power a loudspeaker became possible. The tubes used in 1922 required six volts on the tube filament with considerable current drain. Plate voltage for our early radio tubes was supplied by two or three B batteries of 45 volts each. Bias voltage on the tubes was in the vicinity of 22.5 volts. The cash outlay to operate such a set was considerable, and only more affluent families could afford to listen to more than two hours of radio daily.

In the 1920s at 6:00 p.m., I would guess that at least ninety percent of the radio owners were listening to *Amos and Andy*, radio's first major stars. Later *Lum and Abner* attracted a large listening audience. Lowell Thomas was by far the biggest name in radio news broadcasting. Still, the radio was used carefully, normally when all members of the family could gather in the living room and listen.

∽

Our home, like most others in the state, depended upon the kerosene lamp for light. The mantle lamp, normally referred to as the "Aladdin," came into widespread use about 1930. It was much brighter than the old wick lamps and cost no more to operate. Whereas the wick lamp output was about the same as a 10-watt light bulb, the Aladdin lamp gave out as bright a light as a 100-watt light bulb.

FDR—President Roosevelt—brought many good things to our country. I would rate the Tennessee Valley Authority as one of the greatest things to happen in my lifetime. The TVA electrified the south. In Northwest Arkansas it is known as the REA—Rural Electrification Administration. One can only speculate, but many historians believe that we could have lost World War II if we had not had an electrified southern United States.

In the country, wood was the common fuel used for cooking and heating. Refrigeration, when available, was by the common icebox. In

Spring Valley our nearest ice plant was Springdale; ice was delivered to us by truck. The ice truck stopped at houses and stores along the way before reaching our home. By the time the ice truck from Springdale arrived at our house in Spring Valley, the twenty-five-pound cake of ice had melted until it was nearer fifteen pounds.

Many rural homes were built near a spring. A small building was erected at the spring, usually of native rock construction. The structure was designed so that the cold water entered one end of the house, flowed through the house and out the other side. A heavy wire screen covered the entrance and exit areas in an attempt to keep snakes and small animals out of the house. There is nothing a snake likes better, in the hot summer months, than a cool, damp, springhouse. West of Siloam Springs is a beautiful house built above a spring. The area is known as Rattlesnake Springs. I strongly suspect that the name was chosen after several rattlers were found in the area.

Pails of milk, butter, and other perishables were placed in the cold running water to keep from spoiling. It worked pretty well. It was not unusual for the springhouse owner to share his facilities with neighbors.

∼

Isolated as they were by bad roads and slow transportation, small villages in the '20s bore a striking resemblance to the old feudal states of Europe. Each community was largely self-sufficient: a general store, post office, blacksmith shop, gristmill, church and schoolhouse, and carpenter shop served the needs of the community. Quite often, in smaller villages, the church and school shared the same building.

Spring Valley, so named because of the fine spring beside the road from Springdale to Huntsville, boasted all of the above plus a public stock pen and scales, a tomato canning factory, and a one-pump service station and automobile garage. In the late '30s, they built a fine new split-level school. The lower floor was a community building, while grades one through eight were taught in the second story. Hindsville, five miles to the east, and with a population of over 100 people, had a doctor's office, bank, and drugstore in addition to the usual business firms.

Today they are only names on a map but in 1922 they were thriving communities. Roads, at the time, were shared equally between horse-drawn vehicles and automobiles.

～

This is the world I entered, about 9:00 a.m., February 6, 1922. Very early that morning my mother asked that someone call the doctor. She was staying with her parents in Spring Valley, while awaiting the birth of her first, and only, child. Someone went to the store and called Doctor Hill at his Hindsville office. The doctor assured them that he would be there in plenty of time. He made the five-mile trip in less than an hour, arriving shortly before 8:00 a.m.

In a small village the birth of a child was news. The entire neighborhood came to the house to await the blessed event. My mother told me often that twenty-two people waiting in the living room got to see her child before she did. Within a few days, wrapped in many blankets, I was carried to the 1918 Ford touring car and, with my dad driving over the deeply rutted road, we made our way home, which was at the McDavid Farm about halfway between Spring Valley and Hindsville.

What did those born in 1922 have to look forward to? They would face seven years of lawlessness and crime like the country had never experienced. This would be followed by what is now called the Great Depression—years when many people in our country would go to bed hungry. Most Americans saw their parents work long hours for less than five dollars a week. Mothers wore the same thread-bare coat winter after winter for many years. Fathers went to work wearing patched clothes, with cardboard stuffed in their shoes to cover the holes worn in the soles. Wearing shirts with frayed collars, and old suit coats to keep out the cold, the people of this great land tried to hang on to a thin thread of dignity. The weekly family treat was a five-cent root beer at the drugstore on Saturday night, looked forward to by adults as much as the children. The latest offerings from Hollywood were as close as the neighborhood theater but few could afford the twenty-

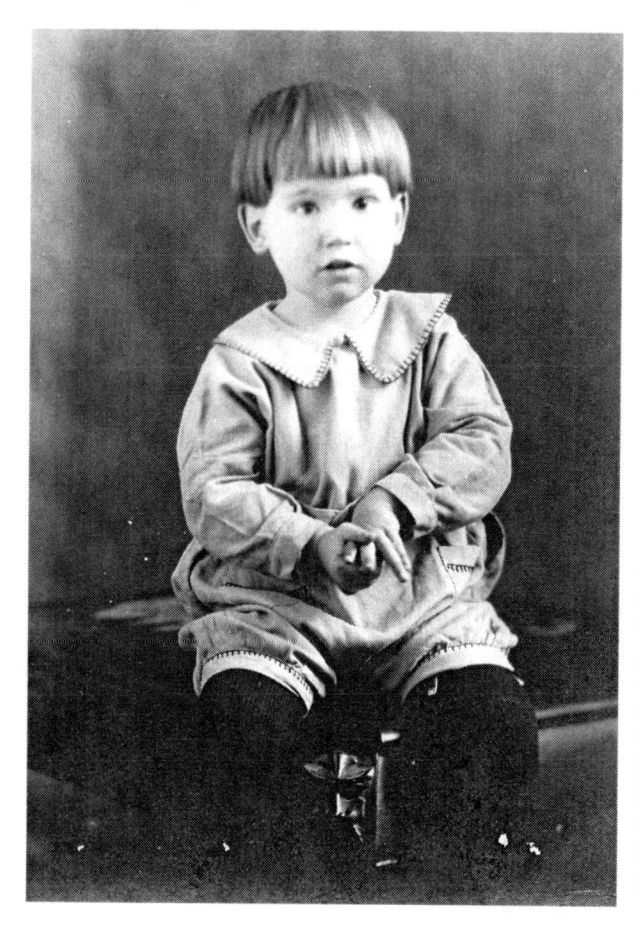

Bruce Vaughan, Jr.

I remember having this photo made at the Davis Studio on the north side of Emma Avenue across from the Famous Hardware in Springdale. It was about 1925. I did not like the experience.

five-cent admission charge more than once a month. Special movies such as *Gone with the Wind* played local theaters at vastly increased prices. The Concord Theater in Springdale sold GWTW tickets for sixty cents.

Most families lived in houses without plumbing—hot in the summer, cold in the winter, with cat-sized rats running around the house at night. Surviving this, you would find that you were the ideal age to fight in the biggest and bloodiest war the world has ever known.

The rest of this book is devoted to the good things children of the '20s experienced. I would not have missed it for the world.

Bruce Vaughan

CHAPTER 1

The Vaughans

They are all gone into the world of light and I alone sit lingering here.

—HENRY VAUGHAN (1622–1695), Welsh poet

There was a chill in the early November air. William "Bill" Vaughan shifted his body to a more comfortable position. Sitting cross-legged on the ground he watched as sparks from his campfire drifted upward into the starlit sky. This was the life he loved. In excellent health, he nevertheless felt aches in his bones—a feeling unknown to him before middle age. Bill wondered how much longer he would be able to live a vigorous life. Thoughtfully, he removed a well-worn pipe from his buckskin jacket, and then tamped it full of Kentucky burley tobacco. Picking up a piece of dry wood, he drew his knife from its holster and shaved off a long splinter. He held the thin piece of wood in the fire until it was flaming brightly, then lit his pipe.

Bill's son-in-law, Phillip Harp, sat on the opposite side of the campfire listening to a story being told by a Cherokee elder. Both Bill and Phillip were well known to the tribe; their visits were an occasion looked forward to by both the Indians and their visitors. Bill was pleased when his daughter married Phillip. Fair-a-bee, (Fereby) Bill's wife, was fond of Phillip and proud of his reputation as a "long hunter"—a hunter who traveled long distances to hunt and trap.

Bill Vaughan, Indian trader, explorer, hunter, trapper, and farmer loved to spend time with the Indians. Now that his sons Daniel and Samuel were grown men and could take care of the farm and their mother, Bill had plenty of time to spend hunting and visiting with the various Indian tribes in his area. It was on such a visit, many years ago, that he met and later married Fair-a-bee. His Cherokee wife understood his need to look for something new—to see what was on the other side of the mountain.

Bill and Phillip had often heard the story now being told by the Cherokee elder. Out of respect for the old man and thinking they might learn something new, they listened again to the story of the "springs that heal" as though they were hearing it for the very first time. The story told of how a beautiful Indian princess was healed by the magic waters. Too weak to walk and with her eyesight gone, she was carried on a litter for many days as the Indians searched for the healing springs. When they came upon the springs, she was near death.

Medicine men had given her up for dead weeks ago. Nothing they tried seemed to slow up the terrible sickness. For days she bathed in the waters and drank from the hillside springs. Slowly her health returned and her eyesight returned to normal, restored by the "magic waters." Before sleeping that night, Phillip and Bill discussed the story and the possibility of the existence of such wonderful springs.

"What do you think, Bill?" asked Phillip, "As many times as we have heard that story there just might be such a place."

"I'll tell you how much I believe it," replied Bill, "If'n yore game we'll shuck out next April and find that Boston water hole." (In years past, one of the Vaughans traveled to Boston on business. The city was so large it literally staggered the mind of the backwoodsman. Returning home, he described the place to his family. Soon the term "Boston" found its way into their everyday dialect meaning anything that was extra large or great in size. Example: "That was shore some Boston bear I kilt.")

"I'll go," said Phillip, "We've got enough carryover crop to do the family, and Samuel and Daniel are as capable as any man in these here parts. If we leave in early spring we oughta be back home before the first snow."

The winter months were spent planning the forthcoming trip, making sure their families were adequately supplied with food and provisions. Fair-a-bee did not want William to leave, but realized it would be useless to protest. On a bright morning in early April, Bill and Phillip said their goodbyes and started their long walk in search of the "springs that heal."

Their provisions for the trip consisted of guns and powder, salt, coffee, tobacco, and furs to keep them warm. They would depend for the most part on game, wild fruits and berries, and edible plants for their food. Where possible they followed old traces left by hunters and warriors. They came to and crossed the Mississippi River in late spring.

Occasionally they encountered a lone trapper or a band of Osage Indians looking for food. Luckily for them the Osages had heard of the healing springs and, while considered hostile, they allowed travelers seeking the springs to pass unharmed. To do otherwise might offend the Gods; the magic powers of the springs could be lost forever. Most nights were spent as if they were back in Tennessee, sitting around the campfire telling stories. Wandering Osage hunters sometime spent the night with them, and while smoking tobacco from Bill's buckskin pouch, and drinking cup after cup of strong coffee, told their version of the story of the healing springs. They assured the explorers that while they were on the right path, the springs were many days travel to the west.

Walking toward the setting sun they passed through grassy flatland and into the wooded foothills of the Ozarks. It was in late September when they arrived at a beautiful valley surrounded by steep hills. There were several springs flowing strong streams of clear, cold water. This was indeed the end of their journey. They were sure they were in the midst of the springs that heal. The area fit exactly the stories told them by numerous Indians from different tribes. Yes, they had found the area that in time would become a famous resort, "Eureka Springs." Somehow, Bill was a bit disappointed; he was expecting something larger and more mysterious.

A group of Indians camped in the area some distance from the springs aroused Bill's interest. Bill and Phillip approached their camp with caution, but the Indians seemed pleased to have visitors. That night they told Bill that it would be unwise to camp near the springs; otherwise, the Gods might be displeased and take away the spring's magic medicine. Bill asked one of the older Indians if they had any objections to them pitching camp where they were. The question seemed to please the Indians. Even then, there was safety in numbers. The area was ideal as a place to winter. Several caves would provide good shelter, and there was more game than they hoped for. Food and shelter would be no problem.

Realizing it was too late in the year to get home before winter, Bill and Phillip decided to winter with the Indians and then return home next spring. Bill and his son-in-law Phillip knew Samuel and Daniel would care for their families while they were away. The winter months would give them time to explore the country more fully when weather permitted. Bill was especially interested in the country about twenty miles southwest. He dreamed of moving his entire family into this beautiful, bountiful, uninhabited land.

After what they hoped was the last snow of the winter here in Northwest Arkansas, Bill and Phillip started their long walk back to the hills on the Kentucky-Tennessee border. Now more familiar with the country, they made better time, arriving home in late August. Bill began making plans for the Harps and Vaughans to move to Arkansas the following year.

He spent many nights that winter telling Fair-a-bee and his children about the plans he had. Samuel and Daniel were anxious to see this new and wonderful country. Bill assured them they would have hundreds of acres of fertile land only a few miles from the springs that heal. There would be abundant game of all sorts—wild turkeys, deer, bear, and more small animals than one could imagine. The streams were deep, clean, and filled with fish. He did, indeed, make it sound like a paradise. Fair-a-bee said little, nodding agreement from time to time. It sounded like a wonderful and perfect place to live.

Travel with this sizeable group that included children, women, and older family members was exceedingly slow. Each man carried as much as he could on his back, sharing the load with their pack mules. There were no horse-drawn vehicles as there were no roads. The older members found the journey especially difficult, progress being limited to a few miles each day. Due to a miscalculation, the group came upon the Arkansas River, upstream from what is now Fort Smith. They realized their mistake and plotted a new route downstream of where they now were. The men built rafts of logs and floated the group to a site near what is now Alma. Now in early November, Bill and Phillip decided that this previously unexplored area of Arkansas would have to wait. Past experience told them that snows often fell in this area from November to late March. They must find a suitable place, erect some temporary shelters, kill some game, and wait until the winter was past before going on to the springs that heal. The group was in need of rest, food, and a few weeks to regain their strength.

Bill thought it best to backtrack across the mountain range to the north, hopefully beating the first snow. Wearily the group once again picked up all their worldly possessions and started their trek in search of a suitable, though temporary, homesite. Deep in the mountains they were caught by an early winter storm. Temperatures dropped well below freezing and a heavy, wet snow covered the wooded landscape in every direction. Some family members, especially the older ones, weakened by the long hard journey, did not survive and were buried along the trail. Descending the range on the north slope, Bill looked backward at the range they had crossed, turned to Phillip and said, "Phillip, those are sure some Boston mountains."

Along their trail they encountered other pioneers and told of their difficulty crossing the "Boston mountains." Today, few people are familiar with this story and are puzzled as to why a mountain range, deep in the Ozarks, is named after a city on the east coast.

Thus in 1824, or 1825, the Vaughans came to a settlement later known as Evansville. They found six families living there: the John Alexander family, two McGarrah families, two Simpson families, and the Shannon family.

The nearby stream should provide all the water they needed and seemed to be alive with fish. The meadows and rich bottom land should provide the party with food. Game seemed abundant and the fertile land offered them a chance to grow some provisions before proceeding on their journey in search of the Promised Land.

From Goodspeed's *History of Washington County:*

> In the year 1826, before the treaty was made giving white people the right of settlement in what is now Washington County, the settlement of those early pioneers was considered a trespass. In August 1826, a command of soldiers was dispatched from Fort Gibson, Indian Territory, to move them off the land. The soldiers, with their sabers, cut down the settlers' corn fields, telling

them to move on. The cabins in Evansville were left undamaged, however the Vaughans had built some distance from the small settlement and were not so fortunate. The soldiers put fire to their modest shelters, burning them to the ground.

In 1828, a treaty was signed with the Cherokees giving the right of settlement to the white man. William Vaughan and his group moved northward to the Cane Hill area, in Washington County. They quickly became involved in politics of the newborn country. Goodspeed's *History* shows that Daniel Vaughan was a grand juror for the county of Washington, Territory of Arkansas, during the spring of 1829. The court appointed Samuel Vaughan a constable of Richland Township, with a bond and security of $400.

The first store building was built on the site of Fayetteville by the Sevier Brothers in 1829. At this time in history it was considered an ideal place to build because of the absence of trees. The rolling hills were covered with tall grasses and provided grazing grounds for herds of buffalo. It was far easier to move buffalo carcasses than to cut down and remove oak trees.

From Goodspeed's *History of Washington County:*

> The Commissioners of the seat of justice were Lewis Evans, Larkin Newton, Samuel Vaughan, and John Woody. They fixed upon the site of Fayetteville, and when the Government survey of land was made, it was found to be upon a sixteenth section of the school section. A special act of Congress was therefore passed transferring the school section of Township 16, Range 30 West to the 20th Section. The patent for the town site was then issued. J.E. Vaughan and Thomas Jennings were, some fifty years later, to establish a livery business here.

There were two principal roads used by the earliest settlers into Madison County. One road followed the Arkansas River to Fort Smith, over the Boston Mountains, through Fayetteville, and then eastward. The other road came southwesterly from St. Louis to Springfield, then south into northwest Arkansas. At this time settlements invariably followed rivers and streams. It is in the more recent history that the population moved out of the valleys and into the mountains.

Madison County was created by the state legislature at its first session in 1836. This part of the state was in New Madrid County prior to 1813, in Arkansas County from 1813 to 1815, in Lawrence County from 1815 to 1820, and in Independence County from 1825 to 1827, when Lovely County was created. Lovely County was abolished in 1828 when Washington County was erected. I hope this will explain some of the references to Washington and Madison counties that might otherwise seem confusing.

The first court in Madison County was held in the barn of Evan S. Polk. Later, the barn of John Sanders was used for the same purpose. Goodspeed shows that B. Vaughan served as sheriff of Madison County for the following periods: 1848–1858, and 1876–1878.

~

A short story about how Ben Vaughan managed law enforcement and order along this frontier might explain why he was re-elected so many times.

A felonious old mountaineer, along with his two worthless sons, stole three hogs from a man in the St. Paul community. There was no doubt as to their guilt, so Vaughan dispatched a deputy to St. Paul to make the arrest. Stealing a man's winter meat was a serious offense.

A week later the deputy returned without the hog stealin' scoundrels—Vaughan asked him why. The deputy replied, "Any man who goes after them three varmints is askin' fer it. They is hid up in them hills with their rifles, and have told everybody in St. Paul that they will shoot to kill iff'n anybody tries to come up there and arrest 'em."

Vaughan said nothing, but the next morning the deputy saw him get his horse from the stable, saddle up, then take off his pistol and cartridge belt, and put them in his saddle bags along with a slicker and some food.

"Where you headin' Ben?" asked the deputy.

"I'm goin' after that old polecat and them two wuthless sons of his'n," answered Vaughan.

"You'll be kilt fer sure iff'n you do," said the deputy. "It ain't worth it Ben, give it up while you are still alive." He should have known that the sheriff had no intention of getting killed. Vaughan knew his job and he knew human nature.

Every year St. Paul had a reunion, and everyone in the area looked forward to this chance to visit with old friends. It was not unknown for some of those in attendance to bring along a jug or two of "white lightning." Ben knew that if anything would entice the hog stealers down from their mountain home it would be the reunion. He was correct in his speculation.

Vaughan rode his horse at a leisurely walk, spending a night on the trail a few miles south of Aurora. He wanted news of his arrival to reach St. Paul well before he did. Word of the sheriff's coming, and likelihood of a gunfight, was news that would travel fast.

When he rode onto the picnic grounds shortly after noon the next day, he could feel the tenseness in the air. News of his arrival went through the gathering like an electrical current. The showdown between the sheriff, the hog stealin' old man, and his two sons promised to be the highlight of the reunion.

Vaughan nodded to the people as he rode to the hitching rack. No sooner had he dismounted than he saw the old mountaineer approaching. From the corner of his eyes he could see the two sons, squirrel rifles in hand, hiding behind the stables.

"Howdy Sheriff," said the hog stealer, "I hear tell you air aimin' on arrestin' me and the boys. Maybe you'd like to tell me how you plan to do that when you ain't even packin' a gun."

Vaughan turned and smiled at the old timer. "I don't need no gun to take sech as you in. I could skin an old polecat like you with my bare hands."

"You'd think you wuz skinnin' a wildcat, 'stead of a polecat," bragged the old man. "Now jest when you aimin' on getting started?"

Vaughan knew full well that if he got in a scuffle with the old timer, one of his sons would shoot him square between his eyes. He also knew that back in the hills a man might be a thief, a murderer, or a bank robber but the virtue of keeping one's word was sacred. In rural Arkansas, once even the lowest of the low gave you their word, it was as good as a written contract.

"No use'n both of us gettin' all bloody and dirty," said the sheriff.

"I'll tell you what. You give me your word that you'll show up fer court next month, and get two citizens to sign fer you, then me and you'll have a little drink from one of the jugs in my saddle bags and enjoy this here picnic. Can you find two people who will guarantee you will show up?"

"Why, shore," said the hog stealer. "My two boys will sign fer me. Is that good enough fer you, Sheriff?"

"It sure is," replied Vaughan. "I know I can count on you and your boys not goin' back on your word." Reaching in his saddle bags he brought out the necessary papers.

The old timer turned toward the stables. "Come on out boys, we got some writin' to do, then the sheriff is gonna' pull a jug outa' those bags and we'uns are gonna' whoop it up."

When word got around the square in Huntsville that the sheriff had not brought in the hog stealers and locked 'em up, but was depending upon their word to show up for trial, he was the subject of a lot of jokes.

"They'll never show," said his deputy "That old scoundrel sure put one over on you, Ben. They laid in on you good and proper."

The morning of the trial, the hog stealers were there bright and early—well before court started. The judge listened to their story, then pronounced sentence: three months in the state penitentiary for the three hog stealers.

When Vaughan heard the sentence he knew he was in big trouble. It was a long hard ride to Little Rock to take the prisoners, and with winter coming on it could be a real problem. A 200-mile trip to Little Rock was not something to be approached casually.

He could talk the judge into letting them stay in the Huntsville jail but that was not without problems. First there would be several trips a day to the outhouse—an experience not looked forward to. Then there was the problem of firewood, and someone would have to cook three meals a day, take the food to the prisoners, then pack the dirty dishes home and wash them. No one in those days bathed daily, but the air in the jail would be getting pretty ripe if the three did not have at least one bath per month. Ben could see that both he and his deputy would be kept busy providing a free hotel for the three lazy prisoners.

To be perfectly truthful, Ben Vaughan was wishing he had let the old timer and his boys get away with the hog stealin.'

Then Vaughan had an idea that would solve his problems. He called the mountaineer into his office. After a few pleasant words he said to the prisoner, "I'm today appointing you as guardian and caretaker of the jail for a period of three months. It is up to you to see that the boys stay in jail, that they are fed, and that the jail is kept clean. I'll come by once a day and give you your ration money. You are free to buy what ever you want to eat at any store you want to visit." So saying, Vaughan handed the keys to the jail to the old man.

Faithfully, the hog stealer locked himself and his two sons into the jail cells each and every night for the next ninety days. It was probably the only job the mountaineer ever had.

Vaughan was elected to the state legislature.

~

In the fall of 1828, Samuel and Daniel Vaughan and George Tucker drove the first wagon into the Richland area. Tucker settled on what was known as the Sheridan Bottom, on the border of Washington and Madison counties. The Vaughans stayed in what was known as the Tuttle settlement.

Samuel moved into a valley (destined to be named Vaughan Valley) in 1831, buying the entire acreage and improvements from a half-breed Indian friend. At the time the Indian was the only occupant of the valley. Samuel dealt largely in government claims. He lived here until his death at 77 years of age. He is buried in Vaughan Cemetery west of Hindsville.

Daniel spent the rest of his life on his first claim in the valley west of present-day Hindsville. William Vaughan, with John Hind, settled in the same area in 1832. John located on the site of Hindsville, while William picked an area about 2.5 miles southeast. There is a discrepancy here—the 1830 census shows William and Ferehy living in the home of Samuel. William died sometime between the 1830 and 1835 census. His gravesite is unknown. I tend to believe they did move in with Samuel so he could care for them in their old age. Elsie

Vaughan, widow of Otis, told me before she died that Daniel was killed by bushwhackers.

The mortality schedule of Washington County, Arkansas, gives the date of Fereby's death as May 1850. She was 105 years old. Her gravesite is also unknown. Samuel died April 26, 1852 and was buried in the Vaughan Cemetery. A beautiful monument, recently erected at the entrance of Vaughan Cemetery, reads as follows:

> VAUGHAN
>
> Samuel and Daniel Vaughan
> Descendants of William Patrick Vaughan
> Immigrant of Tretower Castle, Wales,
> Settled Vaughan Valley in 1831
>
> Legend has it—Samuel Requested to be
> Buried Where He Killed His Last Buck.
> Thus the Founding of Vaughan Cemetery
> Samuel Vaughan, Buried April 1852
>
> The Cemetery Remained Vaughan Family
> Property through Eight Generations from
> Daniel, Grave Site Unknown, to That of
> Buck Vaughan, Buried April 1990
> Who Killed His First and Only Buck Here.
>
> The Alpha and the Omega

It is apparent that both William and Fereby were buried before the Vaughan Cemetery was established. It is certainly possible that they could be buried in unmarked graves, but one other possibility exists. Recently Jim Vaughan of Hindsville told me that a neighbor had uncovered several small headstones while working his fields. Jim moved the headstones to Vaughan Cemetery where they are placed near the entrance gate. Could two of the stones be those of William and Fereby? One can only speculate.

The Vaughans played important roles during the Civil War. From Goodspeed's *History of Madison County*:

> Vaughan, Christopher C., farmer and stock raiser, was born in the County December 7, 1847. He is the Son of Judge G. W.

Vaughan. C. C. Vaughan owns the farm he first lived on. He was a slave holder before the war, but, imbued with a spirit of liberty, immediately joined the Union cause, organizing a Company of men of which he was made Captain, and took an active part in the protection of the lives and property of the people of Madison County.

From Goodspeed's *History of Washington County:*

1863—On January 8, a detachment under the command of Lieutenants Thompson and Vaughan participated in the defeat of Marmaduke at Springfield, Missouri. Lieutenant Vaughan and Sergeant L. D. Jernigan were severely wounded during the engagement.

The oldest congregation of which any record could be found is styled "Friendship Baptist Church." It was organized about three miles southeast of Springdale, in May 1847, by R. C. Hill, and J. F. Mitchell, Joseph Baker, Louis Heath, B. D. Gray, T. B. Van Horn, Asa Brown, and Z. M. Vaughan.

I believe the Z. M. Vaughan mentioned in Goodspeed's book is Zimri Vaughan, who built the first steam mill in the area in 1875. The mill was located about two miles west of Hindsville.

CHAPTER 2

The End of Innocence— The Beginning of Technology

O, call back yesterday, bid time return.

—WILLIAM SHAKESPEARE

December 29, 1882. A. J. Vaughan arose at his usual hour, 4:30 a.m. He enjoyed his customary hearty breakfast of food, which, by today's standards, is considered only slightly less lethal than cyanide: cured ham, pork sausage, fried eggs, hot biscuits slathered with butter, flour gravy made from the ham drippings, and a wide assortment of homemade jams and jellies. All this was washed down with two large cups of black coffee.

Andrew Jackson Vaughan, my great-grandfather, and grandson of William Vaughan, was born in 1815, twelve years before the Vaughan family settled in the fertile valley west of the present-day Hindsville. The area was soon known throughout the country as "Vaughan Valley." The name remains today although much of the original Vaughan acreage now belongs to other owners.

Early in life, A. J. felt the call to become a Baptist minister. Active in area churches, he became acutely aware that one of the more urgent needs of the people was a doctor to treat the ill. Some of his flock, no doubt, would live to a ripe old age while living a life of sin. Others, following the straight and narrow path to heaven, might be surprised to find the road shorter than expected. Brother A. J. Vaughan warned of this paradox often—practically every Sunday morning when he delivered his weekly sermon.

He was painfully aware that potentially fatal infections were always nearby, waiting to strike saint and sinner alike, and that many common diseases were both preventable and treatable—even with the limited medicines available at that time.

I do not know whether he was driven by compassion or by profit, but I do know he "read medicine" according to the custom of the time, and soon became a doctor. To the best of my knowledge, he never attended or graduated from a school of medicine. He never referred to himself as Doctor Vaughan—apparently feeling it was a title he did not deserve. After years of ministering to the needs of the sick and lame, as well as to saint and sinner, many people throughout his area felt differently, and referred to the old gentleman as Dr. Vaughan.

A. J. married his second wife, Elizabeth, about 1857 and their children were Charles Isham Vaughan, my grandfather, and his sister, Mary E. Vaughan.

In the late 1880s Mary married Dr. Edward B. Eddis, a highly skilled, well-educated physician from Great Britain. Dr. Eddis had recently immigrated to America and had difficulty adjusting to frontier life. He always called my grandfather "Charlie, old chap." Being younger than A.J., Dr. Eddis tried to take the long visits to attend the sick.* Dr. Eddis eventually assumed all of Dr. Vaughan's medical practice, leaving A. J. to pursue his church work and tend to his sizable land holdings. Family stories indicate that A. J. was more than pleased to surrender his practice, as he was getting too old to make house calls. Trips at night, especially during our cold winter months, were especially hard on the old man.

For a short time before Dr. Eddis came into the family, A. J. began making his calls on horseback as he thought it might be faster than a buggy. This practice came to a rapid conclusion one night when he rode under a large oak tree. A bobcat, crouching on a tree branch directly over the dirt road, lunged at the horseback rider. The angry feline missed his target but came close enough to knock the hat from

---

* Often Dr. Eddis would be in his buggy for two days without sleep. He found certain pills in his medical bag that would, with vast quantities of coffee, keep him going for days. When he finally got a chance to sleep in a bed he very often took a narcotic, being too tired to sleep otherwise. Before many years of such a routine he was hopelessly addicted. He died in the state mental hospital in Little Rock. I had one of his original medical instruments, a device for pulling teeth. I gave it to my son-in-law, Tom Simmons, who is a Physician's Assistant at the Veterans Hospital in Fayetteville.

Vaughan's head. The good doctor did not stick around to recover his headpiece. After this experience A. J. quit making night calls.

~

My grandfather Charlie tells two stories about his boyhood that should be preserved.

A. J. Vaughan, being a Baptist preacher, often conducted baptizings. In those days the churches had not progressed to an indoor baptistry. People were baptized outdoors in a creek or stream—the way the Good Lord intended. A stock tank placed behind the pulpit with trees painted on the wall in the background was still in the distant future.

These baptizings were something everyone in the community looked forward to. The limited entertainment early settlers had was centered around the church. It was at such a baptizing that Charlie and a few other boys climbed a tree on the creek bank thereby securing for themselves a ringside seat. You never knew what would happen at a baptizing. I once saw a preacher lose hold of a very heavy woman when he leaned her backward into the water. She went completely under with much kicking and flailing of arms. On the creek bank cries of concern were mixed with laughter. A boy certainly did not want to miss anything like that.

Well, Charlie wanted to impress his buddies in the tree, so he filled his pockets with bird egg-sized pebbles. Every time his father lowered someone in the water, Charlie would yell, "Duck 'em under again, Jack," and throw some of the pebbles in the water near the preacher.

My grandfather told me years later that it was a lot of fun, but that his dad "warmed my pants well" and that it was days later before he could sit down on his sore bottom. To get even, at the next baptizing he rode his horse upstream and kept the horse going in a circle to stir up the muddy creek bed. A. J. never knew why the normally crystal-clear creek was running muddy water just about the time he started baptizing.

A. J. Vaughan always kept fine horses and saddles. He even had a surrey with a fringed top. One day Charlie saddled up his handsome saddle horse and, dressed in his best everyday clothes, rode to the Whitener store. There were usually a few young men there telling off-color stories and pitching pennies. Sometimes they gathered under trees beside the store and pitched horseshoes.

Well, on this particular day, Charlie was there with his friends when a "skinny young feller" rode up on an old sway-backed plow horse. His saddle was an old burlap sack and his bridle was made of rope. The faded overalls he had on were patched and re-patched showing many months of hard wear. Here was a good chance for my grandfather to show his friends how much of a man he was.

He walked away from his group and approached the young man. "Climb down off that sorry looking horse," he said, "I'm gonna' whup your butt all over the ground."

The young man declined, saying, "I don't want no trouble. I jest come t' the store fer some salt. I don't want to fight you."

Charlie turned to his friends, smiling, then looked the young stranger straight in the eye: "Either you get down off that old worn-out horse and fight me like a man, or I'm gonna' pull you off."

When the young man hesitated, Charlie grabbed him by the arm and with all his strength pulled him to the ground. Charlie got the fight he wanted, and a whole lot more. He told me that the young man gave him the beating of his life. With a bloody nose and wounded dignity, Charlie mounted his horse and made a hasty trip home.

He told me to always remember two things—don't ever fight unless you have to, and NEVER, NEVER, pull a man off of his horse.

Only five years ago while talking to me, Jim Vaughan put it in a slightly different way: "In Madison County you either speak politely or ride a very fast horse."

∼

The Vaughan family, like other families in the area, arose early, and dressed for breakfast long before daylight. Two flickering kerosene lamps on the kitchen table cast eerie shadows about the large kitchen—a room larger than most living rooms today. The elder Vaughan led his family in returning thanks before breakfast. My grandfather, Charlie, told me many times of the family kitchen and the sumptuous meals served there.

After breakfast, Dr. Vaughan said a few words to the family about his planned trip to Shiloh and stepped from the kitchen into the glassed-in back porch where he took down his warm coat and worn hat from the wood pegs above the cream and egg table. He pulled the coat on over his stooped frame, fished a pair of brown jersey gloves from a pocket, and stepped out into the cold December morn.

Vaughan made his way by first light past the well-stocked smokehouse, down the path by the garden and proceeded to the barn. He harnessed up a favorite horse to the old buggy, which he normally used when traveling alone on house calls to the sick, or for business trips. The large surrey with the fringed top was reserved for Sunday when he and the family attended church services. He seldom used his buckboard; the ride was too rough for his sixty-seven years. His two sons often used the buckboard to make trips to the Whitener store.

Today, the doctor had business to attend to in Shiloh—a rather long trip. He glanced toward the east. An overcast sky could indicate troublesome weather later today. "I better get on the road," he said to himself. "It will be well past dark when I get home even if I wind up my business in a hurry."

It must have been around 7:30 a.m. as the old man guided the horse and buggy along the deeply rutted road past the Spring Valley Baptist Church—the church he and C. S. Fritts founded some years before. "I wish they would quit changing names of places," he mumbled to himself. "This place will always be 'Little Spring' to me." He was proud of that church. Even though their regular services were suspended during the Civil War, the church had shown solid growth since the war, an increase that would continue for another sixty years. "They will need a new church house before long," he mused.

A. J. was pleased to see Anderson Sanders, his son-in-law, up and about. He pulled his buggy off the road and tied his horse to the hitching rail near the old stone wall. He was standing by his buggy as Uncle Anderson[*] came around the corner of the large store building carrying a bucket of water from the spring. "Come on in the store, Andrew, I've got a hot pot of coffee on the stove. It won't hurt to get warm and

---

[*] Anderson Sanders was was known as "Uncle Anderson" by young and old alike, related or not.

have a cup before headin' on to Shiloh. I'll bet Cat (Catherine) saw you comin' down the road. She'll want a word with you before you go."

Within minutes A. J. was back on the road to town. His pulled his horse back to a slow walk as they started up the steep hill west of the spring. As the buggy bounced along the road, dodging a large rock here, a deep hole there, the old gentleman's thoughts returned to that time long ago when the Vaughan family first came to the area. There were few roads then, only traces here and there and most of those were impossible to negotiate with any sort of vehicle.

"Yes, the roads are better now," he mused. Most of the time a horse and buggy could get through with few problems. The biggest aggravation was opening and closing gates when crossing private property. The right-of-way was public for the most part, but often it was nearer, or less muddy or bumpy, to take a shortcut across a neighbor's farm. Near Pilgrim's Rest, he noted that the large walnut tree was still across the road, same as it was three weeks ago. "That old tree probably blew down last September when we had high winds for a spell," he muttered to himself. A new set of tracks had been made around the obstacle by travelers who found it easier to reroute the road than move the tree.

"Heavily loaded freight wagons are another matter," thought A. J., as his mind traced the road from Vaughan Valley to Shiloh, "especially that big mud hole near the Madison County line." He remembered a lot of freight wagons on their way to Huntsville had trouble there. He had seen more than one wagon mired clear up to its axle in mud during wet weather. Freight traffic between Shiloh (Springdale as it is now known), and Huntsville was practically nonexistent until the railroad opened two years ago. Prior to the coming of the railroad, most freight for Huntsville was shipped overland from Ozark, a thriving community on the Arkansas River.

It was obvious the roads still needed a lot of improving if this country was to develop. The importance of the newly developed railroad through Fayetteville and Springdale could not be overestimated. Still, getting freight to outlying towns and communities remained a major problem. He hoped to live long enough to see a hard surface road from Springdale to Huntsville.

His wish was not to be. A. J. Vaughan died later that December day

Ike Vaughan's general store at Whitener, near Hindsville, Arkansas, ca. 1890. There were two Ike Vaughans at that time—one was known as "Store Ike" and the other as "Fat Ike."

in 1882 when his buggy overturned while crossing Brush Creek east of Springdale on the old Upper Huntsville Road. The exact cause of the accident is lost to history but after considerable research, I believe the accident occurred when the buggy hit a large rock or hole, causing Vaughan to lose control. He was thrown from the buggy and suffered fatal head injuries. He is buried in Vaughan Cemetery near his home. As late as 1989, the tracks of that old road were still visible.

This, then, was the small world of my great-grandparents. If they could have seen the future they may well have considered themselves fortunate to live and die in such a time.

∽

The Twentieth Century was foreordained to greatness, and to tragedy, by powers at work long before the Gay '90s drew to an end. Science and invention more or less stumbled its way through the preceding hundred years like a blind man trying to find his way through an obstacle course. Those seekers of new ideas learned much from their failures, perhaps even more than from their successes. During the nineteenth century, a vast pool of knowledge gradually accumulated behind a dam of misunderstanding and doubt. Bits and pieces of information, inventions, scientific discoveries, and dreams filled this lake of progress waiting for men of vision to come forward and forge those ideas into a workable technology. This vast reservoir of learning was more often than not the fruits of labor of men long on vision and short on education. I do not discount the work of our great scientists, but from this pool would come two technologies—communications and transportation—and much of those technologies came from experimenters and tinkerers, rather than from the laboratories of our institutions of learning.

Communication and transportation. Two words, two technologies, which would change the world and every person in it. Even the wonderful advances in medicine would have had little impact without improved communication and transportation.

Communication and transportation, like Jekyll and Hyde, have both positive and negative qualities. Within a few decades improvements in transportation signaled the end for many small towns and villages. Progress moved our population from the country to the city. Progress changed our morals, our standard of living, and the way we worked, thought, and lived.

Only a gifted few, plus a group of science fiction writers, could foresee the drastic changes that were about to descend upon a naive and unsuspecting citizenry. Even fewer would understand what those changes were about to do to our country. Those few who had the nerve to put their predictions and imaginations in writing were considered somewhat strange—eccentrics who let their imagination run wild. Perhaps H.G. Wells and Jules Verne are the best known of this group of writers. As always, there were a few who believed, a few who understood, but often their warnings were buried in an avalanche of political hogwash.

At the dawn of the new century many Americans, even those living in remote sections of the country, had heard talk about strange new devices. Yes, there was talk of instruments that could send messages without wires, machines that might one day enable men to fly like a bird, and horseless carriages that traveled at speeds of fifteen miles an hour. Most dismissed such ideas as nothing more than nonsense, and plenty of brilliant men supported their disbelief. Even those active in the field of science and invention could sometimes become full of doubts. Men like Thomas Edison, who branded the first transatlantic wireless transmissions as nothing but a hoax. Edison felt so strongly about news of wireless spanning the Atlantic that he placed full-page ads in New York newspapers warning the public that such wireless transmissions were technically impossible.

Let's not forget that the director of the United States Patent Office, near the end of the last century, suggested that the government close down that office because it no longer served a useful purpose—everything that could be invented had been invented.

Originally I had meant for this book to be primarily concerned with the impact of transportation upon our area. However, when mail is transported faster, when news is carried quickly from village to village by automobile or motorcycle, when newspapers are delivered in a Model T Ford to rural areas that formerly did not have such service, then transportation becomes integrated with communications. It is impossible to separate the two fields; they are interdependent.

Mack Gibson and his five-string banjo.

Before World War I, there were not many entertainment options in rural areas. With little to do between the evening meal and bedtime, many country folks used the time to learn to play a musical instrument. My grandfather Mack chose the five-string banjo. Music get-togethers were held every few days. Five or six musicians would bring their instruments and "pick and fiddle" until about 9:00 p.m. Continuing any later was past bedtime, as well it should be, because most farm families arose at 4:30 a.m.

CHAPTER 3

Mack and Alice

*A good marriage is at least 80 percent good luck
in finding the right person at the right time.
The rest is trust.*

—NANETTE NEWMAN, British actress

My mother's father had very little money before the Depression, during the Depression, or afterward. He heard talk of hard times but never understood what all the trouble was about. He lived in the same unpainted, oak-sided house he built in the early 1900s, he tilled the same garden, he always had a large woodpile to see him through two winters, the cellar was full of canned fruit and vegetables, three fat hogs were in the pig pen, one old cow had recently "come fresh" and another was about to calf, his chickens were healthy and laying more eggs than he could use. All was right in his world. He thought the stock market was where you went to bid on a new cow, and right now he didn't need one.

Mack Gibson, son of James, grandson of Shadrick, was one-quarter Cherokee and three-quarters mountaineer. He seemed much larger than his five foot nine height. His curly black hair started turning gray when he was forty years old. Now, as I remember him, his curly white hair was tousled and long, standing out from under a well worn old hat. Between soft brown eyes, his curved Cherokee nose was the most prominent feature of his tanned, roughly chiseled face. Mack was an expert marksman, with the strength and determination of a mule. Afraid of absolutely nothing, he was the most generous and gentle man I have ever known.

∼

Shad Gibson was born in Virginia in the late 1700s and migrated to a farm near War Eagle. Most of the family received a little education. Mack was the only one who never attended a day of school. There was a reason why he alone would receive no education at all. He was by far the best rifle shot in the family. It was up to him to keep the family in meat. He started his hunting career early on—about six years old. His first rifle was a cap and ball black powder rifle. When he was twelve years old the family bought him a Winchester. He learned to load his own ammunition and learned gunsmith rudiments. While the other children were in school Mack hunted deer, wild turkeys, and small game. When not hunting or fishing, he was busy shoeing the family horses, repairing farm implements, and loading ammunition for the Gibson family and for others from nearby farms.

When he was nineteen years old, Mack saddled his horse, rode to the Kelly farm near Prairie Grove, and asked fourteen-year-old Alice Kelly for her hand in marriage. She answered in the affirmative. After very few formalities, they saddled her horse and rode to a nearby preacher's house. Hollering out the preacher, they told him of their wish to be married. The preacher went inside his small house and returned to the dusty yard almost immediately carrying his well-worn Bible. Mack and his fourteen-year-old bride never dismounted; they exchanged their wedding vows while sitting on their horses. Constant clucking of the Rhode Island Reds and Dominick chickens as they searched for worms on the dusty ground never ceased during the wedding ceremony.

My grandparents' first home was little more than a shack in the Baldwin community where Mack worked in the coal mines. Arkansas was not rich in coal; the mines paid barely enough to keep food on the table. Accustomed to the freedom of the woods and rivers, Mack disliked being in the dark passages underground all day. However, without an education of any kind, the illiterate backwoodsman's chances of finding a good paying job were practically non-existent. Hoping for a somewhat better life, they moved to Spring Valley in 1895.

Mack's only skills, other than hunting and fishing, were those he had learned on the Gibson farm: shoeing horses, and repairing the farm equipment. He and my grandmother Alice somehow managed to buy an acre of land and a log cabin near the store and spring. He hoped to open a blacksmith shop if he could buy the needed tools on credit.

The young couple unloaded their meager possessions from the rickety wagon. After thanking their neighbor for moving them from the Baldwin community to their new home at Spring Valley, they began carrying their furnishings into the old two-room log cabin. The date was sometime in November 1895, give or take a year or two. From the looks of the cabin they were in for a rough winter. Cracks in the walls where the chinking had fallen out needed to be filled with a mud and straw mixture. The sooner they were filled, the warmer the cabin would be for the coming months.

Large cracks in the floor, some almost half an inch wide indicated that the flooring was laid before the rough sawed oak had seasoned properly. Building with green oak was common practice as it is very difficult to drive a nail in well-seasoned oak. Oak as a building material had two things going for it: it was cheap and it was durable. One major problem when building with oak is its tendency to warp as it dries. That's why barns in this area always have large cracks in the walls—they were built before the wood had a chance to warp.*

Alice swept out the two rooms with a homemade broom while Mack carried in three cane-bottomed chairs, an old iron bedstead and springs, a lantern and kerosene lamp, and a rusty cook stove that would be used for both heating and cooking that first winter. Mack

---

*Perhaps you have noticed that barns always have vertical siding. The same is true of most small houses built in nineteenth-century Arkansas. Only affluent families could afford the more expensive drop siding sold by lumber yards. With terrible roads and slow transportation, the cost of building with pine siding was much more than building with oak. One hundred years ago, one could find a sawmill in practically every small village. Normally sawmills in this area were a family operation. Though it seems ridiculous today, in 1900 it was possible to build a substantial house of four or five rooms for less than one hundred dollars.

The reason for vertical oak siding was that it was sure to shrink as it aged. Knowing this, builders used thinner cut strips of oak about three inches wide nailed over the cracks between boards. When the oak dried and the cracks between boards opened up, the three-inch boards helped keep water and cold air outside. If the boards had been installed horizontally, water would run in behind each board—a problem to be avoided if possible.

carefully placed his double barrel shot gun and his .30-caliber carbine rifle on pegs over the fireplace.

Yes, the cabin had a fireplace of sorts, but the newly married couple had no wood to burn. The cook stove was easy to find wood for—just pick it up off the ground. Small twigs and branches made ideal wood for the little cook stove. There was no front porch. Garden tools, a wood saw, and two good axes were carried inside and leaned in a corner.

Two small packing boxes contained all their clothing, quilts, sheets, and linens. All their sheets, pillowcases, and kitchen towels were hand made from flour sacks.

Alice made their bed and hung their clothes on wooden pegs behind the door while Mack put up the cook stove. When he was finished with the stove, he picked up an ax and walked down to the spring branch behind the house. Gathering up fallen tree limbs along the banks of the little stream, he chopped enough firewood to last two days or so and carried a big armful to the house. It was getting dark now; he would carry in a good supply tomorrow. He built a fire in the cook stove, placing the few sticks of extra wood on the floor behind the stove.

In the dim light of this early winter evening, he filled their one lamp with the last remaining kerosene in their coal oil can. The place was beginning to get warm and the light made the drab surroundings a bit more homelike. By the flickering yellow light they took stock of their meager food supply. It consisted of a small sack of coffee, a half-full box of salt, a small sack of flour, baking soda, and a few hot red peppers. This would have to last them until Mack could kill some meat, or find a job to earn a little money. Fortunately, at this time in history the hills around Spring Valley were full of rabbits, squirrels, a few wild turkeys, and an occasional deer.

"Mack, we don't have a drop of water in this house. You better go fetch a bucket from the spring before it gets full dark. In the morning for breakfast I'll make some water gravy, bread, and a pot of coffee. If you put enough salt and hot peppers in the gravy it will do us until we can do better," said Alice.

"Yeah," replied Mack. "I'll go huntin' first thing in the mornin' and see if I can't bring home some squirrels. Tomorrow night we might

Washday at Spring Valley

have squirrel and dumplins.' I might even run acrost a turkey, or with a lot of luck maybe even a deer."

"I've told you before that the Lord will provide," said Alice. "If you put your trust in Him we will have enough to eat."

"Well, Alice," answered Mack, "that is all fine and well, but I think we'll eat a lot better if I give Him a little help with my old shotgun."

"Mack Gibson, I'll never make a God fearin' Baptist out of you if you're gonna' talk like that," replied his young wife. "You ought to be ashamed goin' on with your foolishness. Just you wait! Someday the Lord will give you a sign—then you'll change your tune."

Within seconds, they heard someone knocking on the door.

Mack took his shotgun down from the pegs over the fireplace— "Who aire you, and what do you want?" asked Mack.

"Open up your door. I've got some fresh meat fer you," answered the stranger.

Mack opened his door. A middle-aged man was standing there with a large dishpan full of fresh-killed pork. Mack could see side meat, a bit of tenderloin, liver, a shoulder, and some freshly ground sausage.

"Mister, I don't know who you aire, but you've sure got the wrong feller. We'uns just moved in today and we ain't got no money to buy no meat," said Mack.

"Who said anything about money?" answered the man. "You don't have no fresh meat, do you? If you don't need it jest say so and I'll give it to some pore person. But if you'uns need it, hit's yours. We jest finished butcherin' and saw you folks moving in."

The neighbor came in and visited for a spell, then returned home. It was easy to see the man was dog-tired. Inside the log cabin, my grandmother carried the pan of meat over to the home-built table, set it down and picked up her worn Bible. She turned and shook the Good Book at my grandfather. "Now I guess you'll believe, you old sinner. How many signs does the Lord have to send you?"

Seventy-five years later, they had changed very little in their religious beliefs. Every Sunday morning during cold weather, Mack got up early, went to the church and built a fire in both stoves so the building would be warm for the 10:00 A.M. service. Just as regular, every Sunday my grandmother was the first to arrive for church and the last one to leave. For over forty years she taught a Sunday School class.

Mack never missed a service either. However, he much preferred in the summertime to sit on the back row of seats so he could spit his "tobaccy juice" out the window and watch the squirrels play in the tall oak trees. In the winter he chose the same seat, but brought a tin can with him to use as a spittoon.

Each worshipped God in their own way. Who was right? I like to think they both made it to Heaven.

CHAPTER 4

The Century Begins

His hair is crisp, and black, and long,
His face is like the tan,
His brow is wet with honest sweat,
He earns what'er he can,
And looks the whole world in the face,
For he owes not any man.

—HENRY WADSWORTH LONGFELLOW,
"The Village Blacksmith"

Mack paused, his heavy hammer at the apogee of his stroke. The whistle of a steam tractor pierced the heavy summer air. From the sound, he judged it was the big Case tractor coming down the road somewhere east of the schoolhouse. He removed the red-hot plow point from his anvil and placed it back among the glowing coals in the forge. The young blacksmith stepped from his coal-smoke filled shop, drew a deep breath of clean air, and sat down on a nail keg under the large oak tree where he could watch the lumbering engine's approach.

Such sights and sounds were unusual enough to bring several loafers out of the dark interior of the store onto the sun-drenched porch. They sought shade near the hitching rack while waiting for the tractor.

The blacksmith watched as the brightly painted tractor rumbled slowly by the store, and across the spring branch, where it began its long climb up the hill. As the front wheels bounced off flint rocks in the road, he could see the steering chains draw taut on one side, sag on the other, and then repeat the action on the opposite side. With

Mack shoeing horse in front of his shop.

This picture was made about two years before I was born. By the time I arrived on this earth Mack had built a new shop that was not in danger of falling down. The small boy is thought to be my uncle, Lee Gibson.

the constant motion of the front axle—first to the right, then to the left—the slow moving steam tractor crawled along the bumpy one-lane road in a more or less straight line.

As the tractor drew even with him, Mack raised his right hand and yanked downward two times. The driver smiled, wiped sweat from his forehead with the dirty red bandanna tied around his neck, then reached for the whistle rope. As a salute to the smithy, he let off two more long blasts.

"Hey, Clive, where you headin'?"

"We're doing the Vol Pullen place, then across the river to John Carroll's. We'll be back through here in a few days if it doesn't rain. We have some work lined up near Mayfield."

"Why don't you stop that thing and cool off for a spell?"

"No, I'm going to push on. I've got enough water in the boiler to make it to Pilgrim's Rest. I'll stop there and take on enough to make it on to the Pullum place before dark."

With a wave of his hand he turned his attention back to the hissing and puffing 12-horsepower engine as it propelled the heavy tractor slowly up the rough one-lane road.

Mack knew the driver well. It had only been a week since Clive stopped at the shop so that Mack could weld the tractor's firebox door hinge. At that time, they were threshing east of Spring Valley on the Puryear and Fitch places. Now the talk was that the threshing crew would work out near the White River crossing. The crew had two tractors, a Case and a Fairbanks. "I guess they pulled the threshing machine through here last night sometime," Mack thought. "It's a wonder they didn't wake up the whole neighborhood as they passed through."

The tractor disappeared from sight over the hill before Mack got up to return to the hot blacksmith shop. The unexpected passing of a steam tractor was a welcome excuse to stop work—he needed a break to cool off and clear his lungs of coal smoke. He finished sharpening six more plowshares, then walked over to two horses at the hitching rack. He lifted up the front foot of one horse, then the other. Yes, they both needed shoes badly. Both horses waited patiently for whatever was to come, occasionally pawing the ground and swishing away flies with their long tails. The horses scarcely paid attention to the blacksmith—they were getting on in years and had always been gentle. Mack patted one on the rump as he walked away.

Mack glanced over his shoulder as he entered his shop. Down behind the springhouse he saw a black chicken snake crawling lazily along the dusty path before it disappeared into the weeds. "No use trying to find it," Mack mumbled to himself. It would be long gone by the time he got there.

He grasped the handle of his blower and slowly turned it until the red fire turned to a brilliant white—hot enough to heat the plowshares. He resumed hammering, beating the edges of the plow points thinner and thinner. Then at the proper moment, he plunged the hot metal into the slack tub. The dirty water hissed and gave off a puff of steam as the sharpened plow point cooled to the correct temperature, thus achieving a proper temper.

While working, Mack was calculating in his mind—five cents a plowshare, and there were ten to sharpen—that would be fifty cents. Then two horses to shoe all around. Two dollars and fifty cents he would have coming if Denny paid in cash. He sure hoped he did—he had a book full of charges that he would never collect a dime on—and Uncle Anderson Sanders, the storekeeper, didn't give the shoes and horseshoe nails away. Mack would have to pay about a dollar for the materials he would use. "Still and all," thought Mack, "Iffen I get paid, $1.50 fer half a day's work is darn good wages for a man who never attended school a day in his life."

~

As late as 1885, horses, and sometimes oxen, remained the primary source of power used on farms and ranches. Though steam power had been around for quite a long time it was not until near the end of the nineteenth century that practical steam-powered tractors began gaining favor as a useful farm machine. By 1900, they were in widespread use. Such tractors were self-propelled, with a large heavy flywheel on the side that provided a power take-off. Slow, rough riding, and quite troublesome to operate, they nevertheless enjoyed their moment of glory. From about 1895 until 1920, steam-powered tractors were widely used especially for threshing, and on very large farms, for plowing.

Quite often around the dinner table, the farmhands discussed the wonders of steam power. It was rumored that two brothers—the Stanley brothers—were actually building a steam-powered carriage that could carry two men. Some said that such a machine was supposed to travel at speeds in excess of twenty miles per hour. Such talk invariably led to discussion of other wondrous inventions—the talking machine, the telegraph, and the speaking telephone. As the workers tried to top each other's stories, the conversation eventually led to talk of a wireless telegraph, and a machine that flew in the air like a giant bird. This usually ended the discussion with much laughter and knee slapping. Everyone knew that such talk was pure foolishness.

It was plain to see that the first storyteller never had a fair chance; someone would always come up with something more ridiculous.*

The drawbacks to steam were many. It took as long as one hour to get up a full head of steam. When threshing, the tractor was often located some distance from a source of water. This meant that one man driving a wagon and team was kept busy supplying the engine with water. Some engines burned straw for fuel, but most in this country used wood or coal. Keeping the engine supplied with fuel took the effort of another man.

Steam tractors and threshing machines were expensive at a time in history when money was scarce. Therefore, few farms or ranches were large enough to justify ownership of such equipment. The answer came in the form of custom threshing. One individual, usually the owner of a large farm, bought the needed equipment and hired enough help to run the operation. His first concern was in doing his own work, but after his crops were harvested, he then recouped his investment and sometimes made a modest profit by doing threshing for farmers in his area. Pay could be in cash but more often was a percentage of the harvested crop.

The area of operation for custom threshing was very limited. As mentioned before, the tractors were slow—very slow—when pulling the threshing machine. Two miles an hour was possible on some roads. Moving from one farm to the next usually took at least one day. The machines were heavy and often more than small wooden bridges could accommodate. This meant long detours to find a place where a creek or river could be crossed. The machines were rugged, but they needed constant attention by the engineer who not only operated

---

*News traveled slowly in 1900. Many, especially rural residents, were unaware of the penny postcard, a recent innovation of the US Postal Service. Rural Free Delivery, or RFD, was still an experimental service not available to everyone. It would not become a permanent service until 1902. Few farm families—and that included well over fifty percent of the U.S. population—received a weekly newspaper. Word of mouth remained the most popular form of news delivery, though its accuracy was often in doubt. Had better communications been available, the threshing hands discussing the wonders of science at the dinner table that day would have realized those "ridiculous ideas" of motorized transportation, flying, and wireless telegraphy were much closer than they realized.

the machine, but also kept the many bearings oiled, belts laced, nuts tightened, and made such repairs as were possible in the field.

Threshing time normally fell during midsummer. It was important that threshing crews move quickly from farm to farm. A rain could ruin the entire wheat crop for a farmer. It was imperative that threshing be done while the grain was dry, therefore, threshing crews were large, often employing a dozen or more workers. It was hard, hot, work with long hours and few breaks during the day. At night, most of the crew slept on the ground near their machines or in nearby barns. The comforts were few and there was the constant knowledge that copperheads often waited until the cool night hours to venture forth in the fields in search of field mice driven from their homes by the harvesting activity.

All men and boys on a farm worked side by side with the threshing crew. The women—and that included any girls over six years of age—were expected to feed the hungry workmen. Farm women put forth their best culinary efforts. Threshing crews spread the word quickly throughout the area as to where the best food was to be found. It was also common knowledge that those farms with the reputation for good food were often moved up a little higher on the waiting list, thus assuring those farmers that their crop would be harvested before a rain soaked the waiting grain and rendered it worthless.

Plans to feed the hungry workmen started months in advance of their actual visit. Fruit was canned with the specific idea of making pies for the crew. Favorite recipes were tested and fine-tuned to perfection. The largest chickens were saved, and often a pig was butchered for the occasion. It was a time of hard work but also a time of diversion, when diversions were rare indeed.

The origin of several phrases once commonly used by farm women are a direct result of harvest hands and their appetite: "I feel like I've been cookin' for the thresher," or, "They ate like a threshing crew," and still another, "I've got enough cooked for the thresher."

There was not only competition between the women from neighboring farms, but there was a competition within the family unit. Sometimes a daughter-in-law was trying to upstage her mother-in-law. In addition, there might very well be a young unmarried woman trying to impress one of the handsome young harvest hands.*

∼

Mack finished shoeing the two large workhorses, and tied the tow sack full of plowshares behind the saddle. He took the horses by their reins and led them across the small spring branch to the store, where he tied them in the shade out near the old rock wall.

He stepped inside where Uncle Anderson Sanders and Denny James were engaged in a slow game of checkers. Over on the hundred-pound feed sacks two loafers were swapping tales about the good ol' days. As was the custom at the time, they had taken the liberty of rearranging the sacks into comfortable seats—one to sit on, and three or four to form a back rest—perhaps not quite as comfortable as today's recliners, but very, very, close.

"Denny, I tied your horses out front. The double shovel points are tied behind your saddle. You owe me $2.50—a nickel apiece for the sharpening the plow shares and twenty-five cents a shoe for the horseshoeing."

---

*My grandmother Vaughan was an average cook. The problem was, she felt—indeed, she was positive—that she was the world's best cook. Somewhere in her past, the Morris genes must have been strongly influenced by her British origin. Most immigrant families soon adapted to the hill country tastes in food. Not the Morris clan—their cooking tasted strongly of British influence. For example, when cooking a big skillet of cured ham for breakfast, she would throw away the drippings, wash the skillet clean, and then make gravy. The gravy was what I referred to as "sterile" gravy—white as snow, tasteless as cotton, and as thin as spring water. Worse still, she taught her cooking skills to her daughters. Her cornbread was light, white, and tasteless. It bore a close resemblance to an angel food cake made without sugar.

Well, my mother and dad had been married about two months when the thresher arrived at the Vaughan farm. My grandmother saw a chance to prove her superiority in the kitchen. She suggested that my mother make a batch of cornbread, while she would make another. It was one of the proudest moments in my mother's life when the threshing crew ate all of her golden brown cornbread, while the plate of my grandmother's anemic-looking cornbread went mostly untouched.

"Mack, you are pricing yourself clear out of business. They say they's a feller over at Mayfield that'll shoe a horse all around fer seventy-five cents."

"Well, Denny, I guess the poor feller is hungry. I've got a good garden and a couple of hogs gettin' fatter by the day. I guess I'll still have to charge you a quarter a shoe. If you can get Anderson to sell me the shoes for a dime instead of twelve cents I might come down a little."

Such haggling and complaining about cost was common at the turn of the century. Offered in a joking manner, there was always a little bit of true feelings that surfaced during such exchanges.

Mack took his money and walked down the dusty road to his two-room log house. Like others in small villages throughout the country, he lived within walking distance of the store and post office.

He knew where he would find his wife and baby—out behind the house in the shade. That old log house got so hot in the afternoon, there was no way you could stay inside.

The baby had been feeling bad for a week now. "This weather is sure hard on little ones. I'll be glad to see fall come. I think we'll all start feeling better," thought the young father as he rounded the corner of his house.

"Alice, I took in a little money today, so I can buy some stuff at the store. What do you need in the kitchen?"

"Well, I trimmed the wicks on the lamps and filled them up. I used the last drop of coal oil we had. We have enough coffee for a day or so—if they have some cheap coffee we could use a pound. I would like to do some canning. If we can afford it, buy some sugar and a gallon of vinegar. I've got the vinegar jug cleaned and sittin' on the table. But why don't you wait until tomorrow to go to the store? There's nothing we need tonight. The *Springdale News* comes in on the mail hack about noon on Friday. If you wait till the mail hack runs, Anderson will read his paper out loud to everyone like he always does. I like to know what's goin' on in the country."

As his wife talked, Mack was looking at their little girl sleeping on an old quilt spread on the ground in the shade of the house. She seemed awfully pale to him.

"Yeah, I'll do that," replied Mack. He turned and walked into the two-room log cabin. Moments later Alice heard the front door slam as her husband left the house. She watched him walking down the dusty road with his old shotgun over his shoulder until he disappeared among the trees.

Less than an hour later, she heard two shots come from some distance away. She smiled; there would be some kind of meat for supper. Rabbit maybe, squirrel most likely, but she doubted there would be turkey. Wild turkeys were mostly hunted out nearby. "You would have to go more than two miles back in the woods to scare one up," she was thinking.

It was rabbit—two of 'em. While the rabbit was frying and the cornbread baking, Mack slopped his hogs, milked the cow, carried in some wood for the cook stove, and went to the spring for a cup of butter and a bucket of water. The springhouse sure kept the butter and milk good and cool.

After supper, Alice "done" the dishes and read her Bible. She had to read a little each night to keep up with the Sunday School class she taught. Shortly after dark, they went to bed.

As was his habit for most of his life, Mack arose at 4:30, built a fire in the cook stove, and while the water was heating got down the old coffee mill and ground enough coffee for the big graniteware coffee pot. By then Alice was up and making biscuits and gravy. They let Hazel sleep until almost 6:00 before waking her for breakfast.

The mail hack arrived shortly after noon the next day. Mack was in the blacksmith shop making gigs when the buggy passed. He put his work aside and picked up the coal oil can and the vinegar jug. He walked into the store and placed them on the floor beside the door. Pulling up a nail keg, he took his seat near the post office window and waited for Anderson to finish putting up the mail. That never took very long—sometimes five minutes or so. He knew the old man would come out from behind the counter, take a seat in his chair and start reading the *Springdale News* to the half-dozen men gathered there waiting.

When the old gentleman finished reading all the items of interest, Mack stood, walked to the door and picked up the two containers from the floor. "Anderson, I need a gallon of coal oil and a gallon of vinegar." Mr. Sanders took the coal oil can to the little storeroom out back where such flammable and dangerous items were stored—items like dynamite (used mostly for removing stumps when clearing land), turpentine, kerosene, and linseed oil. Kerosene and most other liquids were bought in 55-gallon drums. A cap or lid in the top of the drum was unscrewed and a pump with a hand crank attached to the barrel. The storekeeper held the little gallon can under the spout, cranked the pump, and filled the can. He replaced the caps on the can and returned to the store.

Vinegar was bought and kept in large wood barrels. While the barrel was still upright the bung hole plug in the barrel lid was driven into the barrel and replaced with a tapered wood spigot which was hammered in until it fit tight. The barrel was then placed horizontally on a wood rack about two feet from the floor. Once the barrel was on the rack, it was rotated until the spigot was on the bottom.

Anderson held the container under the vinegar barrel spigot and filled the glass jug. The cap of the jug was lost long ago and replaced with a corncob. It served the purpose well and was easier to remove than a screw cap.

"What else can I get for you, Mack?"

"I need a pound of Fox coffee beans, a box of matches, and ten pound of sugar."

The storekeeper gathered up the items and placed them on the rough wood counter. He picked up a short pencil and scraps of paper, and started adding up the bill. "Let's see," he mumbled, "coal oil is seven cents, fourteen cents for coffee, a dime for vinegar, twenty cents for sugar, and four cents worth of matches. That comes to fifty-five cents, Mack."

The blacksmith gathered up his supplies and headed home. "I'll sure be glad when hog killin' time comes," he thought. "I sure would love to have a mess of fresh pork." He became lost in thought as he carried his groceries home. "It's not too early to start a'lyin' in some wood for winter. I want the house warm, especially for the baby."

The little Gibson girl would not survive the winter. If there had been a doctor, if there had been a hospital close by, if the food had been better, if the house had been warmer, if the young couple had known more about raising babies—so many ifs. The baby was placed in a small casket made by a neighbor, and buried in an unmarked grave in the Spring Valley Cemetery. Such sad occurrences were commonplace in 1900. Almost one of every four babies would die before their first birthday.

In April of 1901, Mack and Alice Gibson would bring another baby into the world—that baby was my mother. She lived to be just four weeks short of her 98th birthday.

∽

1904 . . . Mack was finishing up a job, putting a new tire on a wagon wheel. Burl noticed he was ready to shrink the hot tire and came across the road to lend a hand.

"Here Mack, let me pour water on the tire while you hammer it into place."

Mack accepted the help gratefully, but did not bother to say so. He often did the same for Burl when he needed help repairing the bed on a wagon or lifting a buggy.

"Are you and Alice coming to the party tomorrow night at the Shaver's? You oughta bring your old five-string banjo. They's going to be some good fiddlers there."

"We didn't hear about the party till yesterday. I guess we'll go and stay awhile. There's near a full moon, and we can see to walk. Alice has not been feelin' too good and she gets plumb tuckered out after two mile or so and it's near that far up to the Shaver place. I'll carry the baby and Alice can carry the banjo and lantern. I sure would hate to step on a copperhead or rattler out looking for food."

Robert, the man Mack was repairing the wheel for, had been leaning up against the shop door listening to all the talk about parties.

"Heck Mack, we ain't gonna stay any later than that. I'll be going in my wagon and we pass right by your house. You and Alice and the little girl can ride in the back of the wagon with our young'uns. No use walkin' when you can ride. I'll throw a foot or so of hay in the wagon to help smooth out that bumpy road. It's a real booger up there near the Relaford farm."

"I'd be obliged Robert—Alice and the baby will enjoy the ride."

Arriving at the party, Alice took her little girl into the children's room. All the furniture was pushed back against the wall and three old quilts covered the floor. Around the wall were several cane-bottom chairs. There were already a dozen children on the floor playing with spools, homemade dolls, and two balls of yarn. They ranged in age from a few weeks to three or four years old. Several ladies were sitting around the wall, keeping a sharp eye on the young'uns. Some had brought knitting, but most were catching up on talk—who was sick, who was in a family way, who was courtin' who, who was gettin' married, and in very low whispers—what married man was seen coming out of the Widder Riggins' house after dark last Tuesday. They were very careful to make sure that neither the man, nor his wife, was in attendance. It was impolite to gossip about folks if they were in the same house.

Such parties were commonplace up until the late '30s. No invitations were issued by those hosting a party. Everyone was expected to come. Word was spread that so-and-so was having a party. If you heard the news, you were automatically invited. Refreshments were seldom served. Few before World War II drank coffee, other than for breakfast.

I was twenty years old before I ever drank a cup of coffee in a café. Café coffee cost a nickel and we had it at home for practically nothing. Why pay a nickel for something that was available free? The war changed all that. Being in the armed services was a twenty-four hour job. Most service mess halls never closed for coffee. You might not get much to eat in a mess hall, but we always had that greenish-colored G.I. coffee. In addition, most outfits had service clubs run by the Salvation Army, Red Cross, USO, NAAFI,* or simply a bunch of patriotic civilians from a nearby town. Hot coffee soon replaced water as a beverage with servicemen. The habit followed them into civilian life.

~

---

* NAAFI... Navy, Army, Air Forces Institute. NAAFI is a British organization similar to our Red Cross. They maintained service clubs throughout the world for Allied servicemen.

Ice was seldom available before 1930, so iced tea or cold cider was out. Cookies and cake were seldom served, as the lady of the house had no idea how many were coming. Food was expensive and money was scarce. Food simply was not wasted. Some farm families would bring in a bushel of apples, some might have a pan of roasted peanuts, and some would pop several dishpans full of popcorn. Such food was washed down with water from the spring or well, and sometimes with a swig of moonshine.

Usually, some of the men brought a gallon jug hid by a saddle blanket under the wagon seat. Every few minutes you might notice the men drifting toward the front door. Two or three would step outside and return a few minutes later with a rosy color on their cheeks. They pretended like no one knew where they kept sneaking off to, but everyone there over ten years old knew what was going on.

In the living room, people were sitting on the floor or standing with their back to the wall. A few kitchen chairs were offered to the elderly and infirm. It was understood that some, but not all, fiddlers and pickers needed to be seated. Music tonight was played on two fiddles, a mandolin, a five-string banjo, and a harmonica. There was a lot of foot stomping and hand clapping, but no dancing. Spring Valley was a Baptist community. Not many Protestant churches at the time approved of dances. Some were more moderate in their beliefs and could see nothing wrong with dancing itself, but anytime there was a dance in the community you could be sure of at least one or two fist fights, sometimes a shooting or knifing, a bit of hanky panky, and always a lot of serious drinking. And, it seemed there was a certain class of women that seldom attended a house party, but never missed a dance. Needless to say, very few married men got to go to such dances with their wife's approval—although some, by devious means, managed to attend. One of the favorite excuses was a coon hunt. Some of the men planned a coon hunt to coincide with the dance night. Once away from home the coonhounds were tied in the woods while the men sneaked back to kick up their heels.

About nine o'clock families started gathering together and saying their good-byes. By ten o'clock, the last guest had left for home.

∽

1907 ... On Friday afternoon, Mack met the mail hack as usual. Uncle Anderson Sanders sorted the mail and handed Mack a letter. A letter was a rare event in the Gibson household—more often than not, a letter contained bad news of some sort. He was so nervous he did not stay around to hear Uncle Anderson read his *Springdale News*. He hurried home to have Alice read the letter.

"Mack, we are going to have to take in my folks. Pa has the dropsy and can't walk no more. Mama says she just can't take care of him by herself. She is past forty years old, you know. Pa gets his Civil War pension. It is about twelve dollars a month now, and she says there's talk of getting an increase soon—she says she'll pay their way with us. I just don't know how we can handle them in this old two-room house. It's crowded enough as it is. 'Course we ain't got no choice. I can't turn down my folks when they are old and helpless."

"You know Alice, I've been thinkin.' We could build a house if we had just a bit more money. I've got near forty dollars saved up. I think I could put up a pretty good house for less than $120. I can buy good oak lumber from the mill at War Eagle for about six dollars a wagonload. I could buy about three loads of oak for around twenty dollars. I'd need six regular winders and about three little ones. They would cost about fifteen dollars. I'd need some nice pine to frame out the doors and winders and maybe for the inside walls and ceilings. That would be another twenty dollars or so . . . Then there are the shingles, some brick for the chimney, a little cement, some locks and door knobs, and some wallpaper. I'm sure I could get out for no more than $120 and I believe I can get it done for less than $100. I'll trade blacksmith work for the loan of Jack's wagon and team. I can do all the hauling. I'll need two fellers fer a week to help me get the framing up . . . that will be another ten dollars. Yes, I can do it for less than $100."

"We just have to do something," replied his young wife. "I'll write Ma today and ask if they can help a little with the building money."

Her answer was not long in coming back; a money order for sixty-eight dollars was enclosed with a letter. Ma explained that this would still leave her almost forty dollars. "Ma has a man who will move them in his wagon for six dollars," Alice said. "All they are bringing is a bed,

THE CENTURY BEGINS

My grandparents, Mack and Alice Gibson, lived here from 1900 until they moved to Springdale about 1960. Mack is seated in the rocker, with Alice standing behind him. The woman on right is Alice's sister, Myrtle Stanberry. Myrtle's brother and sister-in-law, Lee Kelly and Laura Mills Kelly, are in the swing.

bedclothes, and a few personal possessions. They don't have much of anything. She wants to keep back a little something for medicine and groceries after they move."

"Tell her to hold off a month if she can before moving," said Mack,. "I'll have us a new house built by then. I need to get to moving on it so it will be ready before winter. I know John will let us live with them till I can put up a house."

∼

Not long after the new house was built, Mack was asked to move his shop, which had been located on the highway in a building owned by Henry Sanders. Mack had been allowed to use the building rent-free in exchange for keeping Henry's horses shod and doing a little blacksmith work as Henry needed it. Now Henry was slowing down and selling off his horses. He no longer had need of blacksmith work.

He built a new shop near his house that included a chicken house, smokehouse, and a one-horse stable. Mack never had a well. During the sixty years he lived there, he either got water from the spring or from a neighbor's well across the road from his house.

The shop was nothing much but an open shed. There was no front door and the two windows by his forge were nothing but openings in the wall. They had to be left open to carry away coal smoke from the forge. The same was true of the wide cracks in the wall—they provided needed ventilation. Mack ran his blacksmith shop for over fifty years and never had anything stolen from the shop. I suppose there were two reasons why he never missed anything. One, there was nothing much worth stealing, and two, those passing by the unlocked shop were either too honest or too proud to steal.

The young blacksmith earned a few dollars a month—enough for the bare essentials. At least half the work Mack did was on credit, much of which went unpaid. It wasn't that that his customers were dishonest. Many of them just never got enough money ahead to pay their bills. They knew that Mack would understand. It seemed his friends had the attitude that they would much rather die owing him than beat him out of one penny.

I have many fond memories of the shop. On sunny afternoons, the sun coming through cracks in the wall cast brilliant parallel beams of light on the black coal smoke as it filled the old oak building. How I loved that smell. At the forge stood my grandfather, slowly turning the blower with his left hand while holding a pair of homemade tongs in his right. The tongs might be holding a horseshoe, a plow point, or some other piece of metal, which needed to be bent or sharpened. The sweat stood out on his forehead as he removed the red-hot metal from the forge, then, holding it on the anvil, he hammered it into shape with a definite rhythm.

Every blacksmith had his own beat on the anvil. My grandfather used four regular blows to the hot metal, then moving the hammer to one side, relaxed his arm, and let his hammer fall on the anvil by its own weight—bouncing a few times in a decaying staccato beat. His hammering had a very distinctive sound.

Naturally, I spent most of my time with my grandparents, and for the usual reasons. I was allowed to play with the coal forge and any other tools in the shop when it was not in use. Even though coal cost four dollars per load, I was allowed to use it as much as I wanted. I started out by gathering up all the old discarded horseshoes, heating them red-hot and bending the toes backward to a 90-degree angle. These made very nice and serviceable bookends. When the metal was bent to my expectations I plunged them into the slack-tub where the cold, dirty water cooled them. I shudder to think of how many I made and tossed aside. Today they would sell for at least ten dollars a pair.

Other projects from the forge were stove pokers, garden hoes, potholders, trivets, and of course metal stocks for my bean flips.

Today, neighbors are always complaining that the people living next door are noisy, or some other trivial problem. In Spring Valley, Pete Holmesley and my grandfather lived on adjacent lots. Pete had a gristmill and a woodworking shop, both powered by gasoline engines. When Pete cranked up one of his engines my grandmother would say, "Pete must have some work. I am glad he has a little money coming in."

Pete and his wife, Sally, felt the same way about the blacksmith shop. Though they lived and worked next door to each other there was never a single complaint from either family about noise.

∼

Sometimes we had a radio; other times, there was not money to spare for batteries. Radio was not of much use during the daylight hours but on most nights, you could hear WLW in Cincinnati, KTHS in Hot Springs, and XERA in Mexico. WLW was the nation's most powerful radio station. XERA was the station owned by the famous Dr. Brinkley who offered to restore men's youth and vigor by transplanting goat glands in the man. It was sure death for goats and not much better for Dr. Brinkley's patients. Even listening to those powerful stations' reception was far from perfect, with sounds often shattered by static caused by thunderstorms somewhere along the path between the radio and the radio station. Listening to Mack's old TRF radio is how we learned of the terrible plight facing the country during the Great Depression.

∼

It was 1906 when my great-grandparents Matilda and Francis Kelly moved in with Mack and Alice. Mr. Kelly died soon after in 1908 but Ma lived until 1934. He is buried in the Spring Valley Cemetery. By the time Ma died, the Spring Valley Cemetery was all but forgotten. Most graves were either unmarked or marked with a small stone, and weeds and brush pretty well obscured the cemetery. Furthermore, there was never a road to the little graveyard; you had to pass through a private farm pasture to get to it. While I have not visited the cemetery in years, a local man told me that someone had bulldozed the area, and that all the stone markers were in a large pile at one end of the former cemetery.

I must have been about eight years old when one morning I decided to venture deeper into the wooded area behind my granddad's place. It was an area I had never explored before. As usual, I was alone, and somewhat apprehensive. As I went higher up the wooded hillside, and farther back in the woods than I had ever been before, I was surprised to come upon the Spring Valley Cemetery. Cautiously, I advanced into the graveyard to read the tombstones.

A chill ran up by back. The dead silence, the old moss-covered gravestones and the sudden realization that I, too, was mortal and would someday be covered with earth made me want to run. I visualized ghosts arising from the damp ground, ready to do whatever ghosts are supposed to do—something terrible I was sure. Nevertheless, I stood my ground, even advancing a few feet nearer the largest gravestone in the cemetery. Suddenly an odd piercing sound broke the silence and a figure, unseen up until now, jumped from behind the granite stone. I was petrified for a few seconds, too terrified to run. Then I saw what it was—a large, wild, Tom Turkey.

I got my fear under control and began laughing at the situation. Strangely enough, my need to explore left me and I returned home in record time. I told my granddad about the turkey experience and he had a good laugh. He then told me a real story that sent even more chills up my back.

It seems that Mrs. Pruner had lost a leg in an accident some years past. She had Pete Holmesly build a box to hold the leg and buried it in the Spring Valley Cemetery. After the amputation, her stub of a leg started hurting something fierce. At a quilting, she told the ladies about her painful stub and how terrible the pain was. One of the ladies had had experience with amputations and explained to Mrs. Pruner that the cause of the pain was that her buried leg was turned in the wrong position. She assured Mrs. Pruner that if she would dig up the leg and reposition it in the box, her pain would disappear. Mrs. Pruner was skeptical but still in pain. She had a man go to the cemetery, dig up the leg remains and reposition them in the box. Her pain did seem to be much better—for a short time. As you might expect, the pain returned. Again she had the leg dug up and repositioned before re-burying.

It would seem to me that they had a better solution to the problem right before their eyes. The leg should have been smoked and hung in the smokehouse. Just think of the time and effort saved. When her stump started to pain her all she needed to do was go to the smokehouse and rotate the leg until the pain stopped. Sort of like tuning in a TV picture on one of the 1950 television sets.

CHAPTER 5

Charlie Vaughan

Charles Isham Vaughan married Mary Morris. They had four children: Ethel, Erton, Effie, and Bruce. The family lived on a farm in Vaughan Valley until the World War I period. C. I. had a weakness for fast women and hard liquor. He decided he could have it all if he moved to Springdale and bought the Arcade Hotel. Apparently he had more of both than he needed as he finally lost his farm and most of his money.

During the teens and '20s there were many salesmen or "drummers" out on the road trying to make a living. The Arcade served all their meals family style at two large dining tables—one for ordinary people, and one designated as the drummers table. Meals at the drummers' table cost thirty-five cents. A meal at the regular table cost ten cents less. As expected, the drummers' table had a better variety of food.

After eating, the drummers would often retire to the area in front of the hotel and take a seat in one of the rocking chairs. From their vantage point they had a curbside view of the small town activities. While watching the people—girls mostly—they picked their teeth with a gold toothpick which they carried in a small leather pouch.

Charlie moved back to the country on a fine farm in the Black Jack community that had been in the Vaughan family for years. After a short time he sold the farm to Lawrence Poole. Lawrence bought the farm for a bit over $3,000. The farm, if it ever goes up for sale, will bring many, many times what Lawrence paid for it.

The Vaughans may have been good hunters, avid explorers, and mediocre politicians, but A. J. Vaughan's descendants were never accused of being good businessmen. Charlie recognized the lack of business acumen in his sons. He said this of his son Erton: "If you gave Erton a new Cadillac early in the morning, and told him he had to make three trades before sundown, he would be lucky to come home with a rusty pocket knife with a broken blade."

Charlie moved back to Springdale, and bought a small grocery store near the railroad tracks on Caudle Street. He sold this store in the early '40s and bought a property at the "Y" on Mill Street. He operated this store until his death in the late '40s.

Charlie's half brother George lived on the corner of Holcomb Avenue and Maple Street in Springdale. Uncle George Vaughan and his wife are buried in Bluff Cemetery.

Uncle George's daughter Stella married Roy Joyce, owner of Joyce's "Been Here Always" Drugstore in Springdale.

Erton Vaughan and his wife Nell (Newton) had one son, Charles, and one daughter, Jackie. Jackie married a DVM while in college. She and "Doc" Church live in South Dakota. Charles was a decorated B-17 Pilot in the Eighth Air Force during World War II. When the war was over he returned to college and became a petroleum engineer. He worked for oil companies in the Houston area until he retired to Austin, Texas. He died when he was approximately 82 years old. He is survived by his wife Anne and one daughter, Lynne. Erton and Nell are buried in Memorial Cemetery between Rogers and Bentonville, Arkansas.

My dad told me an interesting story about his days on the farm in Vaughan Valley. He was rather sickly when growing up and it was decided that his tonsils were the problem. He saddled up his horse and rode to Hindsville to see Dr. Hill. He tied his horse to the rail at the livery stable just as Dr. Hill drove up in his horse and buggy. Dad walked over to the old doctor and told him he had come to have his tonsils cut out. Dr. Hill got down from his buggy and said, "Let me take a look at those tonsils now." He backed Dad up against a wall, took some instruments from his bag, and snipped the tonsils out while there in the livery stable. Dad got back on his horse and rode home. The rest of the story is this: the good doctor only got part of the tonsils, and

Dad had to have the job re-done at a later date. It is amazing so many survived frontier medical science.

In 1938 we moved to Springdale where my dad got a job working for Late Chevrolet. In 1955, he and Mr. Late got into one of their big arguments and Dad quit him and worked with me until his death. He died September 23, 1981 and is buried in Friendship Cemetery.

Bruce Vaughan Jr., standing in our 1917 Model T Ford.

This photo of me, circa 1923, was made at our farm home near the Madison County line, about one-half mile north of Arkansas Highway 412. I have very little memory of my life there. Dad bought the Habberton store and home soon after this photo was made.

CHAPTER 6

Habberton

I remember my youth and the feeling that will never come back again . . . the feeling that I could last forever—outlast the sea, the earth, and all men.

—JOSEPH CONRAD (1857–1924)

My memories of life on the McDavid place consist largely of stories told to me by my parents. The only firsthand experience I recall was that of sitting on the lap of a young man who lived with us and helped Dad on the farm.

Marion Henry, the young farm hand, must have been a considerate and patient person. After supper it was our custom to retire to the living room. Like the rest of the country at that time, we had no radio or TV, and very few magazines. I would crawl up in Marion's lap, and by the dim, flickering, yellow light from an old kerosene lamp I would watch as he thumbed through the Sears or Montgomery Ward catalogs showing me the toys. My favorite page was the one with roller skates. It would be some twelve years later before we lived near a sidewalk where I could learn to skate. When the day finally came, the sidewalk was less than one block in length, and we lived there only three months.

While on the farm we had two dogs: a bulldog named Bobby and a hound named Rat. Rat earned his name the hard way—catching rats around the barn. I suppose it was because we had such an abundance of rats and mice that the place was infested with copperhead snakes. No rattlers, king snakes, chicken snakes, or black snakes—just copperheads.

My mother told me about the day she let me go with her to gather eggs. I was around two years old at the time and actually have no memory of this incident. We did not have a henhouse, so the chickens built a nest anywhere they wanted—usually in the hay stored in the barn. To find eggs it was necessary to feel around in the hay. With so many copperheads around, egg gathering was not a chore one looked forward to.

My mother was gathering the eggs when she saw a "whole pile" of copperheads near the south end of the barn. She ran from the barn yelling, "Bruce, Bruce, come here quick! There is a whole big bunch of copperheads in the barn!"

Dad grabbed a hoe with a long handle and came running. He disappeared into the dark interior of the barn and emerged a few minutes later with three dead copperheads draped over the end of his hoe. "That will take care of those," he said, dropping them on the ground. "You can go ahead with your egg gathering, Hazel, but be careful," he cautioned.

My mother reentered the barn, screamed, and ran back out. "You killed the wrong bunch!" she yelled.

Dad went back into the barn the second and time came out with dead snakes on his hoe. He only killed two that time.

It was a rare week when at least one copperhead did not make an appearance somewhere on the farm. Dad decided there was a den of them somewhere.

∽

The Rolla Fitch farm faced old Highway 68, now 412. Our farm joined the Fitch farm on the northwest corner. Early one morning Rolla knocked on our door. He came in our house with a very serious look on his face. "Bruce, you have to come with me and see something," said our neighbor.

Dad knew from the sound of Rolla's voice that something serious had happened. It seems that our two dogs, Rat and Bobby, had paid a visit to the neighbor's farm during the night and killed more than forty of his sheep. The visit cost Dad $175—what he had saved up, plus a small bank loan, paid for the sheep. Dad had little choice—he removed his shotgun from the wall, walked the two dogs to a wooded area, shot and killed both, and buried them in the woods.

At that very moment Dad decided that farming was not meant for him. After two years on the farm all he had to show for it was a loan at the bank that he had to pay off within six months.

~

In the summer of 1925, Dad bought (on credit of course) the Habberton General Store and home from P.G. Henson. It was a very nice place for that time in history. The house was substantially built and average in size. The store building was small and poorly stocked. In addition to the house and store building, the place had a small barn and a blacksmith shop on the two-acre (estimated) plot of ground.

If I remember correctly, the blacksmith shop was rented out for four dollars a month, but it was rarely open for business. It seems that the blacksmith spent more time testing "shine" than working. The shop was torn down soon after we moved there and the site converted to a croquet ground.

Before Dad opened the store for business, he called on his uncle, Albert Morris, an excellent carpenter and woodworker, to double the size of the store and construct a new mill behind the store.

I remember one feature of the mill very well. In the 1920s, nails came in small wooden barrels commonly known as nail kegs. Uncle Albert must have used over a dozen nail kegs as a foundation for the mill building. A hole was dug in the ground about six inches deep, and a nail keg was placed in each hole. When all the measurements were made and placement of the kegs finalized, they were filled with concrete. Two large bolts were inserted in the concrete while it was still wet. The nail kegs made a very solid foundation for the building. When I built my store building on Highway 71, I borrowed the idea and sunk two thirty-gallon iron oil drums completely in the ground and filled them with concrete. A four-inch pipe on top of the drums supported the twelve-inch I-beams of the roof. After standing for over half a century, the concrete block building is still sturdy as the day it was built.

Habberton in the mid-1920s was a dusty crossroads in a fertile valley that reached to Slaughter Mountain on the west to well beyond the White River on the north and east.

The town itself was little more than a general store and post office. A two-room school and one church house about one-half mile south of the store, along with three homes, constituted the entire village. Back then, the Habberton store was about five miles east of Fayetteville. Today the store site is practically in the city of Fayetteville.

Our neighbor, Walter Nelson, bought one of the new Delco 32-volt light systems. Such systems were very commonplace during the '20s and '30s. I suppose there were other manufacturers of home lighting systems but Delco sold so many that the name Delco was used to refer to any home lighting plant. It was a good working system. Buyers of a Delco were furnished with everything needed, from a small building to house the light plant and batteries to wiring for the house.

A typical Delco system used a one-cylinder gasoline engine driving a 32-volt generator. The generator charged a bank of batteries. When the battery voltage dropped to a pre-determined voltage, the gasoline engine started automatically. It beat kerosene lamps by a long way.

Dad made some sort of agreement with Mr. Nelson and they strung a wire along some fence posts to our house and store. Today, I know a bit more about electricity and am sure that Dad and Mr. Nelson overloaded the little Delco power plant.

∼

It was the age of flappers and jazz. Legal whiskey was not available. I remember one illegal still in the area, as well as two men who did a bit of bootlegging on the side to supplement their limited income. Young people from Springdale drove out to country stores looking for Castoria and imitation vanilla extract. Both were largely alcohol and when mixed with Coca-Cola it made a rather potent beverage. Most of those who bought the alcohol-laced liquids drove on east to the White River, built a campfire on one of the gravel bars, then drank and partied all night.

Another popular item in the store was "canned heat." This alcohol-based solid looked a lot like a candle. It was made for portable stoves on which campers could heat their food. Canned heat was dissolved in everything from aftershave lotion to patent medicine to make a dangerous and deadly drink. It was highly toxic and had a kick like a mule.

Another means of getting high during prohibition time was by mixing milk and gasoline—a recipe used mostly by bums and incurable alcoholics. During this time home delivery of milk was made by milk trucks, very early in the morning, always before breakfast. Those desperate for a drink would steal milk from a front porch, pour half of it on the ground, then go to closed service stations and drain the pump hoses into the milk bottle. (Gas hoses often had a little gas left in them from the last use.) Then as now, laws that attempted to make getting high difficult also made it more attractive—especially for young people.

This was in the days before Prestone and other antifreeze liquids. To keep your car from freezing you drained the block and radiator in the winter. Filling your car with water before using it and then draining the water when the car was not in use was a constant aggravation. The answer was to use alcohol. It had all the cooling qualities of water and a much lower freezing point. There was a drawback: in the city especially, there were men waiting to drain your radiator as soon as you parked your car. More fastidious alcoholics filtered the radiator alcohol through a loaf of bread before drinking. Stealing auto alcohol was so common that few even used it in larger towns.

A well-known bootlegger lived on the road between Habberton and Springdale. Across the road from his house was a grape vineyard and strawberry patch. The old strawberry shed, seldom used for its intended purpose of packing berries during the growing season, became a very important part of his illegal sales of moonshine. To place an order, a customer called the bootlegger on the telephone and let their needs be known. At that time they were quoted a price. Immediately after the phone call the bootlegger would take his wares, usually in a grocery sack or a cardboard box, across the road to the old shed. Sometime later the customer would come whizzing down the road and stop his car near the shed. Pretending to look at his tires, or engine, or flowers beside the road, he would make sure no one was watching, dash in the shed, leave his money under a well- known rock, grab the sack, and proceed on his way. So much for law and order.

Is it possible that the "roar" in the "Roaring Twenties" was only the moans of so many people with a hangover?

∼

Now that Dad doubled the size of his store he was ready for growth. Country stores at the time were expected to stock everything from hardware to dry goods. Although not in great depth, Dad stocked the store with nuts and bolts, plowshares, nails, barbed wire, fertilizer, barrels of kerosene and turpentine, rope, paint, hand tools, wagon tires, horseshoes, cotton, work shoes, overalls, shirts, shaving supplies, patent medicine, feeds and seeds, lanterns, lamps, and of course, groceries.

Many grocery items came in bulk. Lard came in five-gallon metal containers referred to as "lard stands." Customers bought lard either by the pound or by price. ("Give me fifteen cents worth of lard.") Scales on the counter read both. Other items sold in bulk were sugar, coffee (coffee also came in packs and tins), pinto beans, and meal. Flour came in sacks made of a printed material suitable for making dresses. Many housewives attended church in a dress made from flour sacks. A lightweight metal scoop was used for everything but lard, which was measured out with a cast aluminum scoop. Something in the aluminum was supposed to release lard without sticking, allowing the storekeeper to drop the lard smoothly into cardboard trays used for delivery to the customer.

We had no refrigeration. When strawberry harvest time arrived, a lot of migrant workers—"strawberry pickers"—arrived. They stayed anyplace where they could find free shelter. Of course they had no cooking facilities and depended upon inexpensive, ready-to-eat foods. Dad always bought a long tube or casing of bologna and a wheel of cheese. The bologna was hung from the ceiling with a piece of heavy string. The wheel of cheese was covered with cloth and placed on the counter. When a customer wanted a pound of bologna, it was unhooked from the ceiling string, laid on the counter and a piece cut off. To make it easy, the bologna maker used a non-toxic ink to put one-pound markers along the length of the casing. The bologna must have been loaded with preservatives. None went bad, even during the ninety-degree heat of summer.

More prosperous families bought beans, meal, sugar, and such by the sack—usually fifty pounds. Kerosene (coal oil) sold for ten cents a gallon. Customers brought their own coal oil can to the store to be filled. Some families bought it five gallons at a time.

One of the new items in the store was sliced bread, available in either a five cent or ten cent loaf. When first introduced, sliced bread was a penny or two higher in cost, but very soon all bread came sliced.

Oleo, or margarine, was relatively new. Without added coloring, oleo looks exactly like lard. In an effort to keep oleo sales from competing with butter, the dairy lobby in our nation's capitol got a law passed prohibiting oleo manufacturers from adding yellow color to oleo. Instead, oleo came with a small cellophane pack of yellow powder. Before using the oleo, the housewife had to put the oleo in a bowl and stir in the yellow coloring. It was quite a chore to get a good mix, and if it did not mix thoroughly, you ended up eating striped "butter." It was years before this ridiculous law was changed.

The Model T Ford was rapidly becoming commonplace on the farm. Dad decided to install two gasoline pumps in front of his store. A large hole was dug for two tanks—one for regular gasoline and one for a "No-Nox" grade. He went with a relatively new company at the time: the Gulf Oil Company. They installed two brightly painted orange pumps near the corner of the store, and hung up a large round sign advertising "Good Gulf Gasoline." The price at the time was twenty cents a gallon—plus or minus a cent or two.

The gasoline pumps were a thing of beauty. Each pump was about nine feet tall with a ten-gallon glass container on the top. A side mounted lever, when moved forward and backward, pumped gasoline from the underground storage tanks into the glass bowl. There was nothing automatic or electric about the pump. The gasoline flowed from the glass bowl into the automobile's tank by gravity.

To announce this new service at the Habberton Store, Dad gave away hundreds of wood rulers that were calibrated in gallons. How could this work? Different cars had different sizes of gas tanks. As it turned out, this was not a big problem as ninety percent of the customers were driving a Model T Ford. The T was a basic automobile, with no money wasted on such things as instrumentation. To know how much gas you had in a T, you had to remove the front seat, unscrew the gas cap, and poke a stick of some sort in the tank and see how high the wet area was. So, the bright orange Gulf ruler worked great on a Model T and not so good on anything else.

I soon learned that by pulling on the gas pump's filler hose, pressure was applied to the nozzle. It was great fun watching the gas squirt several feet from the pump—an experiment both highly dangerous and costly. Dad warned me that this activity must stop immediately. I continued to spray the ground with gasoline any time I thought he was not looking. My failure to do as he said resulted in one of three—and by far the hardest—spankings my Dad ever gave me. I left the pumps alone after that.

We also sold motor oil and kerosene, or coal oil, as customers often called it. Canned motor oil was still some time in the future. Kerosene was pumped out of a 55-gallon drum with a crank-operated hand pump. A spring-loaded return pipe fell back to its position under the spout when you removed your container. You could turn the crank all day long and you were just circulating the kerosene. I had a great time turning the crank and watching the kerosene flow from the spout, back into the return pipe. One day I started thinking—exactly what would happen if I pushed the return pipe to one side, and then turned the crank? The results were a little short of spectacular. I was covered head to foot with kerosene. The volatile liquid began to blister my skin before I got up enough nerve to tell my Mother what had happened. She quickly stripped all my clothes off, filled a #2 washtub full of soapy water and decontaminated me. I had a blister similar to sunburn for the next few days.

Near the McDavid farm was a boarded-up gristmill. It had closed soon after opening because of a lack of business. The equipment inside was like new. Dad bought all the equipment and had it installed in the mill Uncle Albert built behind the store.

Unfortunately, Dad had never bothered to see how many farmers in the Habberton area had cornfields. No corn, no milling. I don't think the mill ever took in enough to pay for the large gasoline engine that ran the mill. When he did have a little grinding to do I was always there watching.

Gristmills in the years before we had electricity were a beautiful sight to behold. Because of exhaust fumes and noise, the engine that ran all the machines was located outside the building. A belt and pulley arrangement from the large one-cylinder engine drove a line shaft inside the mill. Pulleys on the line shaft, in turn, powered each machine: one shelled the corn, another ground the corn into meal, and still another ground up the corn and the cob into a feed for farm animals called "chops." I remember very well the day I climbed atop a pile of corncobs, then on up on one of the rafters. I started across the mill crawling along the two-by-six-foot length of wood. About halfway across I fell, but was saved when one strap of my overalls caught on a bracing bolt. There I hung, about eight feet above the floor. Of course I started screaming. Dad got a ladder and helped me down. In retrospect, he might have been more successful in the store if he had not had me constantly creating problems.

∼

A man in Springdale raised pit bulls for fighting. One day in town he hit my dad up for a forty-dollar loan. It seems he had to have forty dollars in a hurry. I suspect it was to pay off a gambling debt. Dad loaned him the money and promptly wrote it off as a bad investment. On a trip into town at a later date Dad drove by the kennel and asked the breeder to pay the debt. Of course the man had no money, but offered Dad a pit bull as full payment. I suppose Dad thought it better to have the dog than nothing, so he came home with this six-month old "guard dog."

I remember Dad walked the dog to the back of the store, put out a dish of water for him, and left him securely tied to a table leg. He took me aside and cautioned me at great length to "never, never, go near that vicious dog." Felix, as the dog was named, was a guard dog—nothing else. I remember Dad's words: "Harley' (the breeder) told me Felix is the most vicious dog he has ever raised." I looked at the white bulldog and thought how pretty he was. He had one black eye and a black spot on his back. He looked a lot like the dog in *Our Gang* movies.

I waited a long time—perhaps as long as fifteen minutes—for Dad to leave the store to pump gas for a customer. As soon as he was gone I went to the back of the store, grabbed the dog around the neck and gave him a big hug. When Dad came back in the store I was sitting on the floor while Felix licked my ear. Dad gave up. He decided it was impossible to keep a small boy and a dog separated. Felix raised me. Though our yard was not fenced, Felix never left the yard. He allowed anyone to come and go and never even growled. Yet, anyone who came in the yard and touched me was instantly bitten. He also would bite anyone who came in the yard and tried to remove anything. One Sunday we were gone for the day and a neighbor lady decided she needed to "borrow" my wagon to move some flowerpots. As soon as she started to pull the wagon away, she was bitten. In all, Felix bit some twenty people—none seriously, and all were doing something they should not have been doing.

The bootlegger I mentioned earlier always rode his horse to the store. One day he brought his big German Shepherd dog with him. He tied his horse to the hitching post and yelled for Dad to come outside. "Bruce," said the bootlegger, "Lock up that little bulldog of yours. I'm afraid my dog might kill him."

Dad went to the front door. "Don't worry about Felix, he will not leave the front yard, and even if he did he can take care of himself."

The bootlegger was obviously looking for trouble. "I was just trying to be neighborly. I know your dog would not stand a chance against a real dog."

This banter went on until he made Dad mad: "Why don't you take that German Shepherd into my yard under the tree where he can keep cool?"

Felix came charging around the house and made one long leap. He grabbed the German Shepherd by the throat and never turned loose. To keep Felix from killing the dog, Dad got a leaf rake and hooked it into Felix's collar so he could pull him off. Felix never had a scratch. The German Shepherd headed down the road yelping and bleeding.

Mr. 'X' never brought his dog to the store again, and the incident was never mentioned.

When I read all the adverse things written about pit bulls, I remember Felix. Most people just do not understand the breed. No pet is more loving than a pit bull. But they are very protective, fearless, and loyal. This sometimes leads to unpleasant encounters between the dog and those who do not respect the pit bull's home turf.

Felix could be vicious with strangers, and no one dared lay a hand on either my mother or me or they would be bitten before they knew what was happening. Felix died of a broken heart some ten years later, when we went on a trip and left him with my grandfather, Charlie Vaughan. According to him, Felix refused to eat or drink, and while we were gone he died. I will always suspect that Felix was helped out of this world by my grandfather who never cared for the dog.

~

Dad was feeling the optimism and enjoying the flow of easy money that most of the country shared in the 1920s. He drove the Model T to Habberton, but within weeks after taking possession of the store he traded the Ford for a large Buick coupe. I remember the car well because of its much quieter and smoother ride, as compared to the Ford T. From the time he bought the Buick my Dad complained about the five to six miles per gallon of gas it used on those rough, steep, crooked roads.

Within the year he traded the Buick for a 1928 Plymouth, a recently introduced automobile. It got better mileage but the ride did not come close to the smoothness of the big Buick. I did not understand that all this car trading cost a lot of money—I was excited because we had a new car. The feature of the Plymouth I remember best was roll-down awnings outside each window. They were brightly colored canvas and when rolled up fit into a chrome cylinder. Good idea—as long as you kept your speed under 20 mph.

One day Dad drove to Fayetteville in his Plymouth. About once a week he went to the bank to deposit the store receipts. Several hours passed and he did not return home. My mother was running the store and gas station by herself. Though I was only five years old, I could sense her anxiety.*

About five o'clock that afternoon Dad returned home, cold sober, driving a canary yellow, 1928 Chrysler convertible—with the top down, of course. It was a very sporty car at the time. It seems that when he arrived at the bank that morning, everyone was talking about a car race that was going to happen that afternoon. John Graue, a distant relative of Dad's, worked for the Chrysler dealer in Fayetteville. He is the man who sold Dad the 1928 Plymouth. When the Chrysler dealer received the car from the factory he had his mechanics do everything they could to make the car faster. Word of this Chrysler activity reached the Chevrolet dealer. A rivalry developed between the two dealers. The Chevrolet dealer had his mechanics do all they could to hop up the new Chevy. As each dealer claimed to have the fastest car, it appeared the only way to settle the argument was to have a race. The winner of the race was to get the competitor's car. On TV today they call it racing for "pinks," meaning the pink slip of ownership.

---

*When Dad disappeared for several hours you could depend upon him coming home drunk. He did not drink daily, but when he did drink, he made up for his times of sobriety. Sometimes we were lucky; he would pass out somewhere and not come home until he had slept it off.

It has been my experience that alcohol brings out the true personality of the drinker. I have known rough and tough men who, when drunk, seemed to love everyone. During World War II we had a crew chief that you dared not cross. He was a master sergeant and did not hesitate to use his rank to punish anyone who crossed him. Yet when drinking, he was almost sure to start reciting poetry. In reality, his gruffness was a cover for a very sensitive person.

Dad was not like that. When he was drunk he cursed a lot and wanted to fight. He sometimes tried to find his pistol or shotgun that my mother had hidden. He wanted to kill someone who, in his foggy mind, had slighted him in some way. His rampage ended with him throwing up all over the floor and furniture, then passing out and sleeping for several hours. The odor of someone drunk on moonshine whiskey is unforgettable. A few months after prohibition was repealed, he quit drinking and remained sober the last forty-five years of his life.

The straightest section of road at the time was old Highway 71 South by Drake Field. From the foot of the hill in front of today's 142nd Field Artillery Armory, to the city limits of Greenland, is over a mile. The two dealers got the police to post guards at each end of the road, closing the road to traffic for the much-anticipated contest between the two dealers. It was a more laid-back time then and no one seemed to mind the road closing. People were expected to act as individuals, so no one complained about safety, road closing, or gambling. This race had been the talk of the town for several days. I understand that a good many side bets were placed.

The race went as planned, with the Chrysler winning by several car lengths. Dad simply had to own that automobile. I have no idea what he paid for it, but I well remember the day three years later when my dad and mother sat on the front porch of my grandfather's house wiping tears from their eyes as the new owner drove it away for $175.

~

Radio was beginning to appear in homes across America. One day Dad brought home a large table-model radio with a tall horn-type loudspeaker. I was probably four years old at the time. I remember it had three tuning dials and Dad got a writing tablet from the store and when he would tune in a station he carefully wrote down the setting of every dial on the radio. In retrospect, I am sure it was a TRF circuit because sometimes when tuning in a station there would be a lot of squealing, howling, and screeching before a voice or music was heard. The floor beneath the radio table was littered with batteries. One was a lead acid automobile battery. I was cautioned not to go near the batteries because the acid would burn your skin. Surprisingly, I heeded their warnings.

I later learned that the radio used three 45-volt B batteries and a 22.5-volt C battery, in addition to the car battery. The radio was not included in the auction sale when the Great Depression forced the sale of our household furniture as well as all the commercial stock. We took the radio with us when we returned to Spring Valley, but it was never played—we could not afford to buy batteries. We made several moves during the Depression and somewhere along the way the radio disappeared.

Air conditioning was a long way in the future. Electric fans were the primary means of keeping cool in the summertime, but electric fans need electricity and that we did not have. Even though we were tied on to a neighbor's Delco light plant, it was only 32 volts and not sufficient to run electrical cooling. The primary way of keeping cool while sleeping was to open up the bedroom to Mother Nature's cooling breezes. We had two back porches on the Habberton house; Dad screened one in to make a sleeping room. It worked pretty well after about 10:00 P.M. There was one big drawback to the outdoor sleeping room: bullfrogs.

Across the road on our farm was a small stock pond. In the summer if we went without rain for a few weeks the pond lost water and a small island in the center of the pond would appear. It was on this island, and around the perimeter of the pond that the bullfrogs convened. Their nightly serenade started about dark and lasted until daylight.

We also had quite a mosquito problem. Dad mixed up a concoction of chemicals and sprayed the pond weekly. This took care of the mosquito problem but did little to control the mighty voices of the frogs.

One day, after a sleepless night, Dad told my mother he had figured out a way to do away with the frog problem—he was going to dynamite them. He drove to Springdale and bought six sticks of dynamite along with the blasting caps and fuse line. That evening about dusk the nightly chorus of bullfrogs began. Dad put on his rubber boots, gathered up his explosives, waded out into the stagnant water, and planted his dynamite on the island. He made sure he had a long fuse so he would have time to get back to our front porch before the explosion.

He lit the fuse and came stomping through the water, hitting the dry ground at a run. He must have had a surplus of fuse because it seemed a full minute passed before it went off. It was the loudest sound I ever heard—water and mud must have gone fifty feet in the air.

We sat on the porch in dead silence. Not a frog's croaking could be heard. Dad smiled, looked at my mother and said, "I finally got rid of that problem. We should sleep well tonight." The silence lasted perhaps ten minutes before the frogs regained their composure. Then, in their excitement, the frogs let loose with louder croaking than ever before. I doubt that Dad killed a frog, but he sure woke them up. That night they kept not only us but our three neighbors awake all night.

∼

While living in Habberton, I believe the year was 1927 or 1928, a most amazing and unexplainable phenomenon occurred. The Ellerton family lived in a newly built small bungalow on their small acreage about one mile northwest of the Habberton store. The neat home was surrounded by flowers, and they had planted a nice large vegetable garden just south of the new home. The family was well liked and an asset to the community.

I was playing in our front yard when someone came running down the road yelling, "Ellerton's house is on fire—they need help!"

Well, the store had two or three men inside and they came running out, got in Dad's car, and went flying down the road in a cloud of dust. My mother heard the commotion and left her housework and went to the store. Dad had not taken the time to tell her he was leaving.

Some time later Dad and the other men returned to the store. "How bad was it?" asked my mother. "Did they lose everything?"

"No," replied Dad, "we moved all the furniture outside to the yard. Only the wallpaper in one room was burned. We were able to beat it out with brooms and wet feed sacks. They are pulling all the paper off the walls in that one room. When they get that done we will go back and help them get the furniture back in the house."

"I'm so glad," said my mother. "They seem like such nice people. I was afraid their home had burned down."

She had hardly finished speaking when another shout came from the road. "Ellerton's house is burning again. Help!"

For the second time that day all men in the store ran out, jumped in a car, and rushed to the Ellerton place.

"What happened," asked my mother, "did you not put the fire out completely the first time?"

"Yes, we had the fire out," replied Dad. "This time the fire started in a bedroom. I don't understand it at all—there was nothing in there to start a fire. The wallpaper just flared up. A few of us men are going back tonight after we eat supper and keep a watch on things. Walter, 'Whoop,' and Chess are out there now."

Later that evening while the men were sitting out in the front yard keeping watch, a chest of drawers suddenly flared up. "It really surprised us," said Dad, "It was just as though someone had tossed a teacup full of gasoline on a burning match. We grabbed some blankets and smothered it out. Nothing in the chest burned."

That night as the men waiting, two more spontaneous fires erupted on items widely separated. The fires continued throughout the night. The next morning calls were placed to the Fayetteville Fire Department and the University of Arkansas. Representatives from the university's chemistry, agriculture, and engineering departments, along with city firemen, arrived within hours. They were not disappointed; spontaneous fires continued to erupt all that day and into the night. About forty-eight hours after the initial fire, the fires ceased.

No final determination as to cause of the strange phenomenon was ever agreed upon. Two days before the fires the Ellerton family had closed the house up tight and sprayed with an insecticide; the chemistry professor thought that might be a clue.

As usual, there were those who attributed the strange fires to the occult or supernatural. The countryside around Habberton, then and now, is well covered by small churches. The strange fires gave preachers a chance to remind their flock that the Devil is still among us and active in our daily lives.

∽

During the first part of the 20th century many farmers in Northwest Arkansas raised strawberries. A modest-sized strawberry patch often produced several hundred dollars of income every spring. At a time when jobs were practically nonexistent, strawberries were a boon to the economy, providing jobs for those willing to work hard for small wages. Even if you were lucky enough to have a regular job the pay was usually low, less than ten dollars a week. A good strawberry picker could earn more than two dollars a day. Entire families followed the crops. Starting in the south in early April, they followed the crops northward, living in barns, tents, or any other shelters they could find near the strawberry patches. A few pickers had what was perhaps the first motor homes—a crude wood shelter built on the back of a Model T truck.

The average strawberry patch was small—less than twenty acres. One or two women were paid a daily salary to run the strawberry shed. It was their job to nail the strawberry crates together, pack the berries, and, of course, pay the pickers when they brought in a carrier of berries. The usual pay during the Depression years was between three and four cents a quart. Few growers ever paid as much as five cents per quart. The picker was paid in tickets, not in cash. The tickets could be exchanged for cash at the end of the day.

∽

It was sometime in the late '20s when a grocery salesman came to the store and told Dad that the Palace Theatre in Fayetteville had installed a "talking picture" machine. I remember that he said it was so loud you could hear it while walking down the sidewalk outside the theatre. Dad asked him what talking picture they were showing. He told Dad that it was called *The Jazz Singer* and that it starred a fellow named Al Jolson. I did not understand what he was talking about. That night as we were eating supper, Dad told my mother what the salesman told him about the Palace Theatre. My mother seemed very excited and said she would sure love to see this new miracle. So after eating we put on clean clothes, got in the new yellow convertible and went to Fayetteville to see *The Jazz Singer*.

When we parked on the square at Fayetteville, Dad raised the hood on the car and removed a part from the engine. I had no idea why or what he was doing. He told my mother that the only thing he disliked about the convertible was that they were easy to steal. He said that all a thief had to do was slit the top with a pocketknife, unlock the doors, and short across the switch. Later I learned that the part he removed was the distributor rotor.

The movie started and it was loud. I ate about half a bag of popcorn, then went to sleep. I was unimpressed with the movie.

∼

In 1926, sales of the Model T Ford were disappointing. It was plain that the Model T with the puny four-cylinder engine, planetary drive transmission, mechanical two-wheel brakes, limited speed, and even less comfort, was at the end of an era. The public was switching to General Motors and Chrysler products, as well as automobiles made by smaller manufacturers such as Nash, Packard, Reo, Willis, and others.

Edsel Ford, after much effort, convinced his father to shut down the Ford Motor Company and completely redesign their product. Of course this meant months of empty showrooms for Ford dealers across the country. Unconvinced that the public wanted or needed a car better than the Model T, Henry Ford reluctantly agreed to shut down and retool. I'm sure some dealerships with marginal financing went out of business during the six-month closure.

There was much speculation about the "New Ford." The Ford Company was in the papers almost daily; news articles about their closure translated into advertising that would have cost millions. Many coming into the Habberton store talked of buying a new car but said they were waiting to see what the "New Ford" looked like. For several months no one talked of a Ford without the prefix "New."

On December 2, 1927, the first "New Ford," better known as the Model A, rolled off the assembly line. When it finally arrived on dealer floors, many potential customers were disappointed. Clearly the Model A was an improvement, but it was a bit short of what people were hoping for. With its four-cylinder engine, mechanical brakes, and sparse interior, there was little to be excited about.

The Model A offered a three-speed transmission and a choice of exterior colors, but few added conveniences. The gasoline tank in the A was located in front of the driver, behind the dash. It was no longer necessary to dismount and remove the front seat to check or add fuel. Some cars of the period offered hydraulic brakes, a much quieter ride, and a lot more instrumentation. Insulation of the Model A was nonexistent thus making conversation difficult because of road noise.

Although the Model A sold well considering the Depression years, Ford management realized they must offer something new and attractive to the buying public. When Ford introduced the V-8 engine the public finally had what they had been looking for, without realizing it. I remember our next-door neighbor buying one of the first V-8 Fords. He demonstrated to my dad that at idle, you could not hear the motor running from just a few feet away. Within a year, the Ford became the favorite car of police departments and the criminal element alike. It was also the automobile of choice for bootleggers.

~

I remember two events that occurred in the fall of 1927. I started to school, even though I was only five and a half years old, and would complete the first year of school before my sixth birthday. The other milestone of 1927 was attending my first county fair. Of the two, I think the county fair was more educational.

Winnie Stobaugh, the young lady who taught the first four grades at Habberton, lived directly across the road from our home and store. I was very fond of Winnie and anxious to start school. On that first day of school my mother dressed me in a new pair of overalls, tied a shiny new tin cup to one strap of my overalls (our school was sanitary—each student had to furnish his own cup), handed me a bright red school bag complete with a five-cent "Big Chief" tablet and pencils, loaded me in the Chrysler, and drove me to school. I did not carry a lunch as first graders attended only the morning classes.

I was a little shy, and more than a little scared. There were so many strange kids, and I had no idea what to expect once I was inside the school. At 8:30 A.M., Winnie stepped to the porch of the schoolhouse and started ringing a hand-held bell. All the kids ran for the door—well, all of them but me. I decided I had much rather sit on the porch and watch several hawks circling overhead. Winnie came outside and patiently explained to me that all schoolchildren must come inside. I hesitated. Her patience at an end, Winnie picked me up, carried me inside, and somewhat firmly placed me at my desk. While I remained at my desk until recess—and the period between recess and noon—I never found school as interesting as what was happening outside.

The county fair was different. I could have stayed there forever. The things I liked best of all were the midway rides. I remember one called "The Barrel." I wanted to ride it, but my mother thought it better if I observed from a safe distance. I was allowed to ride the merry-go-round, and little cars that looked like ducks. However it was the large barrel, brightly painted, with a door on the side that kept my interest. People would go inside and someone would close the door. Then the barrel started spinning, slowly at first, then gaining speed. Sounds of laughter, then shrieks and screams came from inside the barrel. I tried to imagine what was going on inside to evoke all the screaming. When the barrel riders emerged a minute or so later, none were bleeding, bruised, or limping. I just could not imagine what it was like inside a barrel turning that fast. I really wanted to go inside and ride that barrel.

We returned home near nightfall, and I fell asleep that night thinking of the barrel. Early the following morning I went in the store and asked Dad if he had an empty nail keg I could have. Before World War II, nails were shipped in wooden barrels about fourteen inches wide and two feet high. The store sold a lot of nails, so Dad always had several empty ones. He told me to go in the storeroom and find what I needed. I picked out a nice-looking barrel and carried it to the backyard. I went in the garage where Dad kept his tools and picked out a one-inch bit and a brace. After drilling a hole in opposite sides of the barrel I inserted a broom handle through the barrel, leaving about one foot of broomstick sticking out on each side. I dragged two wood sawhorses to the yard and placed the barrel between them. When I gave it a spin, the broomstick rolled along the top of the sawhorse and fell off the end. I knew how to stop that—I drove a large nail into the top of the sawhorse on each side of the broomstick. Now I could spin the barrel and the broom handle stayed in place between the two large nails. I noticed the barrel turned a bit slower as the broom handle pushed against the nails. Obviously this was a problem that could be solved by a liberal application of another store item—axle grease. There was a big improvement after getting everything well greased. The barrel spun several turns with each push I gave it. One problem remained—I needed a door on the open end. I found an old bucket lid that was a near-perfect fit. I kept it in place by two small egg-crate nails.

I was all ready to go—if only I had a passenger. At that moment he came around the corner of the house—our family cat. I grabbed the cat, put him in the barrel, nailed the door closed, and gave it a big spin. Sure enough, the cat shrieked and made a lot of noise. Since he was having so much fun I decided to give him a nice long ride. When I decided the cat had enjoyed enough fun for the day, I stopped the barrel and let him out. I never saw a cat run so fast—albeit a somewhat crooked path—as he headed for the barn. Somehow, the cat was never quite normal after his barrel ride. I could not help but wonder, did it affect people the same way?

∽

I completed my second year of school at Habberton. Then, quite suddenly, and to the surprise of most Americans, the crash of '29 brought an end to the Roaring Twenties. The next few years would be difficult for everyone—the Great Depression was upon us. Dad spent a lot of time talking to my mother about the store, debts, and money. I sensed that all was not well with our family but did not understand what the problem was. One morning a truck arrived and loaded much of our furniture on board. I was told I was going to a new home in Spring Valley, directly across the road from my granddad Gibson. As usual, when in serious trouble, we ran home to Spring Valley. Here we had food in abundance and a roof over our heads, even though when it rained there were four or five leaks under which we placed pots and pans. Modest though it was—today we would call it primitive—it was always there when you needed a home, and solid as the Rock of Gibraltar. I was very happy.

It was some time later before I realized what was happening. Dad lost everything he owned—the store, mill, home, and forty-acre farm. All he had left to show for his years at Habberton was a truckload of cheap furniture, and that yellow Chrysler convertible. The convertible was sold within weeks to raise a little money to pay off debts. The thousands of dollars that Dad had out in credit from the store was instantly written off. It was not that the people were dishonest—money had simply disappeared.

Only a limited number of country stores ever sent out statements. Customers expected to be carried on the books for months at no interest. The biggest insult the storeowner could deliver to a customer was a bill at the month's end. This is what customers called a "dun." Any customer receiving such a dun would never trade with the merchant again.

Business began moving from country stores to larger, and cheaper, shopping areas of nearby towns and cities. Spring Valley was no exception. Long time customers of the general store gradually began buying nothing there but absolute necessities. Hardware, dry goods, and grocery business gradually disappeared. It seemed not to matter at all that the general store had carried their charge accounts through many a dry summer or cold winter. Customers were quick to forget that the storeowner lived next door to the store, and had opened up at midnight on many occasions, when they needed cough medicine or even a loaf of bread. It was not unusual for the customer to charge the item to his long unpaid account.

My father-in-law, Albano Maestri, had the same unhappy experience when he sold his store in Tontitown. It is easy to see how many merchants went broke. One year, I believe it was in the early 1960s, I wrote off over $12,000 in unpaid bills. This was when our yearly sales were under $200,000. That year the business lost $4,800—enough that the IRS came down on me. After checking my books the IRS agent congratulated me on having a fine set of books and terrible business sense. He advised tightening my credit sales, which I did.

I saw a sign not many months ago hanging over the cash register in a country store: "In God we trust, everyone else pay cash." There was a smart storeowner.

Flat broke after the Habberton store experience, Dad, with no assets at all, bought the Sanders Brothers store in Spring Valley —on credit of course—how else? He continued the same credit business practice that caused his downfall in Habberton. Soon he had to turn the store back to the Sanders Brothers. I assume that Allen and Henry Sanders were the ultimate losers in that transaction.

With no place to live we moved in with my Grandparents, Mack and Alice Gibson. Within a few weeks we (in reality, my Dad and Mother) moved across the road into a house owned by an elderly lady, Mrs. Lissy Pruner. Mrs. Pruner and her 11 year old niece lived in two rooms; my Dad and Mother lived in the remaining three rooms. The rent for the three rooms was $4 per month. I was about to begin the best years of my childhood. I stayed with my Grandparents as much as allowed.

Within months Dad lost the store and we moved to Fayetteville where Dad had a job managing an automobile garage and service station. We lived (read, existed) in a two-room apartment in the rear of the station. It was easy to sweep out—the kitchen was six by six feet, the big room was eight by twelve feet, and the bathroom was somewhat smaller than the kitchen. I am perfectly truthful about the room size.

My mother realized she must do something to keep us from starvation. She started learning to be a beautician. Her apprenticeship at the Beulah Lee Beauty Shop on Dickson Street was to last six months, during which she received no money at all. (Beulah Lee's was in a second-story room in an old building that was later demolished to make room for the Walton Arts Center.) Again it was Granddad Mack Gibson who came to the rescue by keeping us in enough food to ward off starvation.

～

I started school that fall in the fifth grade at Washington School. It was soon apparent that Spring Valley School did not prepare me for the fifth grade in a better school. My teacher was Miss Katz, an overweight spinster with an intense dislike for me. She was not only unsympathetic, but downright hostile at having an ignorant, poorly dressed country child in her class. She may not have made my school year a living hell, but she did her level best to do so. I was kept in after school and during recess each and every day. While I thought it was because I missed a spelling word or some other infraction, in reality it was because she did not want me to be seen with the other children. Washington School, at that time, was in one of the better residential areas of the city. I thought that if I could only get rid of Miss Katz, my next teacher just had to be better. Boy, was I ever wrong.

When my mother completed her apprenticeship and received a license to operate a beauty shop, we moved to Huntsville. Needless to say, I was overjoyed. Little did I realize at the time that my teacher at Huntsville would be a wizened old witch known as "Old Ma Gizeman." She made Miss Katz seem like an angel. Ma Gizeman taught the fifth and sixth grades. Not only was she a sadist, she was little qualified to associate with civilized society. Her daily whippings administered to one or more children were unbelievable. I will never understand why the school board allowed such torture to be administered by a so-called schoolteacher.

Ma Gizeman carefully selected and cut her switches from a row of wild bushes growing behind the schoolhouse. Each switch was about five feet long. The small branches along the length of the switch were deliberately cut about one-quarter of an inch from the limber switch. She was careful to cut those little barbs at an angle so that they penetrated clothing. After one of her orgasmic tantrums the child receiving the whipping would have a very bloody back. Boys and girls alike received these beatings. Very few days went by without one of Ma Gizeman's blood-drawing whippings. She had a special interest in one little girl, Helen. This child's mother always dressed her in pretty, clean, carefully ironed dresses. No matter how good she was, at least once a week Helen would receive a beating until her little white blouse was bloody.

Another favorite trick of Ma Gizeman's was to walk the aisles and try to find a foot sticking outward. When she did she stomped the child's leg and foot. She tried to bring her shoe down about halfway between the kneecap and the ankle. This way she would peel the skin off the leg for several inches before her heavy shoe landed on the child's instep.

Not many years after I moved to Springdale I heard Ma Gizeman finally got what she deserved. The story is that she was whipping the son of a local Huntsville merchant with one of her bondage-type whips and became so aroused that she hit him across the face and damaged his right eye. Realizing that the Huntsville School Board would do nothing, a group of boys in her class decided it was time to act.

The next boy Ma Gizeman called up front to receive his beating waited until she really got excited. He then picked up a metal bookend and laid the old gal out cold. He was punished, of course, but the pattern was set. I was told that she got a taste of her own medicine when several boys held her to the floor while others took turns thrashing her with her own switches—extracting "an eye for an eye." I heard she ran from the schoolhouse in hysterics as blood ran down her back.

It gives me a nice warm feeling all over to think that the story is true.

CHAPTER 7

Medicine Shows, Tent Preachers, Con Men, Hucksters, and Other Entertainment

Every crowd has a silver lining.

—PHINEAS T. BARNUM (1810–1891),
American showman

"Cap Tiller is coming!" Seventy years ago those four words brought smiles of joy to young and old alike in the small towns of northwest Arkansas and eastern Oklahoma.

Beginning soon after World War I and continuing into the mid-1930s, Cap Tiller brought the thrills of western movies to dozens of rural communities. The pictures flickered, outside a small school house an electric generator droned away, and for a short time hard work and poverty were forgotten. The smell of popcorn blended with people odors: some freshly scrubbed, others not so clean. For one brief moment, in dreary one-room schoolhouses across this rural area our citizens caught a flickering glimpse of paradise.

Cap traveled in a home-built motorhome, a crude box-like structure built on a Model T Ford chassis. The interior of his camper was a bit over six feet wide, and about twelve feet long. Entrance was through a door at the rear. Furnishings consisted of two cane-bottom chairs, a bed, and a small flattop woodstove in a rear corner. The stove was used for heating as well as cooking. A stovepipe went straight up, extending a foot above the roof. Attached to the plywood wall were pictures of William S. Hart, Hoot Gibson, and Hopalong Cassidy. Bathroom facilities were provided by trees and gullies beside the road.

In the summer, the rear door was opened to allow the heat to escape during cooking. Drawers under the built-in bed provided storage for food and clothing.

A gasoline-powered generator and some personal belongings were towed behind the contrivance on a two-wheeled trailer. Special padded compartments on the trailer held two 16-mm projectors, several western films, and spare projection bulbs. An aluminum metal tube attached to the top of the camper held the rolled-up silver screen.

Local schoolhouses or lodge halls were usually used for the "picture show." Many country churches, and a few city churches, considered motion pictures sinful and plainly the work of the Devil. Only the most liberal congregations would allow movies in the Lord's House. Cap Tiller and his movies was denounced from many a Baptist pulpit. Ranting of preachers—"yea, even the threat of eternal damnation"—only served as free advertising for Mr. Tiller. Judgment Day was in the future. Buck Jones and Hoot Gibson were here tonight.

In the earlier years of traveling motion picture shows, the projectors were hand-cranked, and illumination was by gas light. Carbide generators for gas was transported from place to place on a two-wheeled trailer much like those that in later years carried electric generators. The generator was normally parked beside a window. Gas was piped to the projector by rubber hoses. Highly flammable, the carbide generators and rubber hoses were treated with respect.

In the early '20s, Cap Tiller made the transition to electric lighting. The gas cylinders, rubber hoses, and pressure gauges were replaced by an electric generator driven by any gasoline engine that could be bought cheaply.

Not many years after "talkies" appeared in city theatres, Cap traded in his hand-cranked, later modified, projectors for 16-mm sound projectors. Though he usually carried two projectors, he considered one a spare and never graduated to dual projector shows. This meant that there was a short intermission at least two times during the show, while he changed reels on the single projector. No one seemed to mind.

The usual admission fee was ten cents. It was not unusual for Cap to have fifty or more people pay a dime to see his Westerns.

MEDICINE SHOWS AND OTHER ENTERTAINMENT

The desire to take medicine is perhaps the greatest feature which distinguishes man from animals.

—SIR WILLIAM OSLER (1849–1919), Canadian physician

Medicine shows were a lot more fun than motion pictures. My favorite was the O'Quaka Indian herb shows. O'Quaka shows visited Huntsville every summer. They normally stayed at least four days, sometimes longer, and came up with a different show every night. I think the "Doctor"—the medicine show owner—called upon his sense of humor when he named the medicine "O'Quaka." I think he purposely picked a name very close to "Quack"—for quack medicine.

O'Quaka set up their stage next to the post office on the west side of the Huntsville square. With large canvas signs on each side, the stage looked a lot like the shows in a second-rate carnival midway. The stage was covered with a bright canvas awning, creating a circus-like atmosphere. An ancient upright piano, situated center stage rear, was never covered. I suppose the slight amount of rain that blew in from the sides was not enough to detune the instrument.

One large banner showed a painting of an Indian chief in a feathered headdress. Under his picture in large letters was the name "O'Quaka." Slightly smaller letters to the side listed all the ailments a bottle of O'Quaka was sure to cure: nervous fits, consumption, colds, catarrh, coughs, night sweats, influenza, nausea, heartburn, constipation, episodic, arthritis, gout, shingles, and biliousness. These maladies were similar to what faith healers claimed to cure by laying on of hands. Of the two, I'd put my money on O'Quaka—at least it was well laced with alcohol.

The other large banner proclaimed that from this very stage you would see comedy, music, magic acts, and drama direct from the stages of America's large cities. In addition, you would see, absolutely free of charge, educational medical demonstrations.

In the '30s, the country was in the grasp of the Great Depression. Medicine shows were free; this fact alone assured them of a large attendance. People gathered an hour or more before show time to secure a good seat. Some came in cars and parked them in places that provided a good view of the stage. Some families brought a picnic lunch and spread a blanket on the ground in front of the stage. Some larger and more prosperous medicine shows even had seating for several hundred potential customers and dressing rooms in trailers equal to some Hollywood movie sets.

You must remember that the Great Depression threw a lot of very talented people out of work. This was especially true for vaudevillians. Out of work and broke, a lot of top talent took to the medicine show circuit to provide them and their family with food and shelter. Some acts were very good indeed, surpassing many of the shows we watch on TV today.

In addition to a strong pitch for their alcohol-laced elixir, medicine shows interrupted the show near the halfway point for candy sales. For those who have never experienced firsthand one of these sales, I'll clue you in. The candy came in a cardboard box slightly larger than the familiar Crack-R-Jack box. Inside the box were a dozen or so pieces of what was called candy, each piece individually wrapped. Even children were unable to eat the contents. It was a tasteless, chewy piece of something that cost very little and would keep forever, under any condition. In those years it sold for fifty cents a box. Adjust for inflation and you have a five-dollar box of something similar to wood putty.

Before the men passed through the crowd with the candy you had to undergo the sales pitch. It went something like this: a large candy manufacturer was introducing a new line of expensive candy. As a sales promotion, the company had cut the price and was putting a nice gift in every box. It was quite a long pitch before the first box was sold.

Very early in the candy sale, a man or woman would let out a loud scream and hold up an expensive looking watch. "Look what I got in my box!" the lucky person would say. The watch bore the trademark of a well-known watchmaker of the day. At that point, candy sales picked up. Most of us got a whistle, a wire puzzle, a key ring, or some trinket that was worth approximately zero.

The following day, like any ten-year-old boy would do, I was snooping around the grass-covered space behind the stage where the show people were camped in two trailers. The lucky watch winner of the night before, and the man now mixing up a batch of O'Quaka, looked surprisingly alike. Come to think of it, the winner of big prizes during candy sales was never a local resident.

I watched as the man mixed up a batch of medicine. He was pouring liquids from gallon jugs into a large dishpan and stirring the concoction with a wooden paddle. When the mixing was completed, he dipped up the "medicine" with a cup and poured it into empty bottles he removed from a cardboard box. When he had fifty or so bottles filled, he wiped each bottle with a dingy towel and applied a paper label to the front of the bottle. I had to admit the bottles looked as good as any in the local drug stores. I noticed that he kept a cup nearby for his personal use. Every five minutes or so he would take a sip of the medicine in his cup and smile approvingly. I suppose he was testing it for quality.

I well remember the night the doctor promised that on the following night he would give a medical demonstration and lecture on the cause and cure of indigestion. He further stated that we would see, by the use of a "glass stomach," the cause of discomfort after eating, and what happened in the stomach when a proper medicine such as O'Quaka was taken.

I looked forward to the demonstration. I had no idea what a stomach looked like. You can imagine my disappointment when the doctor wheeled out a giant Coca Cola bottle—the type used in drugstores to advertise their fountain service. A rubber cork in the top of the bottle had two holes through it with two glass tubes sticking up about six inches above the bottle. Both glass tubes had a small cork stopper in them.

With great fanfare and a sales pitch with a few medical terms sprinkled throughout, the doctor removed the rubber stopper. Then he opened up a can of pork and beans, a can of Vienna sausage, two slices of bread, a cup of coffee, and a few things we could not see. He then took a colorful balloon and stretched the opening over one of the glass tubes, and replaced the stopper. We were astounded when the balloon slowly began to inflate. Within two minutes time the balloon swelled to its limit and exploded with a loud bang. He quickly removed that balloon and replaced it with another. It too swelled to the bursting point.

The stopper was removed from the second glass tube and one spoonful of O'Quaka carefully poured into the oversized Coke bottle. The doctor removed a large pocket watch from his vest and began to count off the seconds: one ... two ... three ... four ... five, as a hush settled over the crowd. The balloon continued to inflate for a few seconds, then slowly started deflating as the medicine did its magic. Soon the limp balloon was draped over the side of the "glass stomach." Sounds of amazement swept through the assembled audience. As the doctor expected, sales of O'Quaka were very good that evening.

It was not until my first year of general science in high school that I learned how easy it was to duplicate the glass stomach experiment. Somehow as I gained knowledge, I felt a bit of disappointment. It is always better when you believe in miracles. So it is with life. Perhaps there is some truth in the old saying, "Ignorance is bliss."

∼

> *I never knew a healthy man who worried much about his health, or a good man who was concerned about his soul.*
>
> —MARK TWAIN (1835–1910), American author

Moving upward on the show business scale, we come to tent meetings and revivals. The more prosperous, better-known evangelists really raked in the money. With tents as large as circus tents, and with far fewer patches on the canvas big top, a preacher and his tent meeting often remained two weeks or more in each town. One such evangelist, the Reverend Royal Riteway, had his act down perfect. Of course I am using a fictitious name to avoid litigation in case a living descendant happens to read this book.

Reverend Riteway always performed in a white suit, white tie, and white shoes. He was accompanied by a Sister—a female member of his traveling congregation. She was a beautiful black-haired young lady in her late twenties, dressed in a white, heavily sequined evening dress and white fur jacket. She played the piano and sang. I often wondered how she managed to maintain her cool, fresh look on those hot summer nights we have here in Arkansas. Her long black hair cascaded down her back, standing out in sharp contrast against the white fur. This glamorous woman drew many a gasp from young male members of the congregation. I noticed a few of the older men had a wistful, faraway look in their eyes. Only in Hollywood could such beauty be seen.

Outside the tent, a portable gas engine droned on as it powered a generator to operate a World War I-era search light. Visible over much of Madison County, the light was like a magnet, drawing folks from their homes and farms to see the miracles performed by Royal Riteway.

Before his fire and brimstone sermon was unleashed upon the capacity crowd, Reverend Riteway's troupe entertained the crowd with a full hour of gospel music selected from the well-worn hymn books scattered throughout the tent. The six-piece band played the songs with a beat, and with a gusto seldom enjoyed outside the Storyville section of New Orleans. The assembled crowd, most of whom thought jazz to be a work of the Devil, clapped hands, stomped their feet to the music—many for the first time in their lives. If it came from the hymnbook, it had to be good gospel music.

From a raised platform near the front entrance, a man moved with precision, pointing the high-intensity colored spotlights on the musicians performing on the stage. The glittering dresses of the women and the gold and silver musical instruments reflected back the colored lights, dazzling the worshippers with millions of red, green and yellow starry points of light. It was a performance designed to make poor farm families drop their hard-earned dollars into tambourines passed down each row of seats by well-endowed and smiling young Sisters.

The Reverend Riteway's sermons were carefully chosen to titillate, arousing dormant emotions that the God-fearing people seldom enjoyed. The titles of his sermons were announced well in advance, assuring a full house, or more accurately, a full tent. Themes of "Flaming Youth," "Sex, the Road to Hell," "The Sins of Adultery," and other erotic subjects were fully explored in Reverend Riteway's sermons. Those who would never think of listening to "that old jazz music" or of reading a racy novel were treated to both without a tinge of guilt.

The largest crowds attending tent revivals came on "healing

nights," when the good reverend, simply by "laying on of hands," cured the sick and afflicted. Everyone was anxious to see if "pore ol' Aunt Sally" would arise from her wheelchair and dance a jig. Perhaps even Uncle Walt would throw away his crutches. Strangely, no one ever questioned why the reverend wore black horned-rim glasses. Could it be that the Good Lord did not do eyes?

The righteous filled the tent quickly, long before dark. Outside, a few who had just "come along 'fer th' show" laughed and talked in loud voices as they passed around a quart fruit jar of white lightning. This invariably brought forth scowls of disapproval from the seated congregation.

Well-known members of the community who had walked on crutches for years would throw them away on those "healin' nights" and dance all over the stage with gusto, and apparently without pain. The following week you would see those who had been healed walking down the street using their familiar crutches. I never fully understood this paradox.

~

A certain portion of the human race has certainly a taste for being diddled.

—THOMAS HOOD (1799–1845), English poet

As much fun as all this was, it never intrigued me like a polished professional con artist. To watch a con man sucker a crowd is pure magic before your eyes—poetry in motion. A well-known truism maintains, "you cannot con an honest man." It is usually the town skinflints and penny pinchers who get hurt. That fact alone was always a source of pleasure to me.

With nothing going for them but nerves of steel, a glib line of patter, and a great personality, professional con artists made their way through the countryside, fleecing hard-earned dollars from those who loved money more than life itself. There were many of them during the Depression years, far too many to cover in these few pages. I will mention the ones that stand out in my memory above all others as truly outstanding pitchmen and con artists.

MEDICINE SHOWS AND OTHER ENTERTAINMENT

One Saturday morning, about 11:00 A.M., an older model car pulled into the unpaved area between the First National Bank and S.R. Wilson's Mercantile store on Emma Avenue in downtown Springdale. I first noticed it when a man wearing a beat-up ten-gallon black hat emerged from the driver's seat, and started pacing back and forth ringing an old rusty cowbell. He was, for the year 1938, a strange-looking man. His skin was very dark; obviously a man who spent his life outdoors, or perhaps there was some truth in his claim that he was a full blood Apache Indian. He had two braids of black hair hanging down his back, reaching almost to his silver Concho-studded belt.

He walked to the rear of his car, opened the trunk, and removed a beat-up #2 washtub. He placed the tub on the ground about ten feet behind his car, then returned to the car trunk and lifted out a large sandstone rock about the size of a basketball. It was all he could do to lift the rock. He placed the rock beside the washtub. He made one final trip to the car trunk, brought out an old water bucket, and approached the gathering crowd. Only then did he speak. "Where can I get some water?"

"Thar's a spicket right over thar to yer right," one man replied. "The bank uses it when they warsh their winders."

The "Indian" walked over to the spigot and filled his bucket, then returned and poured it in the tub. He made repeated trips until the tub was about half full. He returned the water bucket to the car trunk, picked up his cowbell, and began ringing it while dancing in a circle around the washtub. All the while he was yelling and speaking in gibberish, or perhaps in his native tongue. No one in the crowd would have known the difference.

With all the yelling and bell ringing a sizeable crowd soon gathered to see what all the excitement was about. It was then that the Indian called our attention to the very attractive young lady sitting in the car.

"The young lady in the car is a human fly," he said. "In just a few minutes she is going to walk right up the side of that building." He pointed to the two-story bank building, which at that time was the tallest building in town.

Then, kneeling by the stone, the Indian continued, "Before you see this amazing feat, I am going to show you something you will never see again if you live to be one hundred years old. This is something you will tell your grandchildren about. I am going to beat that sandstone into sand with my bare fist. When there is nothing left but a pile of sand, I am going to drink every drop of water in this washtub."

He paused, looked around at the skeptical townspeople and said, "Surely you don't expect to see a miracle like this without offering a small donation. Think of the abuse to my body. Today is a day you will never forget. I am going to ask my companion to pass my hat among you. Please be generous."

The beautiful dark-skinned young lady stepped from the old sedan, took the Indian's hat, and passed it among the crowd. As the nickels, dimes, and quarters were tossed in the hat, she smiled and thanked each donor.

She returned to her accomplice, held out the hat, and let him look at the collection. He frowned, then in an angry voice said, "How can you expect to see the amazing demonstration we are about to do for a few nickels and dimes? I am going to ask that the hat be passed again, and this time I want to see a little folding money in the hat. If I am going to beat that rock into sand, and then drink that tub of water, I want to think it was for more than money enough to buy a hamburger." The lady passed the hat around a second time. I could see a few dollar bills in the hat.

When she showed the Indian the second round of donations, he really got upset. "There is not enough in that hat to get me to smash a grape, let alone that eighty-pound sandstone. Pass my hat one more time." The young lady smiled her best and asked the crowd to be generous. "This is the last time I will pass the hat," she promised each individual who donated to see the show.

While she was making the last pass with the big black hat, the Indian spread an old potato sack on the ground in front of the rock, kneeled on the sack, and rolled up his sleeves.

After the young woman made her last appeal to the assembled crowd, she returned to the Indian, handed him the hat, and then took her seat in the car.

The Indian stared at the money in his hat for a moment, then said to the crowd of fifty or so, "From the looks of this donation, you people don't give a damn whether you see this show or not, and if you don't want to see the show, I am not about to give it." Saying that, he jammed the hat on his head, all the money still inside, quickly jumped in his car, and left town in a cloud of flying gravel and dust.

Slowly it dawned on the crowd they had been conned. At first there were a few sounds of anger, but then someone laughed. The laughing soon spread throughout the crowd and everyone was in a good mood. Most, like me, considered the artistry of the con man more entertaining than his promised feat of physical abuse.

∼

> *No one ever went broke underestimating the intelligence of the American public.*
> —PHINEAS T. BARNUM (1810–1891),
> American showman

In the '30s, as now, stories were told, and retold, about a man who had invented a carburetor that would enable the average auto owner to increase his gasoline mileage to one hundred miles per gallon. According to the story, oil producers bought the patent rights and had no intention of releasing such an invention. The big oil companies intended to withhold the invention so they could continue to sell more gasoline. The story, unbelievable as it was, seemed plausible to a lot of our citizens. A large percentage of Americans remained firmly convinced the story was true. Even some skilled mechanics were willing to believe that science had progressed to the point where anything was possible. Such people were ripe for what I call the "Automobile Con Men."

A favorite con of the times was a "battery-charging pill." The con was easy to work, took very little equipment, and was always profitable for those seeking a dishonest dollar. It worked like this. A car, usually an older model, was fitted with two batteries: its regular battery, and a second, well-charged battery, hidden under a seat or in the car's trunk. The starter was rigged to a well-concealed, double-pole switch. One position of the switch brought the regular battery into use; the other position activated the concealed battery.

The con practically worked itself. The car was driven into town and parked in a highly visible area, usually in front of a bank or a hardware store. The driver casually walked away disappearing into a place of business, usually a bank, where he waited a few minutes before returning to his car.

Springdale, like all small towns, always had a few loafers on the street simply killing time. When the automobile owner returned to his car he would start grinding his starter. His car refused to start; in reality, he had not turned the ignition on. This always caught the attention of two or three loafers. After trying several times to get the car started the battery became weaker and weaker. Eventually the battery ran down and the starter refused to turn the motor over.

By now there were usually five or six men watching and wondering what the car owner was going to do now that his battery was dead. They were much more concerned than the con man. It was a sure bet that some of the loafers would offer to help—either by pushing the car or offering to go get his car and use jumper cables to start the car. Their help was graciously refused. The driver did not seem at all concerned about his dead battery.

Casually he stepped from his car, raised the hood and removed the three battery caps. Then he reached in his pocket, took out a small pillbox, and removed three small white pills. He carefully dropped a pill in each battery cell and replaced the caps, making sure to leave the hood of the car in its raised position. Then he got in his car and switched to the reserve battery. When he hit the starter, the car started immediately. When he stepped from his car to lower the hood, the suckers took the bait.

The con man explained to the gathering crowd that he was an "unemployed chemist," and that until recently, he had been employed by a well-known battery manufacturer. He had invented this simple pill that "restored and recharged" batteries. The big company refused to manufacture or sell the pill as it would ruin new battery sales. He was now on his way to demonstrate his invention to a group of automotive engineers meeting in a nearby large city.

Here he tossed in a few large words like hydrogen, oxygen, catalyst, reactivation, etc. He explained that the pills were cheap to manufacture and that he just happened to have a few extra bottles with him and that he would part with them for only two dollars for a box of one dozen pills. Being temporarily unemployed he could use a few extra dollars until his invention hit the big market.

Was anyone gullible enough to fall for this line? They sure were—my dad brought home two bottles.

∼

The "Spark Intensifier" was another popular moneymaker for those less honest citizens during the late Depression era of the 1930s. As with the battery-pill scam, careful preparation of the automobile was essential. This highly profitable con worked better if the operator worked from a popular, late-model automobile especially modified for the purpose. Looking prosperous was essential if maximum profits were to be realized.

It was essential that the hood, or engine cover, of the car be modified to allow the operator to remove it completely. This allowed a good vision of the spotless engine, and a duplicate instrument panel that included a large six-inch tachometer mounted so anyone within ten feet or so of the engine could read the engine rpms. Most such instrument panels used by the "sparkies," as they were known among other con men, were designed to impress. White dials with red and black numerals surrounded by bright chrome mounting rings.

This duplicate instrument panel had a starter button, ignition switch, ammeter, oil pressure gauge, throttle control, and more—everything the operator needed to operate the automobile engine.

It was absolutely necessary that everything looked scientific and professional. As the huckster would normally be working in sunlight, a large beach umbrella, also brightly colored, was supported by a substantial metal support welded to the automobile firewall. Such brightly colored umbrellas served a double purpose: they were a great attention getter while keeping the con man and his "marks" in the shade.

Let me make it perfectly clear, especially for younger readers, tachometers as standard equipment on cars and smaller trucks were a rarity up until the 1990s. Those buying any automobile engine attachments had practically no way of actually checking whether or not it improved their engine performance.

One more engine modification was necessary before the sales pitch. The distributor cap was reworked so that when the regular lead from the spark coil to the distributor was plugged in, a high resistance was placed in series with the spark coil. This is not nearly as difficult to do as it sounds. When the spark intensifier was plugged in, the resistor was bypassed.

The spark intensifier was a colorful gadget, cylindrical in shape, and about three inches long—slightly smaller in size than an ordinary D-cell flashlight battery.

The demonstration, following a three-minute talk about this amazing invention, was followed by the operator plugging in the regular distributor wire, starting the engine, and carefully adjusting the throttle until the tachometer was reading, say, 600 rpms. Then the engine was turned off and the intensifier was plugged in. When the car was started the tachometer jumped to 800 rpms with the same throttle setting—a twenty-five percent increase in efficiency.

Then, with the regular connection replaced, the engine would be slowed up until it stopped running. Changing nothing, the spark intensifier was plugged into the distributor and the engine started immediately, running smoothly.

It was obvious that with the same amount of gasoline going into your engine, the engine ran faster, offering an increase in miles per gallon of gas. Priced at only $2.50 each (a day's wages at the time) an experienced con man could make more than $100 per day by selling spark intensifiers—more than most workers earned in a month.

The good news was that it in no way damaged your car and that many buyers claimed it was the best money they ever spent. Many claimed their automobiles ran smoother, got better gas mileage, and had much more power.

∼

> *For an actress to be a success she must have the face of Venus, the brains of Minerva, the grace of Terpsichore, the memory of Macaulay, the figure of Juno, and the hide of a Rhinoceros.*
>
> —ETHEL BARRYMORE (1897–1959), American actress

While the circus managed to survive television, large tent shows disappeared with the bombing of Pearl Harbor. Such a pity. I can well remember when Hila Morgan and Company and the Mac and Judy Green Players brought the thrill and excitement of Broadway and the legitimate stage into remote towns and cities of this area. As our city cousins can tell us, there are few art forms more entertaining than a well-produced, well-acted stage show.

For many, many years, Hila Morgan played Springdale for a few days every summer. Weeks ahead of the scheduled shows appearance in town, advance men nailed large posters to the sides of barns and warehouses throughout the area. Of course those owning the buildings were given tickets to the show for allowing such signs to be nailed on their structure. Such free passes did not actually cost the show—it normally made them money. Don't forget the candy sales, advance ticket sales, and sometimes, owners of free passes found that for only a small additional charge, their seating could be upgraded to "front and center." Free tickets were also given to merchants who placed large, colorful show cards in their front windows. Make no mistake—the show was always well advertised several weeks in advance.

The arrival of her company by train was something to behold. A large crowd gathered at the Frisco depot anxiously awaited arrival of the special train. Miss Morgan had a magnificent private coach tastefully decorated in a style befitting such a star. By prior arrangement her coach was parked on a siding near the Railway Express Office where it remained for her entire stay in Springdale.

Once her private rail car was parked on the siding a waiting crowd gathered around the rear of the coach. Everyone talked in hushed whispers while they awaited her appearance on the ornate observation deck. After a respectable period of time, Miss Morgan stepped from her private coach, smiled and waved to the waiting crowd. Our town mayor, stepping forward, placed a large bouquet of roses into the waiting arms of Miss Morgan, a petite blonde of indeterminate years.

The speeches by our mayor and by Miss Morgan were short and often interrupted by noise of the unloading process of the huge tent and show equipment. By nightfall, the tent would be erected, all the stage lighting in place, and hundreds of chairs in place for the opening night crowd.

Sideshow at the Fair.

I never knew a pre-teen who did not enjoy the sights and sounds of a carnival. It did not seem to matter whether it was a state fair, county fair, or a community reunion such as the annual events at Huntsville and St. Paul. The day the show pulled into town was a major event in the lives of young people. *Photo by Bruce Vaughan.*

The first items to be unloaded from the train were the solid-tired Federal Knight trucks. They hauled the tent and equipment to spot chosen for this year's show. Sometimes it was the area west of the city park (now the site of the City Administration Building). The last show I attended was on a vacant block west of Holcomb Street and north of Allen Street.

The show used its own power generating plant—a generator mounted on a four-wheeled trailer. It was parked some distance from the tent so the noise of the generator engine would not interfere in any way with the show.

Due to the lengthy presentation only one show was scheduled for each night of their engagement—normally three or four days. The feature play scheduled for the evening was preceded by a number of vaudeville acts. Shows from start to finish ran about three hours. A different show was presented each night of their agenda.

Families came from miles around came to see the latest Broadway-type show. Many families stretched their budget to the limit and attended two or more nights while Hila Morgan was in town.

A somewhat smaller crowd gathered at the depot to wave goodbye to Broadway as the special train pulled away from the station. Miss Morgan, standing on the observation deck, waved goodbye to the citizens of Springdale until the train was well past the Welch Grape Juice plant. Better known to Springdale residents than most Hollywood and Broadway stars, her death years later was deeply mourned. A friend certainly, indeed a "Golden Era," had passed from this earth.

Circus time was something very special, especially to the young at heart. Children and adults alike turned out to watch circus trains or trucks unload. Watching the tent, or "Big Top," go up was often better than the show itself, and it was free. Some shows used the elephants to help raise the heavy poles that supported the center of the tent. On the outside, long iron stakes were driven into the hard ground by three men wielding large sledgehammers. Standing around the iron stake they struck each blow in perfect time, one after the other. Such timing was a beautiful thing to watch. Their ability to do this was the result of years of experience putting up the large tent many times a month. The safety of hundreds depended upon the strength of those iron stakes, as they were the tie-points for the tent's perimeter. One stake might fail without a major problem, but if several failed, hundreds could be killed. Working with precision gained from years of experience, the men had the Big Top installed within a few hours.

A number of young boys from town always hung around hoping to get a free pass to the show by doing some small job. Carrying water to the elephants was the most popular. Failing to get a free pass, there was always the possibility of sneaking in under the tent flaps. When desperate we talked our parents out of enough money for a ticket. Though we were dirt poor I did not miss many performances when the circus came to town—and that included both the afternoon and evening performances.

Kelly and Miller Brothers and Clyde Beatty played this area often. Both shows were similar in size, but Clyde Beatty featured more wild animals. One of the best shows to play our area was the Tom Mix Circus and Wild West Show. The Tom Mix show came to Fayetteville in 1937. I remember the date well; I was 15 years old and a sophomore in high school. I had recently conned Frank Bunch, the local motor vehicle officer in Huntsville, into giving me a driving license. I remember he said that he "might as well issue me a license as I had been driving around Huntsville for over a year."

My parents agreed to let me and some friends drive the old Plymouth to the afternoon performance at the Fayetteville fairgrounds. Tom Mix arrived at the grounds about one hour before show time driving his white 1936 supercharged Cord 812 "coffin-nose" convertible. I was more impressed with his car than I was with his show. He made only one appearance here. In 1940, he was killed in the same Cord convertible when he missed a curve on a winding road in Arizona.

For those who could afford the long drive, and the higher ticket prices, the big Barnum and Bailey Circus appeared often in Tulsa, Oklahoma, and occasionally in Springfield, Missouri.

During the first part of the 1900s, most of the larger shows traveled by train. As roads became better and large trucks more dependable, the smaller shows switched to trucks and trailers. Only the very largest shows stuck with the railroads; they too made the switch to motor transport in the 1930s. Much of the glamour disappeared when circus trains no longer came to town. It was a rare thrill to watch a circus train unload. The trip from the railroad station to the circus grounds was like a wonderful parade. Some circuses recognized this fact and took advantage of it. Performers, elephants, clowns, and wild animals in their wheeled cages formed a parade often led by beautiful white horses pulling a steam calliope playing circus music. It was a thrill that is gone forever, and we are poorer for it.

Smaller communities like Hindsville, Eureka Springs, Elkins, St. Paul, and Goshen were sometimes visited by small shows. Most of these had few, if any wild animals. This type of show concentrated on trained dogs and horses, trapeze and juggling acts, and tight wire-walkers, with possibly two or three monkeys to round out their performance. It was at one of the small circuses that I saw my first "Punch and Judy" show. I thought it hilarious.

A few down-on-their-luck shows traveled the country by foot and horse drawn wagons. The pitiful elephants, zebras, camels, and giraffes, led by aging and tired circus performers, trudged from town to town. The only persons who rode were those driving wagons. Quite often, the heavily loaded wagons were pulled by the same horses used in acts that night. Sometimes such shows carried a small tattered tent but most had abandoned such covering long ago and now played in open fields, hopefully under a cloudless sky.

I saw my first elephants walking along the dirt road two miles west of Goshen. Someone came in my dad's store that morning telling about the circus that was walking from Fayetteville to Goshen. According to him the walking circus troupe was still some two miles from their destination. My mother put me in the 1928 Plymouth coupe and drove to a spot ahead of the approaching column. I still remember how tired the show people and animals looked as they shuffled past our car.

CHAPTER 8

A Far Better Place

It's not that I am afraid to die. I just don't want to be there when it happens.

—WOODY ALLEN (b. 1935), American filmmaker

We were having breakfast when the phone rang; my mother answered. I could tell she was talking to my grandmother, Alice, and from the sound of her voice I knew it was bad news. Phone calls from Spring Valley to Huntsville cost forty cents. In 1934 it had to be an emergency before you laid out that kind of money. Even though I was only twelve years old, I knew the value of a dollar.

Also, at this time in Northwest Arkansas, placing a long distance telephone call required a lot of patience and a strong voice. To place a call my grandparents would have to walk to the store to use the only telephone in Spring Valley that connected to a long distance wire. Then, if the lines to Huntsville were up and if the local phone company in Huntsville had their equipment operating, and if fresh batteries had been installed recently, the call just might get through. Sometimes the calls would go through but the voice on the other end was so weak, you could never be positive as to what was actually said.

Turning from the phone, my mother said, "Grandma has had a stroke. It's real bad—Mama wants us to come as quick as we can."

I was just getting over the chicken pox, and my first concern was that I would not be permitted to go. Having lived much of my life with my grandparents, I wanted to go if Grandma Kelly (my great-grandmother, who I also called Ma) was sick. I did not fully understand what a stroke was, or just how serious it was, but it must be really bad or my grandmother would not have called for us to come as quickly as we could.

It took us just a few minutes less than an hour to make the sixteen-mile trip. The road had recently been graded and our 1928 Chevrolet sedan moved along at a good clip.

When we arrived we found that Ma was paralyzed and could not talk. Soon Dr. Henry from Springdale arrived. After a brief examination he arose from the old cane-bottom chair. With a nod to my grandfather, they stepped outside and stood talking in hushed tones on the front porch.

"It's only a matter of a day or so," said Dr. Henry. "There is nothing I can do."

My grandfather paid the $5 charge for the house call. I stood nearby thinking that Dr. Henry must be very rich if he charged that much just to make the trip to Spring Valley and back. It was only fourteen miles each way.

Soon neighbors started dropping by. The men dressed in starched white shirts and clean blue denim overalls gathered in small groups on the porch and under the shade trees in the yard. The women sat in straight-backed chairs in the living room, which also served as Ma's bedroom. Mostly they were quiet, but occasionally someone would say, "She was a good Christian woman," or "She's going to a far better place." The women would nod agreement and say, "Yes, a far better place."

Somehow, I found that hard to believe. There was no better place in the world to me. I loved this place. There was my grandfather Mack's blacksmith shop where he let me heat and bend old horseshoes into bookends. A little stream called "the branch" ran behind his garden and outhouse. The branch was full of tadpoles, minnows, crawdads, and more than a few snakes. There were wooded hills to the east of his house where I could play all day. There were blackberry thickets, paw-paw trees, chinquapin trees, persimmon thickets, and grape vines to swing on. I had rabbit traps back in the woods, and minnow traps made from Mason jars and scraps of screen wire in the branch.

Many mornings during the spring and summer months I would fill a burlap sack with my camping gear, which consisted of a fruit jar of water, a knife and fork, a small skillet, some fatback pork, two eggs, potatoes, and an old salt and pepper shaker. Sometimes I'd take an apple, but I much preferred the fatback and eggs.

My grandfather told me long after I was grown that he always watched for a bit of smoke rising from the woods around noon. This was his method of knowing where I was and that I was OK.

My mother, however, would never let me get my hands wet. "You'll be sick for sure if you play in the water," she cautioned. "Don't go back in the woods or you'll get lost, and besides there are a lot of copperheads there. Those woods are full of ticks, chiggers, and poison ivy." If the pioneer women had all thought like my mother, our country west of Boston would still be uninhabited.

When I stayed with my grandparents, I never heard this kind of talk. My grandfather—"Dad" to me—was a typical mountain man. He could see no reason why a twelve-year-old boy should not be allowed to take his .22 rifle back in the woods and spend the day. And there was the possibility I would bring back a rabbit or squirrel for Dad's favorite meal of squirrel and dumplings.

Dad's life was not based on fear, and neither was my grandmother's. One day I watched as she took a two-foot-long stick and killed a four-foot-long copperhead. She only had two fears: mice and high bridges.

If I was not in the woods or playing along the branch, I could go up to Pete Holmesley's wood shop and watch him making rocking chairs, truck beds, or sometimes a coffin. As a baby I was rocked in one of Pete's oak chairs. He made a fine rocking chair from well-seasoned oak, and sold the chairs for $2 each. Pete made it possible for families who could not afford a store-bought rocker to own a really fine rocking chair. I have two of his chairs made from solid walnut. They cost me a bit more than $2, but I would not part with them for $200 today.

Across the dirt road from Pete's shop was Harold Sullivan's garage and service station—if you can call one ancient gas pump a service station. It seemed that Harold knew almost everything about electrical and mechanical work. He helped me build my first working radio— a crystal set with the coil wound around an oatmeal box. In the rear of the garage he was building a racer out of an old Model T Ford. If you stuck around in the afternoon some of the older boys would come around, and if they had a few cents in their pockets they would drink Cokes from the icebox. Eventually the talk turned to girls and by careful listening you learned things you never knew before. Today they would call it sex education.

The gristmill was a wonderful place to visit. I loved the sound of the large single-cylinder gasoline engine. And then there was the corn sheller. You have missed one of life's real pleasures if you have never watched an old-fashioned corn sheller at work. The smell of freshly-ground meal, the feel of the floor slick with meal dust, the beauty of the large wooden wheels on the line shaft, the sounds of wide flat-drive belts slapping against the wooden wheels as the lacings raced over the pulleys—all this and more made the gristmill a favorite place for young boys.

The canning factory, idle except for six weeks every year during tomato-growing season, was never locked. Actually, there was not much there to lock. (Vandalism was not a problem with my generation. That came later when better education, improved living conditions, and better diet became the norm.) I have spent hours looking at the boiler, the big Corliss steam engine, and the big crane used to lift large strap-iron cages filled with canned tomatoes off the floor and into vats of boiling water. After cooking, the tomato cans were put on a conveyor that moved slowly down a table where workers attached the colorful labels.

I can remember the day I finally figured out how the governor on the Corliss engine worked. There were so many things available to youngsters then that would now be forbidden. Too many lawsuits, too much vandalism, too many wanting to find a deserted building to put a meth lab in, too many just waiting for a chance to set fire to a large open building. All these things deprive young boys today of so much fun and education.

Unused can lids scattered over the floor could be used to make windmills, airplane propellers, water wheels, or even for just sailing through the air. Unused dented cans could be made into wren houses, string-and-can telephones, or just to shoot at with a bean flip.

North of the canning factory up toward Bean's Spring were two persimmon thickets where you could climb the slender trees and swing from them, just like Tarzan of the Apes.

When I got hot and tired, I would go to the spring, drink my fill of cold water, and lie in the deep sage grass just watching clouds drift across the deep blue sky. A far better place? I did not believe it then, and still have my doubts today. What could you do to improve a place like I was raised in?

Nevertheless, every Sunday morning at the Spring Valley Baptist Church, a preacher tried to sell me heaven—with little success, I might add. They had their idea of a better life, and I had mine. Somehow, I always left church feeling sorry for the preacher. It seemed to me that he was spending his life looking solemn and hoping for something better after he died. The sinners seemed to have found some joy and happiness here on Earth. I always figured God would not have made so many beautiful and pleasant things if he had not wanted us to recognize and enjoy them. I figured it was an insult to God to go through life looking only at the unpleasant and ugly.

I felt very sad. I had serious doubts that Ma was going to a better place—maybe different—maybe even good—but certainly not better. Three-quarters of a century later, I still feel the same way.

I walked from the house down the road to the oak bridge over the branch, the road that went up the hill to Mr. Welch's place. Sitting on the side of the little bridge, swinging my legs over the edge, I watched the cool, clear, spring water ripple over clean-washed pebbles. Occasionally, a minnow would dart from beneath a rock, swimming and frolicking from the joy he must have felt from being a fish. With tail movements so slight they were almost unnoticeable the fish remained still against the gentle current, then darted beneath another rock. Overhead, the birds kept up a constant chorus of sounds while two squirrels played tag in a large oak tree. Sitting there, I thought of Ma and how generous she was.

~

Born Matilda Catherine Hartley, November 17, 1856, on a forty-acre farm between Farmington and Prairie Grove, she often told me the story of how she was playing with younger children out in their front yard on the morning when the Battle of Prairie Grove first started. When she heard the constant sound of musket fire she became scared and ran to her mother. Her mother told her the sound was nothing to worry about—it was just the hogs cracking corn with their teeth. She was old enough to know better, but felt some comfort at what her mother said, and it seemed to calm the younger children.

During the war, bushwhackers were always a problem. Bushwhackers were nothing but thieves and killers who used the war as an excuse to rob, rape, and pillage farm families. They knew most of the men in the family were away from home fighting for whatever they believed in.

To hide their shelled corn from bushwhackers, and from the advancing armies, the Hartleys went up into the attic and poured corn into empty spaces between the wall studding. The Hartleys, like most families in the area, kept a slave woman. Aunt Sally had been with them since she was a young girl. Now, she was old and blind and no longer able to work, but she was kept as one of the family. The Hartleys had a dug cellar under the floor filled with food. Access to the cellar was through a trapdoor in the floor. They made Aunt Sally a pallet on the floor to cover up the trap door leading to the hoard of food. When Aunt Sally heard someone coming she would run and lay down on her pallet. When the bushwhackers came in she went into her act: "Please don't move poor ol' Aunt Sally. I'm sick and blind and I mean you no harm." The act seemed to work. Ma told me the bushwhackers always talked kindly to Aunt Sally, sometimes giving her something to eat. Thanks to Aunt Sally, and their initiative, the Hartleys never went hungry. They had plenty to eat all through the Civil War.

Two days after the war ended, some bushwhackers came by the farm and asked to see Mrs. Hartley. They told her that her son and her husband were waiting for her at a cabin not far from their farm. They told her she should hitch up a wagon and "go fetch 'em." She did as directed. When she got to the cabin she found both husband and son dead, in a sitting position, leaning back against the log wall. Both had survived the war, only to be killed by the bushwhackers within two miles of their home. Mrs. Hartley recognized one of the bushwhackers as a man named Johnson. She carried a loaded pistol everywhere she went after that hoping to run into Mr. Johnson so she could shoot him dead.

Grandma Kelly married Frances B. Kelly in 1876. Frances had

served in the Civil War as a private in Company G, 35th Regiment, Kentucky Volunteer Mounted Infantry. He was honorably discharged at the war's end. They had four children: Alice, Myrtle, Lee, and Jessie.

Ma often told me how she went through the "Blue-Backed Speller" fourteen times. I believe her story because she was an excellent speller and wrote with a beautiful script.

Ma was a deeply religious person, a Missionary Baptist. As far as she was concerned there were no other churches. West of Spring Valley a few miles is a Freewill Baptist church. Ma always referred to that church as "them old Freewill people." The absolute baddest, meanest, no-account group was "them old Cath-o-licks." It was common knowledge in the Spring Valley church that a former member, who bolted the faith and became a Catholic, was forced by her priest to kneel on rough gravel until her knees were bleeding.

Ma was firm in her belief that Missionary Baptists were the only people chosen to enter Heaven. She explained it this way: John was a Baptist. John was sent. Anyone sent is a Missionary, therefore anyone can plainly see that the only church is the Missionary Baptist Church, and the only people going to Heaven are Missionary Baptists. This seemed reasonable to me. Who was I to question or doubt anyone who had gone through the Blue Back Speller fourteen times.

She often told me that there was "an old Camel Light church near Habberton. Now, I could tell from the tone of her voice that the "Camel Lights" were a real odd group. She never got around to explaining to me why they were so bad, but my eleven-year-old mind filled in the blank spaces. I knew full well what a camel was, having seen one in a circus that came to Mayfield one summer. I imagined they had a camel with a lantern tied around his neck. Just what the Camel Lights were doing to that poor old camel in the evil confines of their church, I could only imagine. To my way of thinking, they were as bad, maybe worse, than the Cath-o-licks. It was many years later that I read of Thomas and Alexander Campbell, their faith, and their followers, known as the "Campbellites."

A deck of playing cards was never allowed in, or near, Ma's house. Checkers and dominoes were okay but those cards with hearts, diamonds, etc., were plainly the work of the Devil. If it had not been for sinful neighbors I would never have learned to play pitch and poker.

Ma and Grandma Sanders, (my grandfather Charlie Vaughan's half-sister and Uncle Anderson Sanders' wife) loved to sit on the front porch and talk about the sins of young people. There was absolutely no doubt that girls who smoked were most surely bound for Hell. During this discourse, Ma would open her purse, remove a plug of Horseshoe brand chewing tobacco, and cut off a chaw with her little penknife reserved for this purpose. She could put a frog's eye out at ten feet with one big tobacco spit. Talking to Ma, I got the idea it was a lot easier going to Hell than most people realized.

Dancing was also the Devil's work. It was, Ma reluctantly agreed, okay to pat one foot, keeping time with music. However, heaven help you if you got carried away and begin to move both feet at the same time. Dances were where you found loose women and drinking. Strange as it seemed to me at the time, loose women and drinking were what a lot of men around Spring Valley were looking for.

Probably the very biggest sin at the time—even worse than dancing —was bobbed hair. Ma bought an Edison phonograph at a farm auction sale. She paid forty dollars for it. No one was allowed to operate the machine but Ma. One of her favorite records was "Why Do You Bob Your Hair, Girls?" I remember the day my mother had her long hair bobbed. Reluctantly she walked into the living room where Ma was seated in her rocking chair. Ma snorted, "Now ain't you a pretty lookin' thing," got out of her rocker, and left the room. It was days before she spoke another word to my mother.

Several records came with the Edison. One was called, "The Preacher and the Bear." I loved that record. Ma said it was not funny to her. She said it was "makin' fun of a man of God." I only got to hear it when she went to town. Then I'd play it over and over, knowing I had plenty of time before she returned from Springdale. With a Model T Ford and a rough dirt road, a trip to Springdale and back took better than half a day. I figured if I played it while Ma was gone it would not lower her chances of going to Heaven, and as for my salvation, I was willing to run the risk.

∽

Ma's phonograph sat in the same corner of the living room from the day she bought it until her death. After she died, my uncle Lee Gibson got the phonograph. Ma was living with the Gibsons when Lee was born—needless to say, he was by far her choice of all her grandchildren. The Edison phonograph was one of the very few things Ma owned that had any value. It was never written down, but understood by all, that Lee would get her phonograph.

Unfortunately, Lee put no value on the Edison and stored it, fully wound, the top raised, and all moving parts exposed, in his barn and henhouse, where it accumulated chicken droppings for years. The chickens loved to roost on the open turntable.

When Lee died, his wife Imogene moved into a small apartment. She called and asked me to pick up the Edison if I wanted it. I was sure it was in bad condition and was reluctant to pick it up. When I did pick it up I was shocked at just how bad the condition really was. The turntable, pickup arm, and controls were completely covered with inches of chicken poop. The oak veneer was chipped and peeling and the front ornate grill was completely missing. It was so bad I did not want it inside my workshop so I put it on the back porch and covered it with a tarp.

A few weeks went by and I decided to put it on the curb for trash pickup. My wife Mary was against my doing so. "After all," she said, "That is your great-grandmother's phonograph. I really think you should keep it." I put an old inside door on top of two sawhorses under a shed where I kept my lawnmowers. This would have to serve as an outside workbench. I placed the Edison on top of the door and begin to disassemble it. I used my shop vacuum to remove as much chicken poop as I could, and then removed the mechanical parts from the cabinet. I placed the mechanism in a large plastic pan and poured a gallon of kerosene over it. I let it soak for a few days, turning it several times a day to allow the kerosene to penetrate. A paint brush was used to work the kerosene throughout the machine. The kerosene was changed three times. Finally, it was clean enough to test and see if it would run. When I flipped the "run" lever, there was a sickening sound of a spring breaking. Two things ruined the spring—being stored in a fully wound condition, and rust brought on by the acidic runoff from bird droppings.

A search of the Internet turned up a gentleman in Canada who buys spring steel in large coils and will custom-make a spring for any phonograph. All I had to do was remove the spring housing (cartridge) and send it to him along with $125, and in a few weeks I'd have a new spring.

While waiting for the spring, I went to work with my orbital sander and sanded it completely. Chipped and missing veneer was replaced using razor blades to cut the wood for an exact fit. I found a piece of oak veneer that was a perfect match and sawed out a new grill for the front. I had to create a design as I could never find a picture of the original. Grill cloth was another problem. It must be heavy enough to stretch tightly, dense enough that you cannot see through it, and thin enough to allow the sound to come through. The fabric store had material that worked okay. The felt on the turntable was filthy and rotten. I removed the felt, cleaned and polished the turntable, and then covered it with green felt.

I now had a clean, perfectly restored motor and turntable. The cabinet restoration was relatively simple. After thorough sanding, it was given four coats of satin varnish. I wet-sanded the entire cabinet between coats. As a finishing touch I used 0000 steel wool and rubbed the cabinet until it was glass-smooth. My final coat was done with Kiwi neutral shoe polish, the best polish for furniture I have ever used.

The machine is now in my bedroom and working perfectly. I think Ma would be pleased if she could see it today. I even have some of her old thick Edison records. Most are badly scratched but you can find many of them in good condition on eBay. Now if I can just find "The Preacher and the Bear."

∼

Short skirts, according to Ma, were so bad that they should not be mentioned in mixed company. She believed in women being well covered at all times. She wore seven petticoats, winter and summer, and her dresses covered not only her ankles, but her shoes.

Though stern and somewhat stubborn, Ma was very thoughtful and generous. The presents under our Christmas tree during the

Depression years were few and inexpensive. The best present I received every Christmas was always from Ma. She received a Civil War pension check every month for forty dollars. When her check arrived she had her grandson Lee drive her into Springdale for shopping. She only went to one store—S.R. Wilson Mercantile—where she spent over half of her check on our family needs.

Sometimes a merchant would take advantage of Ma's advanced age and poor eyesight and unload items they had been unable to sell for years. One such transaction is engraved forever in my memory. It was early September, and time for school to start was fast approaching. I was in the fifth grade and had no shoes to wear. Ma assured me that I would have shoes before school started. Being a practical woman, she decided to buy me a pair of lace-up boots. The storeowner sold her a pair of ladies high-top shoes obviously left over from the period before World War I. I suppose I was the only boy who ever attended the entire school year wearing ladies high-top shoes. I never told Ma what she had done. I did not want to hurt her feelings.

During the Hoover era we had a lot of peddlers who brought merchandise to those living in the country. Some such vendors provided a valuable and needed service. Country stores normally carried a very limited stock. It was nice to have a wider selection to choose from, especially when buying such things as spices and patent medicines. We looked forward to monthly visits of the Raleigh and Watkins salesmen. They carried large cases which opened up to display their wares. The salesmen always left with a good order from Ma. Raleigh's Liniment and Watkins Salve became staples in medicine cabinets of most country homes.

Ma was always an easy mark for salesmen with religious books. She never could resist buying a book if it had a picture of Him in it. It mattered little what contents were in the book as long as it had a picture of a man with long hair, dressed in a flowing white bathrobe. These books were never read but put on display on top of the library table for visitors to see.

Speaking of books, when Ma saw the preacher coming down the road for a visit, my job was to grab the Sears and Ward's catalogs and hide them under my bed in the bedroom. Ma would take care of placing an open Bible on her chair-side table.

It's difficult today to realize how quiet it used to be in the country. Spring Valley is at least fourteen miles, as the crow flies, from Fayetteville. The Budd brothers operated a hardwood and wagon factory out near the old Washington County fairgrounds. At six o'clock in the evening they would blow the whistle on their large steam boiler, signaling quitting time for their workers. Most afternoons in the summer months, sitting on the front porch in Spring Valley, you could hear the "hardwood whistle."

Somehow, Ma got the idea that whoever was blowing the whistle had a better clock than the Seth Thomas hanging on our living room wall. Every time she heard the whistle she arose from her rocking chair and walked to the front door where she could see the clock inside. If it was a couple of minutes off, she would go inside and set the clock. I never understood her preoccupation with knowing the exact time.

One afternoon our old hound dog Sam was sleeping behind Ma's rocker. About twenty minutes before the six o'clock whistle a chemical reaction occurred in Sam's stomach, caused no doubt by the large meal of cornbread and fat meat he had enjoyed only thirty minutes before. Sam expelled a large amount of gas, accompanied by the appropriate sound. "There goes the hardwood whistle," said Ma. She jumped up, walked to the door, and looked at the Seth Thomas clock. "Mack, this clock is twenty minutes slow. I told you yesterday it was time to get a turkey feather and give it a good oiling."

∼

I started laughing thinking about ol' Sam. Looking to the west, I could see the sun sinking behind Wes Holmesley's barn. It was later than I realized. I walked slowly up the dirt road to the house.

"Come on in, Son, and eat," said my granddad, Mack. He always called me Son, and I called him Dad. "The neighbor women have been bringin' in food all afternoon." I did not feel hungry, but with all the fried chicken, pies, and cakes, I managed to eat "a sizeable meal."

That night I slept on a pallet on the floor. I awoke occasionally and looked in Ma's room. Some of the neighbor men were "sittin' up" with the patient—a custom in our area when someone was near death. I remember a time when my granddad Mack walked four miles every night for weeks to sit up with a sick man near Hindsville.

I could hear hushed voices and see grotesque shadows on the wall cast by the flickering light of the kerosene lamp. Sometime after midnight, I heard Dad get out of bed, go to the kitchen, and grind coffee. I knew he was making coffee for those sitting up all night with Ma.

The following day Ma continued to weaken. She died the morning after the second day, about 9:00 A.M.—almost exactly 48 hours after her stroke. I left the house and went down to sit on the bridge. When I returned an hour later I found the quiet house was now a beehive of activity. It seemed everyone had a job and was going about their work.

"Alice, you go out on the porch and sit a spell," said Sally. "We will take care of getting Mrs. Kelly ready."

"I have her clothes all laid out," replied my grandmother. "Ma picked them out several years ago. They may need ironing. They have been in the bottom of her trunk for a long time."

"Don't worry, Alice," replied Sally. "I've prepared a lot of bodies for burial. Do you want she should wear her black and silver pin?'

"Yes, she would like that," replied Mama Alice. She walked to the end of the porch and eased herself into the porch swing, turned to me and said, "I would like a cup of hot coffee. Run in the kitchen and bring me one."

I was glad for the chance to do something useful. I had felt out of place for the last two days. As I handed her the coffee, Dad walked up and said, "Alice, I better get up to Pete's and see about getting the box made. He needs to get on it right away. Have Hazel call Lee's family at Muskogee. We better have the funeral about one o'clock day after tomorrow. Lee and Myrt's family will want to drive back to Muskogee after the burial. I suppose they will leave direct from the cemetery. It's a hard four-hour trip to Muskogee."

"That's fine with me. If I know Pete, he is probably making plans right now," answered Mama Alice.

"Can I go with you Dad—up to Pete's?" I asked.

"Come on, Son," he said.

Pete was in his shop when we got there. "I figured you'd be needin' a box," he said. "I was just lookin.' I have enough pine to do the job. I will need to go to town and pick up the coffin hardware at the Famous, and I'll need some cloth for the inside and outside of the box."

"How much do you figure this will be costing?" asked Dad. "We want to put her away real nice."

"Well, Mack," said Pete, "I can buy real bronze handles and hardware for the box for about eight or nine dollars. Figure five dollars for the sateen lining and cotton padding. Then a nice grey material, with raised flowers, to cover the box will run another seven dollars or so. Mine and Sally's labor will run about ten dollars, and the pine I use will be less than two dollars. I'll guarantee no more than forty dollars—probably less. If this is all right with you, I'll get my old Model T cranked up and head for Springdale. I'll have to get movin' if you are to have it by tomorrow night when the Muskogee folks arrive."

"I'm obliged," replied Dad, "I know you will do a first-class job. Let me give you twenty now to buy material with. I'll have the rest of the money tomorrow."

We walked down the dusty road to the house. I was anxious for Pete to go to work on the casket. I knew he would let me watch he and Sally doing the building. Minutes later I heard Pete's 1924 Model T coupe climbing up the long hill on the way to Springdale.

The odor of Lysol was strong. I could smell it the moment we left Pete's shop. I found the women had moved Ma to a bed in the small back bedroom where they were fixing her hair and dressing her in her Sunday best.

Other neighbor women knocked down her bed, then scrubbed the bed and entire room with Lysol. After the scrubbing, the bed was "put out to sun" in the backyard. One of the ladies gathered up all the bedclothes, along with Ma's nightgowns, and tied them up in a sheet. "I'll do these the day after the funeral, Alice," she said. I suppose the scrubbing of all bedding and floors with a strong disinfectant, sunning the bedding, etc., was a custom left over from the time when sicknesses such as smallpox, typhoid, and influenza were easily transmitted.

Ted Sanders came down the road and stepped onto the front porch. "Alice," he said, "I will be glad to haul Mrs. Kelly to the church and cemetery in my truck if you would like."

"Thanks, Ted, I was going to ask Mack to go up and see if you would do it," she replied.

"I'll pick up the coffin when Pete and Sally are done with it," he said. "Then I'll bring it down here and help put Mrs. Kelly in it."

In Spring Valley, when there was a death, no one worked until after the funeral unless it was absolutely necessary and the work could not be postponed.

Ma was buried in Friendship Cemetery, about three o'clock on a beautiful sunny afternoon. She had a nice funeral, and was buried in a casket handmade by close friends. She was carried to the church and then to the cemetery by a man she had known since the day he was born. The church at Spring Valley was filled with friends and family. Store-bought flowers may have been absent, but there were dozens of bouquets, picked with care, and arranged with love, by her many friends. She had lived her "three score and ten," with eight years thrown in for free. What more can one expect from life?

CHAPTER 9

The Depression Years

Mary had a little lamb,
Its fleece was white as cotton,
Every time it wagged its tail,
It showed its Hoover Button.

—A popular poem from 1928

A salesman—known then as a "drummer"—on his weekly trip to the Spring Valley general store, recited the little verse above for those sitting around the woodstove awaiting arrival of the mail hack. It was repeated often during the coming months. It is, perhaps, the first poem I ever bothered to commit to memory.

President Hoover, one of the most unpopular men ever to occupy America's highest office (other than George W. Bush) was the subject of many harsh jokes. History since then has done little to change his image. Then, as now, Americans blamed their leaders for whatever misfortune came their way. The principal reasons for the crash of 1929 and the Great Depression are today well known. Nevertheless, in 1930 most Americans blamed President Hoover. Then, as now, with the small correction we are going through today, people refuse to place blame where it belongs: squarely on the shoulders of the average greedy American citizen.

On Wall Street brokers leaped to their deaths from their plush offices in high-rise buildings lining both sides of the street. Unemployed businessmen, broke and hungry, stood in line with out of work laborers at soup kitchens across this great land. "Hobo Jungles" on the outskirts of our major cities were wryly called "Hoovervilles." In smaller towns and villages fewer people were out of work. However, with the "bank holiday" and a general tightening of the economy, the Great Depression was beginning to touch the lives of everyone. Our country was ripe for a president with new ideas. Franklin Delano Roosevelt was ready, and waiting in the wings.

~

> *And while I am talking to you mothers and fathers, I give you one more assurance. I have said this before, but I shall say it again and again. Your boys are not going to be sent into any foreign wars.*
> —FRANKLIN D. ROOSEVELT (1882–1945),
> October 30, 1940

In the rural areas of Arkansas things went along pretty much as usual. In eastern Washington County and the less populated counties, well into central Arkansas, lay the so-called backwoods areas of the state. The lives of those living in this area were less dependent upon the national economy. Most of the population continued to live as they had for years, growing much of their own food, and trading and bartering with neighbors.

The average farm family had two or three cows, a henhouse full of chickens, a pigpen with a few fattening hogs, a large vegetable garden, and a few fruit trees. During the spring they worked in their garden. From midsummer until late fall they canned food in glass fruit jars and stored their winter food in cool cellars. Wild blueberries and blackberries could be had just for the picking.

Two things were needed when picking wild berries: a strong back and a sharp eye. It took a lot of bending and stooping to pick berries, especially blueberries, as the wild variety, while superior in taste, is also smaller than the commercial variety. It takes a long time to fill a gallon bucket.

A sharp eye was needed to watch for snakes. If there is a snake within a hundred miles you can be sure he will head for a berry patch. The best explanation I have heard about this is that birds feed on the berries and the snakes lie in wait for the birds. It sounds reasonable to me.

Ray Shaver and his wife Margaret went huckleberry (blueberry to city folks) hunting a number of years ago. After finding a fine patch of berries Margaret started filling her bucket from a heavily loaded bush. Ray was some ten feet or so away working on another bush. Suddenly Margaret yelled, "Ray, come here quick! There is a big rattlesnake!" Ray dropped his bucket and ran over to Margaret. Sure enough, not five feet away was a coiled rattler. Ray started throwing some rocks at it. "No, no," said Margaret, "over here is the snake."

"I can see it," said Ray. "I'll kill it if I can find enough rocks."

Well, it turned out that there was not two, but actually three snakes visible to the berry pickers. Ray turned to Margaret and said, "I think my bucket is full." Margaret agreed. They left the berry patch with not even enough berries to make a pie.

Preserving foodstuff for the winter was an art. A hole dug in the ground and lined with straw provided a good storage bin for both turnips and potatoes. Fresh, crisp vegetables could be enjoyed all winter long. The hole was covered with boards and a layer of dirt shoveled on top of the boards to keep the vegetables from freezing, and to protect them from curious animals. When you needed the vegetables the dirt was raked away, and reaching down in the hole you removed enough for the week ahead. The hole kept the vegetables as fresh and solid as they were the day they were stored. Some farmers dusted the potatoes and turnips with lime to keep down moisture.

They made soap, hominy, and apple butter in large outdoor kettles, heated by wood they chopped on their place. When winter came they had a smokehouse full of meat, a cellar full of food, and enough wood chopped to last through a long winter. Money was scarce, but only the lazy went into the winter without a plentiful supply of wood for heating, and more than enough food. Potatoes, onions, apples, sweet potatoes, and turnips could be kept all winter when properly stored. About the only expense they absolutely had to bear was a few dollars a year in property tax. I am sure that the average backwoods family ate better than their city cousins that had well-paying jobs.

When the ladies met for their weekly Ladies Aid Society meeting they gathered around a quilting frame. While quilting, they bragged about how many jars of kraut, beets, peaches, etc. they had canned, and shared their favorite canning recipes. Farm women did not rest until all available shelving was filled with canned food. My grandparents canned peaches, green beans, sugar beets, corn, hominy, tomatoes, cucumbers, tender greens, and several different jams. They also had cans of green tomato and cucumber relishes. Practically every farm family had a barrel of apples stored for the winter. They had to be kept cool, but not allowed to freeze. Glassed-in back porches made an ideal place for apples and pickled food such as kraut and meat.

It is easy to see how those living in the country withstood the Depression much better than their counterparts living in the city.

A few years ago my wife Mary and I were fortunate enough to be afternoon guests at an old farmhouse near Cane Hill. We had never met the old couple living there. A grandson, whom we knew very well, asked us to go with him one Sunday to visit his grandparents and photograph them while we were there. It was just one of the perks of being professional photographers.

The cordial grandparents were genuine hill-country people. They were perfectly content and happy living as their parents and grandparents had lived before them. In a large, clean kitchen we noticed a brand new gas range. On the opposite wall was an old wood cookstove with a well-filled wood box sitting beside it. The kitchen floor was covered with a nine-by-twelve foot piece of bright linoleum. The center of the kitchen was occupied by a wooden table, obviously used as both a dining table and a food preparation area. The two remaining kitchen walls served as backdrops for a kitchen sink, crude but serviceable cabinets and shelving, and more food preparation space. Hanging on the wall was a large calendar, a bunch of dried sage tied with a string, and a long string of garlic.

I wanted a picture of the grandmother standing at the old wood cook stove. She gladly posed for the picture. In an effort to make conversation, I asked when they were going to take the old stove down.

The elderly lady replied, "Oh, I never use that newfangled stove. The grandkids bought it fer us five year ago. Pa and me jest don't like food cooked on it. We'll jest stick with the one we was raised with. You jest can't beat a good woodstove fer cooking." She continued, "Pa, build a fire in the cook stove while I whip up some pie dough."

Turning to me, she asked, "How long has it been since you had a mess of fried pies?"

"Much too long," I replied. "I don't think I've had a fried pie since my great-grandmother Kelly died."

In a bit less than one hour we had a large platter stacked with fried peach and apple pies. Now these were not the sterile healthy kind that tastes like cardboard, they were the real thing, fried in hog lard and full of all sorts of things damned by modern medicine. I ate six of them and Mary did equally as well.

I am sure such food contributed in a large part to my grandfather Mack's early demise. He desperately wanted to live to see his 100th birthday. If he had left off his "chewin' tobaccy," fat meat, and fried food he might have lived another three weeks and made the 100 mark.

Mack dearly loved his fried ham and redeye gravy. To be sure he had plenty of meat for the winter he kept and slopped three hogs all summer. He looked forward to "hog-killin' time" like a kid looks forward to Christmas.

On a chilly late November morning when it appeared that winter had arrived to stay, neighbors gathered at a farm picked weeks before for the annual hog killing. Refrigeration was unknown in the country, so a warm week in the winter could spoil your winter's meat. The honor of having your place chosen for the event was not to be taken lightly. Each farmer tried his best to provide good hog-killin' facilities and good food for the workers. Next year a different farm in the area would host the event. No matter where the butchering took place, some of the same equipment would be used. Not everyone owned a vat large enough to scald a hog; the same was true for the sausage mill, and block and tackle hoist.

Before daylight, or more likely the evening before, the vat was placed on stones so that it was several inches off the ground. Then many buckets of water had to be carried from the spring or well to fill the vat about half full. Kitchen wood was placed under the vat with a few kerosene-soaked corncobs used for kindlin.' The first chore of the morning was getting a good fire going under the vat. It takes a time and effort to get the water to the boiling point before sunup.

An A-frame, built from poles usually cut just for this event, was in place over the vat. A block and tackle hanging from the A-frame would be used to lower the hog carcass into the boiling water. Most hogs butchered would weigh around 250 to 350 pounds.

Nearby, long tables made from sawhorses and two-by-twelve foot oak boards were scrubbed clean with lye soap and boiling water from the vat. After scalding, hogs were scraped to remove all hair. The scraped carcass was then carried to the scrubbed table for butchering.

About 6:30 or 7:00 A.M. families started arriving in loaded wagons. Hogs, shot through the brain that morning, their bodies still warm to the touch, were piled inside the wagon along with children, pots and pans, sausage casings, and butcher knives. The spring seat of the wagon, or the cab of the truck, was reserved for the farmer and his wife.

Upon arrival, the ladies retired to the house to start preparing a large dinner (for you Yankees, "dinner" is the noonday meal). While catching up on local gossip they brewed pots of hot coffee and carried it to the working men. Outside, the young children played games, their breath crystallizing in the cold morning air. Boys over ten years old were expected to work alongside their father to learn the art of butchering.

All of the actual butchering would be finished about noon. The men, up since before dawn, were now ready for a little rest and a lot of dinner. Along the back of the house a long low table, normally used for washday, had been scrubbed clean and was, for today, an outdoor washroom where the workers could scrub up before eating. Nails driven in the unpainted oak siding served as handy places to hang hats and coats. The women carried teakettles of hot water from the kitchen to fill pans for hand washing.

After a big meal and a few minutes rest, the men returned to work. There was a lot of cleanup to be done before leaving for home. Each man loaded all of his butchered meat in the wagon with the exception of a washtub half-full of trimmings—that was meat for sausage.

Inside the house, or sometimes on a back porch, another improvised table was ready and waiting for grinding sausage. This was not done by an electric motor—FDR's Tennessee Valley electric service was still a few years in the future. Everyone took turns cranking the sausage mill. Good sausage depends upon the proper mix of lean and fat meat. Once the sausage was ground it was placed in large dishpans, covered with clean dishtowels, and carried to the wagons and trucks. Final work of mixing and stuffing the sausage meat would be done after they arrived home and completed their daily chores.

After supper, the fresh-ground pork was mixed with salt, sage, pepper, and sometimes with sodium nitrite as a preservative. There were few families that seasoned sausage the same way. In this area very few families used natural casings for stuffing the sausage. Most families made casings from a porous white cloth sewed into cylindrical tubes about sixteen inches long. After it was stuffed, the sausage tube was tied with string and either kept at low temperature or smoked. Some families preferred sausage with a bit of bite in it. Those families often used dried red peppers ground into flakes instead of conventional black pepper. Final curing and processing of the meat might take another two days work.

None of the hog was wasted. The feet were pickled, and the head ground up into head cheese, which was sometimes called "souse meat." Hams, shoulders, and side meat were cured according to the wishes of the family. Some liked the sugar cure while others preferred smoke-cured meat. My grandfather used a lot of salt to cover and preserve his meat. Later, after being covered with salt for days and when the winter got much colder, the hams and shoulders would be hung from rafters in the smokehouse.

One family of German descent who lived in the Black Jack community pickled their meat. They sliced side meat and put it in a five-gallon or larger stoneware container of brine solution. This was kept on a back porch or storeroom without heat. A weighted cover was placed on top of the meat to keep it well submerged in the brine. Believe me, if you have never tasted pickled side meat, sprinkled well with black pepper, rolled in flour, and then fried a deep brown, you have no idea what you are missing. This has to be the very best meat I have ever eaten.

It's a hard fact that those who suffered less in the Great Depression were those who lived in rural areas. They were used to hardships and knew better how to get by as our pioneers lived years ago. It was my pleasure to drive Mack and his hogs to the event described above. It was his last 'hog killin.' For the remainder of Mack's life, he would have to make do with meat from the butcher shop or supermarket.

Lee Gibson, Bruce Jr., and school bus.

All school buses at the newly-constructed Huntsville State Vocational School were driven by students. Lee drove this Model A Ford bus all four years he was in high school, from 1932 through 1936. The school operated about five buses and I do not believe there was ever a serious accident. This photo was made after Lee finished washing the bus in the spring at Spring Valley.

CHAPTER 10

The Magnificent Model T

In the early '20s, the rough and often muddy road linking Springdale and Huntsville became State Highway 68. It was graded, graveled, and widened enough to let two cars pass anywhere along the thirty-mile stretch. New one-way concrete bridges replaced the old wooden bridges that were subject to rot and washout. Former mud holes, impassible in wet weather, were filled in, graveled, and graded, turning the new highway into an all-weather road.

The contractor building the road offered work, at a good salary, to those living along the right of way. Unused to a paycheck, most men felt the money was a gift from above and theirs to spend on luxury items they had never thought of owning. Some families bought a nice ornate pump organ for their living room. Others bought phonographs and radios. The item of choice in Spring Valley was the Model T Ford. Pete bought a new Ford coupe. His brother Wesley, Spring Valley's other blacksmith, bought a two-seated enclosed sedan. Mack bought a two-seat touring car.

Now for those born since World War II, a touring car is what you would call a two-seated convertible. I use the term with reservation. To convert the open car to one in which you got only moderately wet in a rainstorm was quite an operation. The cars came with side curtains that were carried under the backseat, along with iron support rods that had to be inserted in holes in the doors. The curtain installation is as difficult to explain as it is to execute—which is plenty difficult. When installed there were cracks and openings everywhere. However Mr. Ford tried to think of everything. There was a flap by the driver that could be pushed open to allow him to spit his tobacco juice out.

Mack took delivery of his new 1924 Ford in Springdale. The seller gave him a few verbal instructions and assured him that driving a Model T was "as easy as fallin' off a log." That may be true, but not many people are anxious to fall off a log. Everything went along smoothly until Mack reached Sonora. Somewhere east of Sonora, but before he got to the White River bridge, he lost control of the car and it jumped a small ditch, coming to rest in a plowed field. Nothing was hurt but my grandfather's pride, but that must have been a terrible wound. He, with a little help, got the car back in the road, drove it to Spring Valley and never drove it again.

Wesley Holmesly must have had some sort of similar experience. His Ford was parked in his barn, covered with a tarp, and never driven again. Pete used his Ford coupe on occasion. I remember once when Pete and Sally invited me to go with them to Fayetteville to a church service that was supposed to be something special. I remember the trip taking a bit under two hours each way. At no time did our speed reach 25 mph. I realize the church service was probably two hours long or so, but it was the longest two hours I ever spent. I still shudder thinking of those hard seats, and the preacher talking for what seemed to be hours.

∼

My uncle, Lee Gibson, was born twelve years after my mother. The new Model T Ford sitting in the garage was a temptation to Lee. He started driving the car when he was twelve years old, and became a very good driver. Once every month he drove his grandmother, Ma Kelly, to Springdale where she cashed her forty-dollar Civil War pension check and bought necessities for the Gibson family. Without the forty-dollar check each month, the Gibson family would have been hard pressed to make it through the difficult years.

It became a ritual in the Gibson household to make an annual trip to Muskogee for a three-day visit every fall during the Muskogee State Fair. Ma's son, Lee Kelly, had moved to Muskogee, Oklahoma in the World War I era. (He had met, courted, and married a young lady, Laura Mills, fresh off the large Mills Ranch in Big Piney, Wyoming and together they had four daughters: Mabel, Opal, Erma, and Mildred. He managed to keep his job even though he was often "in his cups" during working hours. Lee hated work almost as much as he loved his cigars and hard liquor.) Six of our family always made the trip: Grandma Kelly, Mack and Alice Gibson, my mother and I, and Lee Gibson. Lee did the driving even though he was not yet fourteen years old.

One year, for reasons I no longer remember, the trip was planned for late spring instead of early fall. The annual trip was planned as one would plan a trip to Australia today. First the car was thoroughly checked down to the minutest detail. Not wanting to be a financial burden on the Kelly family, we always took along a lot of food: a bushel of potatoes, some canned fruit, and a side of bacon or a ham. The Model T was loaded with about all it could carry. Those of you who remember the car will recall the narrow body size. Three sitting in a seat was not a very comfortable trip.

The Gibsons believed the success of any trip, especially a long trip like from here to Muskogee, depended upon an early start. We arose at 2:00 A.M., ate a big breakfast, packed a picnic lunch to have somewhere along the long 100-mile trip, double-checked the cars tires, radiator, and gasoline supply, and were off and running by 3:30 A.M. If all went well, we would arrive in Muskogee early that afternoon.

By good daylight, we were approaching Westville, Oklahoma. As we passed through Westville we noticed black clouds in the west. It was obvious we were going to drive through some rain. It was now time to prepare for wet-weather driving. Lee pulled off the road and we all got out of the car to install the curtains. When we looked under the back seat for curtains it dawned on us they were in the garage at Spring Valley. They had been removed from the seat to make room for a bushel of potatoes, a pork shoulder, and a dozen jars of canned fruit.

Before we were all back in the car the rain started coming down in torrents. Everyone in the car was soaking wet and speed slowed to about 10 mph. By 10:30 A.M. we were about ten to fifteen miles from Tahlequah, in the valley east of the Cookson hills. The road in front of us disappeared into a lake of water. In the distance we could see a train stopped on the tracks, the rails disappearing into the same lake of water. In language of the time, we had a "washed-out roadway." We found out later that flooding of the roadways in that area occurred often. Obviously, the lake was not going to drain anytime soon, especially with water coming down in torrents.

My grandfather got out of the car, stood in the heavy rain, and said, "We passed a house back down the road a piece. Son, back this dern car back down there, and I'll ask if there is another road we can take to Muskogee."

By now we were all soaking wet and getting a bit discouraged at travel by automobile—if the Model T could ever be considered an automobile. Obviously we had but two choices: backtrack to Arkansas, or find an alternate road to Muskogee. Lee put his foot on the middle pedal, and backed the Ford down the narrow dirt road. He stopped in front of an unpainted old farmhouse. An old-timer was sitting in a badly worn rocking chair on the porch. His overalls were well worn and not very clean. He had no shirt on, just his long underwear under the overalls. He was barefooted. Even so, we could not help but envy him, for he was warm and dry. Mack got out of the car and walked onto the porch to get out of the heavy rain. When he asked about another road to Muskogee the old fellow replied, "Yep, thar's another way, but hit's a rough 'un. You jest take this here road beside my house and go about two mile up Turkey Holler. Thar's a ford up there acrost the creek. Hit's shore to be up today with all this here rain, but you might make it acrost. Iffin you can ford that creek, the road winds around a bit and comes out on high ground. From there on hit's a clear shot to Tahlequah."

Mack thanked the old gentleman and returned to the car. After talking it over it was decided to push ahead. Lee turned the Model T up the dirt road toward Turkey Holler. Before we had gone a mile up the hillside, the trail tilted to a steep and dangerous angle. If the car rolled over we would end up in a raging stream beside the road. Mack got out of the car and had my mother do likewise. They stood on the running boards on the high side of the car, gripped the metal bows of the canvas top, and leaned backward in hopes of balancing the car to keep it from rolling, or sliding, down the steep hillside. About six miles up the dangerous road we came to the creek. It was running swift and full. We had no idea at all how deep the stream was. There was another farmhouse a short distance up the hillside. "Honk the horn, Son, I'm gonna go up there and see if I can find out how deep that river is. Since that feller lives right by it, he oughta know whether or not we can ford it. It may not be very deep—but then again it might be over our heads."

The door of the house opened and a man stepped out onto the porch. "You folks lost or something?" he asked.

"We are tryin' to get to Muskogee," replied Mack. "How deep you figure the creek is?"

"I don't think it would be smart to try to ford it," the man replied. "You might make it, but it will be mighty close. I am afraid you might get your feet wet and drown out your motor. Tell you what. Let me go hook up my team of horses to the wagon. I'll take the womenfolk and the kid across in my wagon, and then I'll come back and hook a chain to your car and pull it across."

We loaded into the wagon, and with my mother near panic, the farmer pulled us across the stream. Sitting in the wagon, the water was inches below the wagon bed. I remember reaching over the side of the wagon and putting my hand in the water. Once he unloaded us he returned and hooked a chain to the front axle of the car and pulled it through the water. Lee was near panic and crying as he steered the Ford across the river. The floor of the Ford got good and wet. It took some time to get the engine dried out and started.

Here is where the story gets unbelievable. The farmer would not accept any payment at all for his work in the rain. When we offered him money for all his help, the farmer, now soaked to his bones, refused payment. "It's the least a man can do," he said. "I am always glad to help somebody in trouble." We thanked him profusely. He wished us luck on our journey and drove his team back across the raging creek. My, how times have changed. We arrived in Muskogee before dark.

The Model T was also used to take us to the annual Fourth of July picnic in Springdale. The picnic grounds are now occupied by the City Administration Building. Near the center of the grounds, southwest of the water tower, was a bandstand. During the annual celebration the

Springdale High School band usually played a concert in the morning. Politicians, most of whom were running for office, took up most of the afternoon making long and dull speeches. Thankfully this was before loudspeaker systems became available in our city. Often the speeches were barely audible over the laughing and visiting of people in attendance.

The water tower in the center of the park was there long before I was born. It was years before the city discovered that an insurance agent, who was also a city office holder, had the water tower more than adequately insured against fire damage. I have always wondered what the odds were of a metal tower filled with water catching on fire and burning.

My grandparents started planning for the Fourth weeks before the occasion. When the big day finally arrived my grandmother would arise about 4:00 A.M., prepare a big breakfast, then fry two chickens killed and dressed the night before. In a large basket she packed the fried chicken, biscuits, boiled eggs, some fruit of some sort, and a bowl of potato salad. We always brought two fruit jars of water to the picnic because we could only afford a small amount of money for cold drinks. We were ignorant and did not know that you cannot keep potato salad for hours in a hot automobile without it becoming dangerous to eat. We dined on hot potato salad and chicken in perfect safety. Sometimes a little knowledge can be a terrible thing to bear.

Normally we left home about 7:00 A.M. and arrived at the picnic grounds within the hour. Such early starts assured us of our favorite parking space under a large oak tree on the southeast corner of the grounds.

The jingle of change in my pocket was like music to my ears as I walked around the picnic grounds. I'd saved my strawberry picking money and today I had thirty-five cents to spend on the picnic. I can assure you the money was not spent without careful consideration. In my ten-year-old mind I tried to work out a budget. Ten cents would go for two large glasses of lemonade—one in the morning and another about mid-afternoon.

The wonderful smell of hamburgers frying covered the grounds like a fragrant blanket, which made this budget thing very frustrating.

Mack and his great-grandson, Mike, circa 1960 at Monte Ne.

Which had I rather spend a dime on—a ride on the Ferris Wheel or one of those good-smelling hamburgers? I pondered the choice; the Ferris Wheel won out. There was still a lot of chicken and potato salad in the back seat of the Model T. Then I made a major decision. I'd not spend a dime on the Merry-Go-Round and enjoy a big hamburger instead. After all, the Merry-Go-Round was more for small children, not ten-year-old boys like me. That settled my dilemma. I'd ride the Ferris Wheel, enjoy two glasses of lemonade, eat a big, good-smelling hamburger, and have a nickel left over to buy a United States flag on a stick. I could hold it out the side of the car on the way home and watch it flap in the breeze. Everything considered, I think I spent my money wisely.

By 4:00 P.M. I had to be back at the car. My granddad Mack had to be home in time to do his chores. I always suffered a great feeling of sadness as we pulled away from the picnic grounds and headed home. The day looked forward to for so many weeks was now a thing of the past and it would be an entire year before the next picnic. I pondered relativity: why did the trip home seem so much longer than the trip to the picnic grounds?

CHAPTER 11

The Discovery Years

These dark days will be worth all they cost us if they teach us our true destiny is not to be ministered unto, but to minister to ourselves and our fellow man.

—FRANKLIN D. ROOSEVELT, (1882–1945)

Our country in the midst of a Great Depression was looking for a savior. Then, even more than now, people were discontented and disillusioned with their representatives in Washington. It seemed that Roosevelt might have ideas that would lead the country out of its financial crises.

In the spring of 1932 we moved to Huntsville, county seat of Madison County. With an economy better than many larger cities, Huntsville did not have one foot of paved roads in the city. Electric power, at best a fluctuating intermittent service, was supplied by a private power company. Huntsville's water supply, primitive in nature and privately owned, reached most homes within the city limits. Sewer service was nonexistent.

According to Goodspeed's *History of Madison County*, Huntsville was beginning its second century as a county seat. Original copies of Goodspeed's are hard to find and when found demand rather high prices. Therefore I feel the following paragraphs copied directly from my reprinted copy of Goodspeed's should be of interest.

> Courthouses: The first court in the county was held in the barn of Evan S. Polk, northwest of Huntsville about one fourth of a mile. The barn of John Sanders was used for the same purpose.
>
> The first courthouse stood upon the public square in Huntsville, which has been occupied in this way ever since. It was

built of hewn logs, which, to facilitate ventilation or for some other purpose, was never chinked and daubed. There was one room, about thirty feet square, open to the roof. It was entered by two doors from the north and south, while the judges table was at one end. There was neither stove or chimney, nor need of any, as the sessions were held late in the spring and early in the fall. The benches and tables rested on terra firma for several years, when a puncheon floor was added. This building was erected in 1837–38, at a cost of $150, provided by a tax levied at the rate of $1.28 per forty acres of improved land.

The next courthouse was built in 1845. It was a brick building forty feet square and two stories high. The lower floor was used as a courtroom. It was entered by doors on the north and south; the judge presided at the east end; the floor was of brick; the stairway was in the northwest corner, and a narrow hall extended east and west through the second story, communicating with the offices of the clerk and sheriff, the jury rooms and several other apartments. There were three windows on the east and west, an equal number on the north and south in the second story. The roof sloped north and south. The contractor was Evan S. Polk, who burned the brick on his farm adjoining the town. The cost was about $4,000. This building was burned by Northern vandals in 1863. The records were taken to Springfield, Missouri, and there lost or destroyed, in great part.

The first sessions of the court, at the close of the war, were held in the house of John Vaughan, now owned by W.J. Sams, and in the Masonic Hall, January 28, 1867. James A. Jay, commissioner of public buildings, was directed by the county court to sell the bricks of the old courthouse. April 27, 1868, the court resolved to build a new courthouse, and appointed John Carroll to draft a plan for a suitable building. May 1, 1868, he reported a plan of a brick building to cost $6,000. October 30, 1868, Charles W. Raymond succeeded Carroll, and on the following day he reported a plan, which was adopted, and $10,000 appropriated for its erection. November 14, 1868, Richmond and Carroll were directed to let out the erection of the building by contract.

The bids for this structure exceeded the budget. A frame building, because of its lower price, was built in 1872. It burned to the ground seven years later.

In April 1879, a two-story stone building was erected on the north side of the square. To the best of my knowledge this was the courthouse was still in use in the 1930s.

Immediately west of the courthouse, on the northwest corner of the town square, was the hotel. The two-story stucco building seemed strangely out of place with architecture more appropriate for a small western town. Large letters across the front of the second story proclaimed simply, "HOTEL."

Huntsville's post office and two large billboards filled the entire west side of the town square. As the billboards were set back from the street at least fifty feet, the weeded area in front of the billboards made an ideal spot for medicine shows. The city was very pleased to have free entertainment for its citizens and gladly allowed shows to occupy the space.

Hawkins Drugstore, Teague's Café, Warren and Culwell Hardware, the city's only theater, an automobile garage, and some smaller businesses lined the south side of the square. Some business firms came and went on a regular basis. When we moved from Huntsville, the Brashears family had just opened the city's only undertaking establishment between Teague's Café and the automobile garage. On the east side of the square was Guinn's Hardware, Harper's Café, Coger Drugstore, and the Brashears furniture store. Mr. Harper was badly crippled and walked with difficulty. The tall, pleasant gentleman could be found working in his café from daylight until well after dark. The rumor was that he had been injured years before in a gunfight. I believed the story. In the years prior to World War II, it was very easy to become involved in a gunfight at Huntsville.

I well remember one day when I was riding my bicycle across the square, I suddenly became aware that I was the only person moving. Where was everyone? I looked to my right toward the Hawkins Drugstore and found myself looking down the barrel of a .45 revolver. I turned, looking northward to see who Junior Hawkins, son of the store owner, was aiming his revolver at. I found out. I was looking down the barrels of two more guns held by the Holland brothers. I decided to retreat to our home one block west of the square. When I started west my path was blocked by an older model touring car.

Sitting in the driver's position, an elderly gentleman was aiming a double barrel shotgun in my direction. I quickly made a 180-degree turn and headed east only to find Sheriff Virgil Weathers standing in front of Coger Drugstore, gun drawn, and again aiming more or less my direction. I took the only path available to me. I left the bicycle and dove under a pickup truck.

It seems that the young Holland boy had gone in the drugstore and gotten into an argument with Junior Hawkins, the storeowner's son. The Holland boy left with the vow to come back with his brother and shoot Junior dead. Junior believed him. He got his dad's old .45 revolver from under the cash register, carefully checked it to see that it was fully loaded, and waited. Mr. Hawkins, expecting a gunfight, wisely called Sheriff Weathers. The sheriff checked his guns and took up a position in front of the Coger drugstore where he could see the road leading to the Holland home and the drugstore.

Sheriff Weathers was at home when he received the call. He turned to his father and said, "Junior Hawkins is about to get himself killed. I'm going up to the square and see if I can stop this gunfight."

His father, a rugged old-timer with a snow-white handlebar mustache, decided he would back up the sheriff. He got down his trusty double-barrel shotgun, got in the old open car and drove to the west side of the square. If anyone got in a gunfight with his son, he would blast them into eternity. It was especially tense because everyone knew the Holland boys did not make idle threats. They were not to be dismissed lightly. Mr. Weathers stopped his old car in front of the post office. The car had no windows, just a canvas top. This gave the old gentleman a wide range of fire. He pulled his Stetson lower over his eyes, cocked his shotgun, and aimed it in the general direction of the dreaded action.

As promised, the Holland boys returned, and called out young Hawkins. Junior, defending his honor, stepped from the drugstore with his .45 in hand. The Holland boys appraised the situation. When Sheriff Weathers called for them to drop their weapons, they slowly complied after seeing it was sure death if they fired the first shot. Everyone involved was greatly relieved, especially me, as it was getting very uncomfortable under that pickup truck. Apparently the problem was resolved between Junior Hawkins and the Hollands, and nothing more was said about the incident.

A short time later, the Holland boys had a get-together with friends in their home. Early in the morning one of the boys left the room, came back with a gun, and killed his brother, girlfriend, and a young Boatright boy. It was reported that he then called the sheriff, and calmly took a seat on his front porch and waited to be arrested. He offered no resistance.

Older residents told me that at one time there was a water pump and a bandstand in the center of the square. Apparently they had been neglected and Nature allowed to proceed uninterrupted. The only thing I recall in the center of the square was a lot of weeds, a few empty bottles and tin cans, and sleeping hound dogs.

The great bank robbery occurred the year before we moved to Huntsville. It was still a popular topic of conversation when we arrived. Dalton Dotson, sheriff at the time, could have played in any John Wayne western without make-up of any kind, and he would have been perfectly at home doing so. Tall in the saddle, lean and strong, he was the idol of not only every boy in town, but of their parents as well. He dressed and looked much like Matt Dillon of the *Gunsmoke* TV series.

Back to the robbery. One morning, two men walked into the First National Bank, whipped out their revolvers, grabbed what cash they could, pushed bank employee Uncle Dave Anderson around a bit, then ran to their car and made a fast getaway.

Someone ran from the bank yelling, "We've been robbed and they hurt Uncle Dave!" Dalton had just left the jail and was walking up to the square when he heard all this. He quickly jumped on to the running board of the first car he saw and instructed the driver to give chase.

A few miles from Huntsville, the robbers decided to leave the car and take off on foot. They started running up a dry creek bed. With Dalton gaining on them they decided to fight it out. Taking cover behind a fallen log, they started shooting at Dalton—a serious mistake. Dalton never bothered to take cover. Planting his feet wide apart he lifted his heavy gun and took careful aim. Every time one peeped over the log he got a face full of splinters. One of their bullets hit the stock of Dalton's gun, but he stood fast, firing slowly and with grim determination. The criminals soon decided they were no match for such bravery. They threw out their guns and surrendered to the young sheriff.

This is the story I heard many times during our seven years in Huntsville. I strongly suspect that it was the Hindsville bank that was robbed instead of Huntsville. I have no idea how Uncle Dave Anderson got into the story, if it was the Hindsville Bank. I knew both Dalton and his son X Dotson. I do not for one moment doubt the story could be true, but I do know that sometimes after repeated telling, stories are embellished a bit. After years and years of retelling a story can become a legend.

~

In 1931 my parents, driven by sheer desperation, opened a beauty shop in Huntsville. They raised $175 by selling their Chrysler convertible. I have no idea where they obtained the rest of the money needed. I remember they bought all the equipment and supplies from Max and Betty Cox for a total selling price of $300.

Betty had been operating the shop from her home south of town, just north of the Lon Garrett home. (In 1992 I checked and the house was still there.) Max, a highly intelligent young man, about thirty years old at the time, was one of those rare individuals who could do practically anything he tried. Always thinking, it would take more than the Great Depression to keep Max out of work. He would create a job where none existed before.

Though separated in age by more than twenty years, Max and I became good friends, and our friendship lasted until he left the area. During the years I knew Max he was engaged in many different enterprises: a motel, drive-in restaurant, appliance repair, dime store, building contractor, and theater manager in Huntsville and Springdale. At the time of his death he was living in Roswell, New Mexico, where he built and managed a large mobile home park.

Now that Betty had sold her beauty shop Max decided he needed something to add to their income. After thinking it over, he discovered that Huntsville did not have a dry cleaning service. Max opened a shop offering seven-day dry cleaning, the actual dry cleaning being farmed out to a firm in Eureka Springs. He bought a brand new Model A roadster (today it's called a convertible) with which to make the weekly trips to Eureka.

All went well until Max and the owner of the shop in Eureka bought a quart fruit jar of white lightning from one of the Eureka natives, and proceeded to sample its contents over a period of hours.

The road from Eureka to Huntsville, unpaved at the time, was narrow, very crooked, and like riding on a washboard—very rough. The road was just wide enough for two cars to pass, provided they both slowed up and pulled to the right. The road was wide enough for the small number of cars using it during the Depression. Seldom was there a problem, but one unfortunate day all this changed.

Max lowered the top of the roadster and put his load of dry cleaning in the empty front seat. Feeling no pain, he was cruising along at a good rate of speed when he suddenly found himself on a collision course with a 1928 Chevrolet sedan. The Chevrolet driver did not wait to see what Max was going to do—he took immediate evasive action, left the road, drove through a barbed wire fence and came to rest with the radiator firmly embedded in a sizeable oak tree.

Max brought the little Ford to a sliding stop, ran to the Chevrolet, and helped the shaken driver from his car. He was relieved to see that the driver was only scared and had suffered no injuries. There was, however, considerable damage to the sedan. The driver was in a very unpleasant mood—especially when he smelled the moonshine, and noticed that Max was having great difficulty in walking in a straight line.

Though both drivers were equally at fault, the Chevrolet driver proceeded to file suit against Max for the extensive—and expensive—damage to his car. Max retained the services of a well-known if somewhat eccentric local defense attorney. To avoid any possible embarrassment to descendents of the attorney, I will refer to him as Mr. Jones.

The trial date was set for late spring. As usual, jurors were picked from the group of loafers who spent their days hanging around the town square. By mid-afternoon Max realized he was in deep trouble. Under oath he admitted that he had been drinking, and was driving in the middle of the road at an excessive rate of speed. As he had invested the money from Betty's beauty shop in the new Ford convertible, he had very little money available. It looked grim indeed. Max figured that he was looking at a time in the local jail.

Mr. Jones was also concerned, because he had a reputation of winning, not losing, damage cases. He asked the judge for a ten-minute recess. His request was granted.

Mr. Jones called his client into a deserted corner of the room and said, "Max, I can win this case if you have six dollars on you."

Though it almost broke him, Max dug deep in his pockets and handed the attorney six one-dollar bills. Grasping the money, Mr. Jones slipped downstairs and walked around the corner of the courthouse. Two minutes later he returned with two-quart fruit jars of the best Carroll County white lightning.

Two and three at a time, Mr. Jones took the jurors into the men's restroom where they all had a double shot of the high-octane colorless liquid. When the court reconvened there was a different attitude among the jurors. Starting at the feet the 'shine worked its way upward in the tired bodies of the jurors. Gradually the wooden seats seemed softer as the normal aches and pains that afflict most people over fifty disappeared, replaced by a contented, generous feeling for one's fellow man.

Mr. Jones, his tongue now well lubricated, gave a masterful if somewhat rambling summation. It was a soliloquy worthy of Shakespeare. He had never been more eloquent. After what must have been one of the shortest deliberations in the history of the court, the jury rendered its verdict of "not guilty."

Young as I was, my education was off to a good start. Our court system in America is a wonderful thing, indeed.

One of the more colorful Huntsville attorneys at the time was Lon Garrett, a portly gentleman of many years. Mr. Garrett was well liked by practically everyone, and was the subject of many stories told around the courthouse. A smooth talker with a booming voice, Mr. Garrett prefaced his statements with "Yep, yep."

One story about Mr. Garrett concerned the occasion of his first automobile ride. His son Howard brought home a new two-seated touring car. He talked his father into going for a ride in the country. A few miles from town the car sputtered a few times, backfired once, and stopped dead. Howard took a measuring stick the dealer had given him, pushed it to the bottom of the gas tank, and withdrew a perfectly dry stick.

"Yep, yep, son," said Mr. Garrett. "What seems to be wrong with it?"

"I'm out of gas, Dad," answered Howard.

"Yep, yep, son, let's just drive it back to town and buy some. I don't think driving it a few miles will hurt it."

∽

The following year, much to my delight, Bill Sonneman of Fayetteville reopened the theater in Huntsville. Max Cox was hired to act as manager, projectionist, janitor, and maintenance man for the small theater. The projectors were the old Powers 6B silent film projectors, retrofitted for optical sound. The projection room was small, so small that the projectors, when pushed against each side wall, left barely enough room between them to thread the 35mm film. A rewind and splicing shelf on the back wall took up even more room. Only fourteen inches separated the Powers projectors from the walls. There was no way for Max to oil the machines properly. I was extremely skinny, the lightest student in my sixth grade class. To my embarrassment I weighed only sixty pounds. Max gave me a free movie pass to help him oil the ancient machines. I had no problem at all crawling behind the projectors.

The Powers 6Bs dated back to World War I. When optical sound was introduced in 1928–29, conversion kits were made available to add sound to the old silent film projectors. In reality, the conversion was rather simple and well-maintained projectors had a long life span. Light was by carbon arc. Extremely bright and very hot, the arc would burn a hole in the film within milliseconds if and when the film broke, stopping motion through the film gate. Nitrate film, extremely flammable, was in use during the '20s. It literally burned like paper soaked in gasoline. Not the safest thing to be playing with in a crowded building.

It was to be expected that every theater, sooner or later, would experience fire damage. The theater in Huntsville and the Concord Theater in Springdale both suffered fires in the projection booth. The only answer for a time was to line projection booths with sheet metal. It was not until 1951, with the introduction of acetate film, that the dangers of projection room fires were relegated to history.

Like most youngsters of the '30s, I never missed a Saturday matinee. Ken Maynard, Buck Jones, Hopalong Cassidy, and a newcomer, John Wayne, appeared in dozens of B-grade Westerns shot in seven days or less. Hollywood cranked them out by the hundreds to take care of the Saturday movie trade. The feature film was almost incidental, as most of us really went to see the serial. Week after week, at the end of each episode, the hero or heroine faced certain doom. Only a miracle could save him. You could be sure we all returned the next Saturday to watch that miracle take place.

I remember one serial especially well—*The Three Musketeers*. It was a story of the French Foreign Legion, whose fight for right and justice brought them into weekly conflict with the villainous El Shaitan. I followed the serial weekly, never missing a Saturday matinee, up until the very last episode. My dad and mother, insensitive to my schedule, planned a weekend trip to visit relatives in Oklahoma. I would have to miss the final episode.

Max heard about my problem. Around 4:00 P.M. Thursday our telephone rang. It was Max. "Come on down to the theater and help me oil the projectors," he said.

When I arrived at the theater Max was waiting at the ticket booth. "How would you like to see the last chapter of *The Three Musketeers?*" he asked.

"Boy, would I!" I replied.

"The film arrived on the mail truck at noon today," Max said. "Come inside and I will run it for you."

I sat in the balcony, just outside the projection room, while Max ran the entire final chapter for one skinny kid dressed in ragged overalls.

(Twenty years later, I hired Max to build a business building on Highway 71. He built me a sturdy, attractive building that has aged well, and he stayed within my very limited budget. One of my most treasured possessions is a small model of a steam engine built by Max using nothing but hand tools.)

Mr. Sonneman owned the Ozark and Palace theaters in Fayetteville, along with the Concord, Shiloh, and Apollo theaters in Springdale. I believe he owned other theaters in Northwest Arkansas, as well. The Shiloh Theater was built on the cheap, in a small downtown business building. Unlike most theaters, in the Shiloh you entered the front door, walked down a narrow walkway and emerged with the screen behind you. The projection booth was in the back of the building.

The Shiloh's matinee showings were not for the critical movie fan. On each side of the screen you were distracted by the street scene outside. You could watch a western and see people walking up and down Emma Avenue at the same time. When you stepped into the darkened theater from the sunny street outside, you were blinded by the flickering image being projected. It was never meant by the motion picture industry for patrons to look directly into a projector, but such cost-cutting methods used in this third-rate movie house were not uncommon.

The floor of the Shiloh was made of cheap unfinished white pine. The seats were a bunch of secondhand seats purchased from one of the early movie houses. They were never built for double features. One needed a well-padded behind to sit through a newsreel, four or five previews, a cartoon, and a full-length movie.

While building the Shiloh, Max gave me a job after school and on Saturdays working on the seat installation. The old seats were bolted together with one-quarter-inch machine screws. The bolt ends were a hazard that was sure to injure someone or tear a hole in their clothing. My job was to saw off all the bolt ends and file them nice and smooth. Otherwise, lawsuits were sure to be numerous when people scraped the skin off their legs or tore holes in clothing.

One hot Saturday afternoon I was working on the seats and wiping sweat from my eyes. The building was not air-conditioned. As a matter of fact, it was not even ventilated. Max was showing the ill-tempered Mr. Sonneman around the construction project when suddenly he stopped dead still. Pointing to me he asked, "What in hell is that damn kid doing?"

Max explained about the danger from the protruding bolts, and that I had been sawing them off and filing the ends smooth to avoid someone getting hurt.

Mr. Sonneman watched me a few minutes and then said, "I hope to hell you ain't paying him much."

Always close with a dollar, Bill Sonneman and Max carried on a love/hate relationship. Max really thought a lot of Mr. Sonneman but found it very difficult to get his boss to do a job right. He would cut any corner he could, even when it was a matter of safety.

In the period prior to World War II, Mr. Sonneman decided to build a really nice theater near the University. It was a large building for the time with a large restaurant and some smaller shops on each side of the flagship UArk Theater. A number of apartments on the second floor were built to supply additional income from the prime piece of real estate. To facilitate moving furniture and fixtures up to the second floor a service elevator was installed.

Max pleaded with Mr. Sonneman to put a safety guard rail on the second-story elevator shaft. The guard rail idea was turned down immediately: "That elevator is not for general use. It is for moving furniture and equipment only—anyway only an idiot would walk into an open elevator shaft."

Max reluctantly gave up the guard rail. I am sure you know where this story is going. Within weeks, Mr. Sonneman walked into the open shaft, fell one story to the floor below, and was in the hospital for some time.

∼

When I read, or hear on TV, about the sad state of education in America, I think of the Huntsville High School, or Huntsville State Vocational School to be more correct. Operating with a very limited budget during the Depression years when I was there, the school was far ahead of most institutions of learning today.

When I completed the eighth grade, I was bored with school

and had no idea what to do with my life. Within weeks my attitude changed: I was interested in school, I became an avid reader, enthusiastic about learning, curious about everything, constantly seeking knowledge about our universe and its inhabitants. One teacher, Murphy Mears, ignited a spark within my empty skull. Thankfully, that spark still burns today.

Mr. Mears did not have an advanced degree at the time. He had a bachelor of science degree and a natural talent for inspiring students—qualifications, in my opinion, adequate for any high school teacher. Mr. Mears taught general science (a required ninth grade course), and physics for those brave enough to stick with him. I remember my very first day in general science class. He looked over his class, thought a minute, and asked, "What is wind?"

Most of us thought it a stupid question. One student, smarter than the rest of us, replied, "Wind is nothing but air in a hurry."

Perhaps a rather flippant answer, but it pleased Mr. Mears as it gave him a lead to teach the class a bit of meteorology.

Mr. Mears had three requirements his students had to meet to pass general science: they must build a working radio, telegraph set, and electric motor. Furthermore, the student had to demonstrate his projects before the class, and explain fully how it worked. All construction had to be from scratch—no commercial kits involved.

I could sense an opportunity to make a dime, maybe even a dollar, on this radio project. I sketched out a schematic of a very simple crystal radio. After studying my trusty Allied Radio catalog I figured I could get the needed parts for about sixty cents. The school had an old pair of earphones, so students could use them for their demonstration. I could sell all needed parts for one dollar and make a tidy profit. By putting my crystal set on display in the science room students could look at my radio and build a duplicate. They could not go wrong.

The deal worked so well, I followed up with an electric motor. My armature and motor shaft were sawed from two different-sized nails. The large piece had a hole through the center; the smaller nail fit through the hole and became the shaft. Magnets were found on old Model T ford magnetos.

Teaching methods at the Huntsville High School during those

Depression years achieved maximum results with a minimum budget. For example, every freshman male student was required to take three weeks of home economics. Home ec girls traded places with the boys and took three weeks of shop and manual training.

The home economics teacher, Miss Bennett, a refined southern lady, was very conscious of our absence of good manners and complete lack of social graces. She was determined to civilize an entire class of unsophisticated young country boys. I often remember the dignified Home Economics teacher and have to admire her courage in undertaking such a difficult task.

I recall very clearly some of Miss Bennett's words: "Chewing gum in public is as bad as eating a cold biscuit in public. Chewing is acceptable only at meal time." She also told us, "Using a toothpick in public is a form of dental hygiene. You should no more pick your teeth at the dinner table than brush your teeth at the table while others are eating. These things are done in private."

Here are some other gems of wisdom from Miss Bennett: "It is highly insulting to a young lady to drive your car up in front of her house and sound the horn. [You would think that most of the class would know this, but they did not.] You drive to your girlfriend's house, leave your car and knock on the door or ring the door bell. You speak to both Mother and Father if present. Tell them where you intend to take their daughter, and what time you expect to bring her home. Then walk the young lady to the car, open the door for her, and when she is comfortably seated, close the door. Do not, under any circumstances, lay a strip or spin your wheels in gravel when leaving."

To further civilize her band of ruffians, Miss Bennett had her girls convert the classroom into a restaurant. The home economics girls prepared a meal and acted as waitresses. Tables were set with napkins and silverware. Each and every boy was required to take a date out to the improvised restaurant. Dates were arranged by Miss Bennett from among the girls in her classes. You had to go through the entire routine. Woe to the boy who did not help his date with her coat and hold her chair when seating her at the table. Your grade suffered if you did not place your napkin properly, if you did not eat your salad with a salad fork, or if you chewed with your mouth open. The teacher missed very little.

During the meal, another couple was sure to come by and had to be properly introduced. It did not make gentlemen of us but it was a step in the right direction. It is true you can't make a silk purse from a sow's ear, and you cannot make a suave gentleman out of a insecure, fifteen-year-old country boy. However, Miss Bennett made a lasting impression on every boy that spent those required three weeks in her classroom. From that day forward I have been unable to enjoy chewing gum anywhere, I have never sounded my car horn in front of any house, and I never use a toothpick in public. I always made dates at least three days in advance and have tried to treat others with kindness and respect. This is not to say that I always succeed in all these things but at least I make an effort. I consider the three weeks spent in her classroom as the most important three weeks in my high school career.

Meanwhile back at the Agri Building girls from the home economics class were learning how to check and replace electrical fuses, replace float balls in toilet water tanks, change washers in water faucets, replace cords on small electrical appliances, adjust hinges and locks, sharpen scissors and knives, and change a car tire.

Tell me anything taught in schools today, more practical and valuable than what we learned in those three weeks.

∼

Certainly I know very little about education, but it's obvious that our poor educational system could be vastly improved by the application of a few simple measures. I believe the ideas below would be a start in the right direction.

> Get rid of troublemakers and those who do not want to learn. Our country should see that qualified, ambitious young people are guaranteed a good education. On the other hand, a college degree is not necessary or even desirable in many professions. If you think I am wrong, the next time your sewer stops up and you

are standing in raw sewage up to your eyes, try and get a Ph.D. to come to your rescue. Society requires a balance between skilled workmen, laborers, craftsmen, and those in so-called white collar professions. Each requires training, but not all require the same level of education.

Forget No Child Left Behind. Replace this with No Child Kept Behind. The first concept will guarantee that we become a second- or third-class country. The second will make the U.S. a country that leads the world.

Teach to the upper half of the class, rather than the lower ten percent. All students are capable of far more than they realize.

Spend more tax dollars for good teachers and less on frills and palaces of learning. Give scholars the same recognition and encouragement that is now given to athletes.

Institute a national examination to be administered yearly to every student in America. Withhold federal aid from schools whose students fail to achieve a certain level of competence. If school administrators and teachers know that their salary is directly related to test scores turned in by their students, you can rest assured that test scores will improve.

~

Mr. Mears encouraged students to follow their interests. I became interested in hydrogen gas. It was simple to make, and we had all the necessary items in our physics lab. I was curious as to what effect it would have if someone inhaled large quantities of pure hydrogen. I mentioned this idea to a few friends but strangely enough, I did not recruit a single volunteer.

My problem was solved, rather unexpectedly, when a student captured a live mouse in one of the school rooms. The mouse was deposited in a one-gallon glass jar until I could work out the final details of my experiment.

I obtained permission from Mr. Mears to use the lab that afternoon. I decided to use a five-gallon bell jar to feed the hydrogen into. A small flask with a glass stopper would be my hydrogen generator.

With such a large area to fill and with a very small flask, I realized it would take a bit of time. When I poured the hydrochloric acid on the zinc filings in the flask the reaction did not last long. This meant I would have to disconnect the flask, refill it, and connect it back to the rubber tube going into the bell jar.

I was on my third flask when James Brashears came down the hall and decided to take a look at the great experiment. James smoked. When I removed the flask from the rubber tube I turned around to refill the flask when I saw a disaster in the making. James lit his cigarette, and then casually held the lighter to the open rubber hose. Yes, hydrogen burns very well. There was an explosion, the like of which I had never heard before. Glass flew everywhere.

It was reported that one obese female student in study hall was sitting in her chair with it tilted backward, the front legs off the floor, when the experiment was suddenly terminated. Reports said that she threw her books in the air, yelled, "Oh my God," and remained tilted at a 45-degree angle for a full two seconds before falling backward in the floor.

It was a mess. The miracle was that not a single student was injured. Broken glass was found thirty feet from the explosion. By the way, I still don't know how the hydrogen affected the mouse. He was never found. I suspect that not enough of him remained to be recognized as a mouse.

First to come rushing in the room was Mr. Mears, followed closely by school superintendent John Baggett and at least 100 students. I knew I would be expelled but not a word was ever said about the damage. It seems everyone was so relieved to see that no one was seriously injured.

The following day Mr. Mears scribbled the following equation on the blackboard:

$$2 \, HCl + Zn \rightarrow ZnCl_2 + H_2 \uparrow$$

That pretty well summed it up. I have but two regrets about the event: I wish I could have seen the study hall incident, and I often speculate about the demise of the mouse. He may have been so full of hydrogen that he was lifted into mouse heaven.

After this brief excursion into the strange field of chemistry I decided to return to something less volatile: electronics. Floyd and Boyd Roberts, two young men with ability bordering on genius, built a radio transmitter. They brought it to school and demonstrated it to Mr. Mears' class. Mr. Mears decided that this wonderful broadcasting set must be demonstrated to everyone in school, and to every resident in Huntsville.

In a dressing room on one side of the stage in our auditorium, the Roberts brothers set up their broadcast set. The stage of the auditorium was the broadcast studio. Every day at noon, radio station HSVS presented a one-hour broadcast. Our home near the square was probably one mile from the school. By listening carefully the broadcast came through, but not terribly loud. All of this was as illegal as it was educational.

The bell system in HSVS was primitive. A large bell in the hallway was controlled by a simple doorbell-type push button located just outside the superintendent's door. One teacher was assigned the job of official bell ringer. When I was there the honor was assigned to Dean Baldwin. Mr. Baldwin taught typing and some business courses. The reason the job fell to him was because his classroom was the one closest to the bell button.

About three minutes before the hour Mr. Baldwin approached the bell with his large pocket watch in his left hand. His right hand was the button-pushing hand. When the watch indicated one minute until bell-ringing time, he extended his index finger and held it in readiness approximately three inches from the bell. At the exact time—well, the time according to his watch—he would jab the button good and hard with that extended finger.

My best friend at the time was James Deer. James had an exceptional I.Q. and went on to become a successful engineer and physicist. One day when James and I were exploring behind the stage of the school auditorium, we found an access door to the attic. At the moment we had no idea how to use this newfound discovery. Then an idea came to us like a lightning bolt: we would screw up the bell-ringing. As we talked it over we refined the plan somewhat.

Directly over the push button in the hallway we made a very small hole in the Celotex ceiling, which gave us a clear view of the push button. Then we wired another push button in parallel with the hallway push button. We waited anxiously for Mr. Baldwin to ring the bell. As usual, three minutes before the hour, he approached the button with watch in hand. When the hour was up he aimed his index finger at the button. The bell started ringing before he touched it. He jumped back, looked surprised, and slowly moved the index finger toward the button. Again, when his finger got within two inches of the button it would ring, and when he withdrew his finger, the bell became silent. We worked this two more times that day, then removed our button and destroyed the evidence.

When we graduated the mysterious ringing of the bell had not been solved. Mr. Baldwin told and retold the story, but few put much stock in such an occurrence.

Dean Baldwin (Dean was his name, not a title) resembled a dignified Charlie Chaplin. He was a small man, about five feet seven inches tall and must have weighed about 145 pounds. Very fastidious, he always dressed in a dark suit, white shirt, black shoes and socks, and a derby hat. He kept his Chaplin-like mustache carefully trimmed and tried to look older than his thirty-three years. He taught typing, bookkeeping, and shorthand. No one in school would ever know he was a serious contender in collegiate wrestling.

Our star running back for the Huntsville Eagles was Merritt Wentz. Merritt was responsible for the winning streak Huntsville enjoyed in the mid-1930s. Merritt was big and he was fast. Standing about six feet two and with a weight of 220 pounds, when Merritt got the ball he was likely to score. His size and his speed made him one of the best football players in the state.

One day at school someone mentioned that Merritt should go in for wrestling—that he would be absolutely unbeatable. Dean overheard the statement. Knowing that there was a lot more to wrestling than physical size, he said, "I could whip Merritt in a wrestling match. He would need a lot of coaching and training to become a wrestler." Merritt heard about the comment and approached Dean in the classroom. "I hear that you think you could beat me in a wrestling match," he said. "There would be no contest," replied Dean. "You would not stand a chance."

"I guess I'll have to prove you wrong," said Merritt.

Well, that afternoon after school, word of the impending match between Dean Baldwin and Merritt Wentz swept through Huntsville like a grassfire during a drought. You must remember, Huntsville was a small town, it was during the Depression, and very little entertainment was available other than medicine shows. Both Merritt and Dean were well-liked and everyone was getting a big laugh about a wrestling between the small teacher and Huntsville's star running back. It had soon gone too far for either to back down. The only decision left was to figure out where the match would take place.

It was decided to build a ring in the courthouse for this one occasion. There would be an admission charge of ten cents for children and twenty-five cents for adults. Proceeds would go to the school.

The courtroom was jam-packed that night. What a sight they made as they came into the ring. Merritt was a ten to one favorite. Price Fritts, the Huntsville football coach, would act as referee.

By the third round the crowd realized that Dean was simply playing with Wentz. The small teacher was right. There was really no contest. Dean pinned him down in the fourth round, providing a topic of conversation in the town's barber shops for months to come.

I now look back on those years with envy. Never again will this country see such innocence: a time when a county courtroom was, without any reservations at all and with the blessing and enthusiasm of the entire town, turned into a wrestling arena for a match between a high school teacher and one of his students. Somewhere during my lifetime people have lost their zest for living, and take themselves far too seriously.

CHAPTER 12

Clarence

Any activity becomes creative when the doer cares about doing it right, or doing it better.

—JOHN UPDIKE (1932–2009)

The year was 1937. As the Great Depression gave way to an improved economy, our nation's youth danced its way into an unknown and horrifying future. Big bands, the likes of which will never be heard again, perfected a sound that defined the times. The Swing Era was upon the country. With the fiery crash of the Hindenburg, Nazi Germany's flagship, the era of lighter-than-air passenger ships came to a tragic end. The world's largest and most luxurious airship disappeared within seconds when it exploded while landing at Lakehurst, New Jersey. FDR, in frequent radio addresses, offered the nation hope with his fireside chats, even as the rumblings of war reached our country from both Europe and the Pacific. As late as 1940, FDR assured the nation's mothers and fathers that no American boy would ever serve on foreign soil. The latest Technicolor movie was *Ebb Tide*, a swashbuckling epic starring a beautiful young girl named Frances Farmer. Television, according to daily reports in the media, was just around the corner. However, that corner would not be reached until the industry abandoned its crude and cumbersome scanning disc technology and embraced the modified cathode ray tube. Talking pictures, radio, and television were still very young. So was I.

I was sixteen years old, in my second year of high school at Huntsville, and much more interested in *Short Wave Craft* and *QST* magazines than English Literature and American History. I had discovered ham radio. I did not know exactly what amateur radio was, or how one earned the title "ham." But my curiosity had become aroused by radio magazines full of pictures of impressive-looking equipment and ham stations with broadcasting sets that occupied a whole wall or even an entire room.

Otto Grubbs, a slender young man about twenty-two years old, was the town's only radio repairman. I asked Otto what amateur radio was. He was not thoroughly familiar with the hobby, but explained to me that even he would have to spend a lot of time studying in order to pass the FCC amateur radio operator examination. He went on to say that every ham must know how to send and receive Morse code, and must pass an exam that covered FCC rules and regulations as well as radio theory.

Otto also pointed out, "The Federal Government gives examinations at different locations throughout the country. I believe our closest examining point is Kansas City." Both Otto and I were unaware of the Class C license available to those who lived more than 125 miles from their nearest examining point. This entry-level license could be administered by any Class A license holder.

I reluctantly put ham radio on hold. However, I kept buying all the radio magazines I could afford, and building receivers from published articles, some of which even worked. Listening to the 160- and 75-meter phone bands I began to acquire a basic understanding of ham radio.

Featured in large display ads in *Short Wave Craft* magazine was a beautiful little regenerative receiver called the AC-4. It was a stripped down, less expensive brother to the *RSR* (Regenerative-Super Regenerative) Clipper. The full price, including coils for four bands, was $17.50—a lot of money in 1937. I began trying to devise a way to own one of those fine short wave radios. I believe that if you sincerely desire something, sooner or later you will get your wish. Boy, did I ever want that radio.

I raised four dollars by selling my .22 rifle and my Sears beginner's guitar. Odd jobs around town eventually supplied the remaining fourteen dollars. I remember the agonizing decision I faced: now that I had the money should I really spend it on a radio, or should I be practical and put it away for my college education. After wrestling with my adolescent conscience, the radio beat out college by a wide margin.

I mailed a money order to Radio Construction Laboratories. Anxious for the radio to arrive, I marked off each passing day on the large calendar over my future operating desk. To my impatient young mind ten days seemed time enough to allow for shipping. My estimate was off by a few weeks. Today I have a better understanding of the mail order business. I would wager that actual construction of the radios began after orders were received. Anyway, it was eight long weeks before the postman delivered the long-awaited box.

My hands were shaking as I eagerly unpacked the black crinkle cabinet beauty, and gently placed it on my desk. Its two German silver dials sparkled like diamonds. I plugged in the ten-meter coils, hooked up the aerial and ground wires, plugged the set into the wall receptacle, and waited for the set to warm up. Was the radio dead? There were no signals anywhere on the dial. I was completely unaware of sunspot cycles, or their relation to HF propagation. It would be several months before there were enough sunspots on old Sol to enable communications on the higher frequencies.

I replaced the ten-meter coils with twenty-meter coils. Now, it seemed there were signals at practically every division on the shining dials. It took me a few minutes to find the amateur phone band. Gee, this sure was a great receiver! It was obvious I had made a wise decision. College was intangible; it existed only in the distant future. Ham radio was here and NOW.

About this time, in a desperate attempt to find employment, my parents moved to Springdale. Less that one week after moving into our three-room apartment on Shiloh Street, I learned there were six amateur radio operators in town. Better yet, a ham near my age lived within one block of our apartment. I lost no time in becoming friends with Wade Luckett, W5GWA. Wade was already an old-timer—he had been licensed for over a year.

Tall and somewhat heavy-set, Wade was larger than most fifteen-year-old boys. His handsome face had a serious, inquisitive look common to those possessing an exceptionally high I.Q. Before his eighteenth birthday, Wade earned his class A amateur license as well as a commercial radiotelephone license. Soon afterward, long before he was old enough to vote, he obtained a job as chief engineer with a radio station in Alaska.

Wade and I spent many hours in his attic shack among boxes of radio magazines, including issues of *QST* from the '20s and '30s. Our daily experiments revolved around several old junk radios and a badly abused Sky Buddy, all gifts from older hams in the area.

Shortly after our first meeting, we were in his attic trying to get a 47-crystal oscillator to oscillate. The quality of the crystal we were using was in doubt, but let's be honest, every part in the circuit was in doubt.

"Bruce," said Wade, as he hung the loop of wire-tail-light bulb RF indicator over his ear, "if you really wanna become a ham, you just gotta meet W5BQI. Clarence works at that crummy-looking auto repair shop over on Meadow Street. Let's walk over there—if the boss is not around I'll introduce you to one of the best hams in town. That grouchy old coot he works for gets mad as a hornet if Clarence stops working long enough to talk to anyone. If I see the old man around, we'll leave and come back another time."

Walking inside the dingy garage, I could see only one person—a mechanic with his head buried under the hood of an ancient Ford sedan.

"Is that Clarence?" I asked.

"Yes," answered Wade, "That's him. The boss goes home most afternoons and takes his nap. We'll only stay a couple of minutes. I'll ask Clarence if it's okay with him if we drop by his house tonight."

We walked across the oil-soaked dirt floor of the shop. The odor of gasoline, oil, and carbon monoxide hung heavy in the stagnant air; the only ventilation was the open doorway. With the August sun bearing down on the corrugated sheet iron roof, the temperature must have been near the 100-degree mark.

"Hi, Clarence," said Wade. "I have a new ham here I want you to meet. He doesn't have his ticket yet. I was wonderin' if you could give him a little help."

Clarence pulled his head out of the Ford's insides, turned, and looked at me. Well, he sort of looked at me. In reality, one eye looked at me. His other eye seemed to be looking at the far corner of the garage. Smiling, he extended a greasy hand in my general direction. With his left hand he brushed a lock of black hair away from his eyes, leaving a greasy streak across his sweaty forehead in the process. I noticed blood on his knuckles where he had knocked off the skin seconds before we entered the door.

"Hope you are not afraid of a little dirt," he said, shaking my hand. "So, you are interested in short wave radio."

"I sure am, Clarence. Wade tells me you might be willin' to give me some help," I said.

"Well, I can't spend the boss's time talking radio, but if you fellows would like, you could drop by tonight after supper for an eyeball QSO," he replied.

I was excited as we left the dilapidated building. Clarence was going to help me become a ham. "Eyeball QSO," he had said, talking to me as if I was already a member of the ham fraternity.

After our evening meal I walked over to Wade's house, where I found him sitting on the front steps waiting for me. Our conversation, confined exclusively to radio, made the two-mile journey to the section of town referred to as the East Side seem short. Clarence lived in a two-room house near the edge of town. Later I would learn one room was the bedroom for Clarence, his wife, and three daughters, while the remaining room served as a combination kitchen and sitting room.

Wade stepped up to the door and knocked four knocks, followed by two knocks; Morse code for the letters H I.

Clarence was expecting us, and he opened the door and invited us in. We stepped into the clean kitchen. I looked past the white enameled table, still covered with food and dishes, toward Clarence's shack—a small wooden table in the corner of the room. His transmitter, housed in a standard size nineteen-inch rack, stood about thirty inches tall. I had looked at many pictures of ham transmitters, but now I was looking at the real thing. I never realized they would be so beautiful.

Clarence explained to me that he made the rack from old bed railings picked up in our city dump. The transmitter's glossy black panels were made from hardboard. The secret of making hardboard look like Bakelite was wet sanding and multiple coats of black enamel. The chassis for the RF deck and power supply was made of wood and hardboard painted with several coats of aluminum paint. Double-spaced condensers (capacitors, to you youngsters) were made by removing every other plate from old BC radio-tuning condensers.

Number ten copper wire from the same town dump was used for winding oscillator and buffer inductors. Clarence first heated the wire to make it easier to remove the insulation, after which he cleaned the wire with gasoline. Once clean, the wire was pulled straight, then polished with fine steel wool before winding into coils. Tank and antenna matching coils were wound from polished copper tubing. Clarence explained it was also available for nothing at the dump. The junkyard always contained a number of old wrecked cars; it was an easy matter to remove the gas lines. He cautioned us to be careful to not scratch or kink the tubing during removal. Needless to say, the tubing was also polished to perfection. I learned that hardboard was available for nothing behind furniture and hardware stores. It was used to protect mirrors and windowpanes from breakage during shipping. The stores discarded it along with their corrugated cardboard boxes.

Clarence had fashioned professional-appearing tuning indicators from white dime store protractors, and pointer knobs salvaged from discarded battery radios. Antenna tuning components, mounted directly to the hardboard panel above the RF deck, were connected with more of the polished number ten wire. Two large beehive insulators protruded from the center of the top panel. Parallel copper wires, connected to the insulators, passed through porcelain tubes in the wall above the rig, on their way skyward to the Zepp antenna.

As I stood admiring the workmanship, Clarence beamed with pride. He explained that the rig used a 47-crystal oscillator, a single 2A3 for a buffer-doubler, and push-pull 45s in the final. The rig was capable of operation on 80, 40 and 20 meters with almost 40 watts input. I was curious to know how much a transmitter this elegant might have cost, but I thought it best not to ask.

Sitting beside the transmitter was an old RCA tombstone radio. "Is this your receiver?" I asked.

"Yes, it covers the 80 and 40 meter bands," answered Clarence. "Of course it doesn't have a beat oscillator, or any type of bandspread. I am trying to figure out whether to rebuild it, or to keep gathering up parts and build a regenerative receiver. I work stations on 80 meters almost every morning before breakfast. By tuning the set carefully, I am able to copy CW."

After talking ham radio for two hours, Clarence said, "Fellows, I am enjoying this QSO, but us poor folks have to get up early for work. Why don't you fellows come over Sunday afternoon and we will get into this business of getting Bruce licensed. I have two more boys who are rarin' to get a license. I'll get hold of Carl and Raymond and we will get us a class goin.'"

With the coming of fall, W9BSP in Olathe, Kansas started his code and theory lessons on 160 meters. "Fellows," said Clarence, to his three eager students, "I have one requirement if I am going to help you get your ticket. You must listen to W9BSP every night. I am dead serious about this. If you want a license, you must learn, and there is no faster way to learn code than by listening to W9BSP. I don't mean when its convenient, I don't mean every other night, *I mean every night.* Listen to Marshall Ensor, do what he suggests, practice every day, and above all study your ARRL license manual. When you go up before the radio inspector, I want you to look him square in the eye and pass your exam."

We understood perfectly and did exactly as Clarence said. In addition to the W9BSP sessions, Clarence had us draw schematics of power supplies, RF amplifiers, crystal oscillators, self-excited oscillators, and antenna matching networks. All of these circuits and more were etched in our mind. Within weeks each of us could draw the diagram of a complete three-stage transmitter without referring to the handbook. Before long, we began to acquire a basic understanding of radio.

One of Clarence's favorite assignments was to have each student draw a diagram of an amateur station, including both transmitter and receiver, complete with antenna and power supply. All components had to be marked with their approximate values and approximate voltages to be expected on all tube elements.

One Sunday afternoon in early October, Clarence met us at the door. His normally pleasant face was beaming. It was obvious something wonderful was about to happen.

"Come in fellows, come on in," he said, opening the door with a flourish.

We all noticed his new receiver at the same time. On the table, beside his transmitter, was a bright, new, Hallicrafters Sky Champion. The glossy gray cabinet and the receiver's large silver tuning dial made a perfect foil for the black transmitter. It looked like a picture from *QST*.

"Got it yesterday," said Clarence. "Ordered it from Bob Henry just four days ago. Now there is a real receiver! Worked a K6 in Hawaii this morning about 4:00 A.M. I heard him loud and clear. We had a 100% QSO for over twenty minutes."

We cut our class short that Sunday, as Clarence was anxious to get on the air with his new receiver. The Sky Champion was the only piece of new gear he ever owned.

I realized I could not afford $44.95 for a Sky Champion, but with my janitorial job sweeping out our family doctor's office every day, I could afford to make payments of $2.50 or so each month. I decided to write Bob Henry and see if he would sell me a new Sky Buddy, the one with electrical band spread, on monthly payments. Within two weeks I had the new receiver sitting on my operating desk. It was not much better than my old Raco AC-4, but it was roughly calibrated and easier to tune. I felt I had hit the big time. I owned a genuine Hallicrafters radio.

Our radio classes continued, winter arrived on schedule, and Christmas music greeted shoppers throughout our modest business district. Clarence told us we were ready for our amateur radio examination. "I can't give you the exam," he said. "I only have a class B license, therefore I am not eligible to act as an examiner. However, I have talked to Alan Glass—he has a class A license, and says he will be happy to give you fellows your class C exam."

On a cold afternoon in early December, Alan came to our house carrying a large manila envelope. "Clarence says you are ready to pass the exam," he said. "Do you feel ready?"

A lump came up in my throat. Would I know the answers to the ten questions? Could I copy thirteen words per minute of code?

"I would sure like to give it a try," I said.

"Sit down at that Sky Buddy and tune in some 40 meter CW," ordered Alan.

Nervously, I started tuning the receiver. Finally I found a QSO in progress that seemed near the required thirteen words per minute. I picked up a pencil and started writing. Alan stood behind me reading the words as I wrote them down. After what seemed like ten minutes he tapped me on the shoulder and said, "You just passed the receiving part of your CW exam. Now, get on that practice oscillator there and send me something."

Sitting by the coal stove in our parlor that dreary afternoon, I passed my ham radio examination. After dinner that evening, I hurried across town to tell Clarence the good news. All was right with the world as I climbed the now-familiar steps and knocked. Clarence opened the door. The look on his face is difficult to describe. Sadness, defeat, hopelessness, despair—it was all there.

"Come in, Bruce," he said in a low voice as he turned away.

I stepped inside and pulled a cane-bottom chair up to the dining table. Clarence took the chair opposite me. I noticed he seemed to be avoiding looking toward his station. Then I saw the empty space by his transmitter, the space only last week occupied by the Hallicrafters Sky Champion.

"Where's your receiver?" I asked, thinking it might have developed a problem.

Clarence turned away, stared at the floor a few seconds, then looked up and said, "I had to send it back. I know $3.40 a month don't sound like a lot of money, but I'm only making $14.00 a week. I was depriving my family of things they need. The girls and my XYL need winter clothes. Then there was the doctor bill last month. It was better to give it up now before I really became fond of it. It's what I have left that matters," continued Clarence. "I wouldn't trade my wife and girls for a brand new Super Pro, with a HRO thrown in for good measure."

I didn't sleep much that night. What could I do to help my "Elmer"?* Without him I would never have passed my ham exam.

---

* Someone who acts as advisor and instructor to a new ham operator. Often this means help from the very beginning until the newcomer is on the air and capable of becoming an Elmer himself. It is then his turn to help some aspiring newcomer.

Clarence seemed to always be giving, but so far he was not receiving much in return. Then, just before dawn, I had an idea.

That evening, I picked up the heavy cardboard box and walked the route I knew so well. With aching arms I set the box down on porch, stepped up to the door, and rapped out H I.

Clarence answered the door. "Clarence," I said, "I need help. Look through this box of parts, then tell me what else I will need to get a rig on the air."

He started removing the parts from the box, placing them on the worn pine flooring. He was laying out a transmitter in his mind as he inspected each part.

"All I see that you are going to need is a crystal and holder, and maybe a couple of filters for your power supply. A crystal will cost you about $2.50 and you can use 450-volt filters and connect two of 'em in series," said Clarence. "That should handle a 600-volt power supply with room to spare. Burstein-Applebee has filters on sale for forty cents each; you need at least four of 'em. It looks to me like $5 to $7 would get you on the air in good shape. I have a lot of old junked radios we can salvage for the rest of the parts."

"Well, I was kinda hopin' you would build it for me," I said. "I can't pay you what it's worth, but I will trade you my Raco AC-4 and dig up the money for crystal and filters if you will put the rig together for me."

"Sure," answered Clarence. "I'll put it together this coming week. I'll bet you have it ready to go before your ticket arrives from the FCC."

The rig was indeed finished some three weeks before I received my license. My 40-meter Zepp was suspended high (at least 20 feet) in the air, my Sky Buddy was in place, the rig was neutralized and loaded into the antenna—all I needed was a license to make operation of the station legal.

My friend, W5GWA, had been urging me to try out this new station. "Get on the air and work someone," he told me time and again. "Use my call—who's ever going to know the difference?" One afternoon after school I was listening to 40 meters on my Sky Buddy. Temptation finally overcame conscience and I decided to send a short

My ham station circa 1938–39.

This is the station I was using the morning of December 7, 1941, when the Japanese bombed Pearl Harbor. I heard the distress call direct from Hawaii several minutes before news networks broadcast the event to the nation. Within hours, all ham operations were shut down in the United States and most of the world.

CQ, bootlegging Wade's call. I was confident that no one would reply as I pounded out a two-minute CQ on my ancient hand key. When I finished the CQ I started tuning the entire band, from the low end up. My crystal at the time was cut for 7209. THERE HE WAS! W5HHR was answering my call. I almost went into cardiac arrest. When he finished his long call I threw the three necessary switches to change from receive to transmit, and nervously answered his call. I stood by. He came back to me and gave me a 579 report, but I was so scared I missed his name and QTH. I tried one more time and then gave up the QSO. I was simply too scared to complete the QTH. I received his QSL, addressed to W5GWA of course, one week later. He was using a 45 self-excited oscillator, and a type 30 regenerative detector. There were few elaborate stations back then.

My license soon arrived and I gained confidence. I made hundreds of contacts and many friends on the air during the next few months.

One station, W5HMV from Baton Rouge, Louisiana, was operated by Windy Bill Waller. Bill and I had many QSOs during the late afternoon hours. Bill worked nights and slept during the mornings. He usually got on the air a couple of hours before going to work—the hours from 3:00 P.M. until 5:00 P.M. I got in from school at 3:15 P.M. and usually worked the rig until my folks came home about 5:30 P.M. So it worked out just great that Bill and I met almost every day for a short exchange of greetings. I have his card in front of me as I write this. He was using an SX-16 Sky Rider for a receiver and Utah kits 1, 2, and 3—quite a fine station. We became such friends that we exchanged a lot of snapshots of our stations and ourselves.

My little transmitter, a 47-crystal oscillator, into push-pull 45s, nicely constructed on a hardboard chassis, worked perfectly. I soon added a pair of T-40s in the final and used this rig until Uncle Sam closed us down right after Pearl Harbor. With the little RSR regenerative receiver beside his rig, Clarence was once again on the air.

I left for the Air Force in 1942. Occasionally I found time to write to Clarence. Soon after I left he moved to Jay, Oklahoma. I have his Jay, Oklahoma QSL card. Then my letters started coming back to me marked "Address Unknown." Someone said he had moved the family to the west coast where he was working in an aircraft factory. When I returned home I looked, unsuccessfully, for his address in every call book I could find. Local hams could not help me in my search. W5BQI had disappeared.

I regret I did not write more often; perhaps then we could have kept in touch. We all have one Elmer in our lifetime that goes the extra mile, helping us become good hams, sharing his knowledge and experience. Clarence was my Elmer.

The story above is true. Otto went on to become W5ZJI. Bruce Vaughan, ex-W5HTX, now is NR5Q. Carl Owenby, W5HTD, soon lost interest and dropped out of ham radio. Alan Glass, N5AG, Raymond Lewallen, W5HTV, and Wade Luckett, W5GWA, are all silent keys.

CHAPTER 13

Pearl Harbor

That strange feeling we had in the war. Have you found anything in your life since to equal it? A sort of splendid carelessness, it was holding us together.

—NOEL COWARD (1899–1973)

Sunday, December 7, 1941 was a dreary day in Springdale. A gloomy overcast sky covered the city. A temperature in the low- to mid-forties kept the heavy mist from turning into an ice storm. It was a very good day for everyone to remain at home by the fire, and that is exactly what happened. Activity on Emma Avenue was zero. The town was deserted.

In the kitchen my mother was cooking a pot roast. Dad, not feeling well, decided to spend the day inside. Normally on Sunday mornings he attended the Holcomb Street First Baptist Church. "No use spreading my germs around," he said, "I think I might be coming down with the flu. I'm sure I have a little temperature."

I was reading the latest issue of *QST* magazine, daydreaming of owning the new SX-28 Hallicrafters receiver and a KW transmitter. My daydreaming was interrupted "It sure don't look good over there," Dad observed, his head still buried in the paper. In the kitchen my mother continued rattling pans and dishes.

I was in my third semester of college. I planned on spending all afternoon working on my physics lab notebook. I was in no hurry to get down to serious study. Earlier, about 8:00 A.M., I had fired up the rig and spent an hour rag-chewing on 40-meter CW with hams in Kansas, Missouri, and Texas. Little did I realize that these three contacts were the last I would make until more than four years later.

The old Majestic console radio in our small living room was tuned to an NBC station featuring its regular Sunday morning program of big band music. I believe on this particular program they were featuring the Blue Barron Orchestra whose tag line was "Music of Yesterday and Today, the Blue Barron Way." I even remember the song they were playing: "Dear Mom." Understand that even though we were not at war until that fateful Sunday, the U.S. had been preparing for war for some time, and a lot of young men enlisted months before Pearl Harbor. The song was most appropriate for the time—even more so today. I remember a few of the words:

> The weather today,
> is cloudy and damp,
> your package arrived,
> but was missing a stamp,
> your cake made a hit,
> with the boys here at camp,
> I love you, dear Mom.

I am sure a lot of families listening to the radio had sons or husbands in the service. I thought the song a bit too sentimental and returned to my radio room, and turned on my Breting 9 radio receiver to see if there were some good 20-meter openings.

In an effort to save two dollars per month rent, Dad spent over $100 to move to a cheaper place. He was always a great businessman. But I digress.

I had not installed a good antenna at the new location. I was using a sixty-six-foot-long Zepp antenna with quarter-wave feeders. The antenna was tied between two trees—one in our garden patch, and the other in the tree of a neighbor. The entire mess was about twenty feet above ground. Signals had to be good or I'd never hear them.

This was one of the good times—the band was wide open. I listened to some CW for a few minutes, then tuned down to the phone section of the band. At first there were the regular QSOs talking of radio, weather, antennas, and the usual chatter. I cannot remember whether I was on the 20-meter amateur radio frequency, or the 19-meter commercial broadcast band. I do remember the voice, near panic, repeating over and over, "We are under attack." Then the operator would describe some of the scenes of damaged ships and installations. "The death toll must be in the thousands," he commented at one point. I hurried into the living room to tell my parents what I had just heard.

Dad never had much tolerance of ham radio or ham radio operators. To him, anything you enjoyed was too expensive and probably sinful as well. "It's just some of those kids playing with radios," he said. "Nothing to it at all. Let's eat."

Before we were seated at the dinner table, the old Majestic radio in the living room came alive. They gave a little news about the bombing but mostly they repeated the same message over and over: "All military personnel return to base immediately." I remember they repeated this message at least once every two minutes. Between times, we started getting a bit more coherent news analysis. I knew it was useless to discuss this at home so I put on a light water-resistant jacket and cap and walked the two blocks to downtown Emma. Not one car was in sight. I walked to the Citizens Newsstand and found that Mr. Dyes was open. He had not heard the news. I told him what I had heard. Like me, he had no idea where Pearl Harbor was or how important it was. He assured me that the news was of little importance. "The United States could lick those Japs in two weeks," he assured me. "They would not dare attack us."

The belief in the possibility of a short decisive war appears to be one of the most ancient and dangerous of human illusions.
—ROBERT LYND (1879–1949), Anglo-Irish essayist

The following morning, about 6:00 A.M., I drove to the University of Arkansas campus. Normally at this hour, the campus would be all but deserted, but not this morning. It seemed that many students and professors had stayed up all night listening to the news. Classes that Monday morning were mostly confined to discussions of the impact this would have on America, and especially the college students of America.

At noon, Kay Brogdon, Brushwood Nelson, Dick Cantrell, and I walked downtown to have lunch at Ralph Ferguson's Blue Mill Café. The restaurant was especially popular because of their great forty-cent plate lunch. After eating we walked up to the square. A sizeable group was milling around on the southeast corner of the square in front of Guisinger's music store. I asked what was going on. "The President is going to make an announcement in a few minutes. Everyone seems to think he is going to declare war."

The music store had a large speaker temporarily tied to the small canopy over the corner door. It was hooked up to a large radio inside. We did not have to wait long before the speaker came alive with the address from the Capitol. "The day that will live in infamy" address was short and to the point—the United States was now at war. Slowly we walked back to the campus.

Most male students had already registered with the draft board. The U.S. had known for some time that war was inevitable. The big surprise for most of us was that our nation had been caught with its pants at half mast. We could not see why the government had been so irresponsible. When I registered for the draft I was immediately classified 1-A, which means you are in the very first group to be called up.

Like most sane young men I was in no hurry at all to stand up while a lot of people shot at me, but I also had a strong dislike for the term "draftee." I realize that my thinking was somewhat flawed but in my mind, the word draftee was closely related to conscientious objector. I admit I was wrong, nevertheless this was my feeling at the time, probably the result of too many B-grade movies.

At the time, I was dating a young lady who worked at the local draft board located in the basement of the old post office building on Emma Avenue. I asked her to let me know when my name was coming up. I wanted a head start on the draft board. The alert came very quickly. I remember the details very well. We were sitting in the UArk Theater one night watching the latest Bogart and Bergman movie, *Casablanca*. About halfway through the movie, my girlfriend whispered in my ear, "You are going to get a letter from me tomorrow. I won't tell you what the letter says, but the opening line is 'Greetings.' I put the letter in the outgoing mail when we closed at five."

I smiled and said, "Thanks for the warning. I am awfully sorry, but I think your letter is going to arrive too late. You've given me the head start I need."

The following morning I went to the PMS&T (Professor of Military Science and Tactics) office in the old ROTC building. Sergeant Major Greathouse was at his desk as usual.

"I would like to enlist in the Army, Sergeant. Can you get someone to swear me in?"

"Get your damn hands off my desk," he snapped. I did not realize I had placed four fingers of my right hand on the corner of the worn oak desk. "I'll see if Colonel Gray has time to do it."

He stepped into the colonel's office and returned immediately. "Go in, report to the colonel, state your wishes, and for God's sake, act like a ROTC cadet. Don't lean on his desk the way you did mine."

I went into the colonel's office, snapped him my best hand salute, and stood rigid as a stove poker in front of his desk. "Colonel Gray, sir, Private Vaughan has permission of the sergeant major to speak to the PMS&T. I wish to join the Army, sir."

The colonel returned my salute and said, "At ease." Then he shuffled some papers on his desk, knocked his pipe out in an ashtray, refilled and lit the pipe with a kitchen match, looked up at me and said, "Hold up your right hand and repeat after me."

Once I repeated the oath, the old colonel smiled and said, "By GOD, son, you are in the Army now. Wipe that smile off your face and come to attention. From now on look and act like a soldier. Sergeant Greathouse has a paper for you to sign. Dismissed."

I signed the papers for Sergeant Greathouse. With a scowl on his face he inspected the papers and said, "Dismissed." I never saw Sergeant Greathouse smile in the two years I was in ROTC.

When I arrived home that afternoon, I had a letter waiting for me from the draft board. I returned it unopened with a notice to address all communications to Pvt. Bruce Vaughan, serial number 18113200. I never heard from them again. In the Army they had a phrase to describe those who enlisted to stay ahead of the draft: handcuffed volunteers.

Shortly afterward I realized I had paid a big price just to outwit the draft board. I had volunteered myself into the infantry. All that walking and sleeping in the snow did not appeal to me in the least. With my colossal ignorance of the military, I asked for, AND RECEIVED, a transfer into the Air Force. I had the stupidity to send the commanding general of the Eighth Corps Area a telegram about 8:30 A.M. requesting a transfer. I had a reply, by telegram, that same afternoon. I still cannot believe it.

My hopes were to be stationed someplace close to home if possible. Then I found that the University of Arkansas had a flight training program to prepare pilots to become ferry pilots. It was an outgrowth of the old Civilian Pilot Training program that was in existence several years before December 7, 1941. The program was now known as WTS, or War Training Service. The program involved colleges across America. It would assure me of at least ninety days training—primary flight training—before being shipped to another school for secondary, then ultimately, advanced training. At the end of nine months those in the program would receive a commission and wings. I really wanted in that program. It was a chance to fly many different aircraft and to see a lot of the world.

I applied for, and after many physicals and written examinations was accepted into, the program. My first assignment was at John Brown University for primary school and flight training. We would receive about 400 hours of ground school and 50 hours of flight training, before moving on to secondary school.

Ground school included studies in meteorology, navigation, general service of aircraft, and CAA (now FAA) rules and regulations. Our days began at 6:00 A.M. and ended at 10:00 P.M. There was no ground school on Saturday, only flight training. After 4:00 P.M. on Saturday, cadets received a pass until 6:00 A.M. Monday morning.

John Brown's flight training school was without frills, but solid. The airport commander was Pop Allen, a former barnstorming pilot who had reached old age because he understood the pilot's axiom: there are old pilots, and bold pilots, but there are no old, bold pilots. At the airport safety was the number one priority.

I was on my eighth hour of dual instruction. As always, Moose (T.K. Moose), my instructor, was flying from the front seat—I was in the rear. There was a reason for this seating. The center of balance in a J-3 makes it much easier to fly from the rear seat if there is only one person in the plane. The instructors knew if students became comfortable in the rear cockpit they would do better when they were allowed to fly solo.

Moose and I had been up for twenty minutes or so when he turned his head to one side so I could hear, cut the throttle, and said, "We will spend the balance of the hour shooting takeoffs and landings. It's all yours."

I opened the throttle to 2300 rpm and headed for the field. Checking the windsock I saw we still had a north wind. I made four or five takeoffs and landings. I carefully entered the landing pattern on my downwind leg on the first landing. After that I simply made a large circle of the field. I felt I was doing okay. As we rolled to a stop after a landing Moose swung around in the seat and said, "Taxi this crate back to the hangar." When we reached the hanger I locked my left brake, and with a gentle blast of the prop, swung the little J-3 around so its tail was toward the hangar.

Moose jumped out of the plane, and with an angry look at me said, "Those were the worst landings I ever rode through. If you keep that up you are going to kill yourself. I am not going to die with you. Get back out there and do three more by yourself, and try to get at least one right."

"Well, this is it," I thought. "This is what I have dreamed about since I was five years old."

I felt fear well enough, but only fear that I'd do something stupid. Like most young people I felt I was immortal. I feared I might wash out a landing gear, maybe the airplane, but at no time did I think of getting injured of killed.

Advancing the throttle, I taxied to the end of the runway, parking the plane at a 45-degree angle so I could see incoming traffic, if any. I pulled the stick back, locked my wheel brakes, and ran up the engine—first on number one magneto, then number two magneto, then both magnetos. Again I visually checked for incoming planes. Locking the left wheel I swung the nose of the plane northward, pushed the stick full forward and hit full throttle. The tail immediately came up and I moved the stick to neutral position. I was watching air speed as well as the runway. Thirty, thirty-five, I could feel the plane trying to lift off the ground. I kept the stick slightly forward to keep the plane from getting airborne until I saw at least 45 on the airspeed. At I gently eased back on the stick and the ground dropped away. I kept the nose down until the airspeed indicated 65 mph. Off my right wing was the 450-foot KUOA radio tower. I passed the tower then made my 180-degree turn to the base leg and flew southward parallel to the runway. Two more 90s and I would be lined up with the runway. All too soon I was on the final approach. I could see Moose watching my progress. I'll bet he was sweating more than I was. I passed over the south end of the short runway; it was obvious I was at least fifty feet too high. I powered up the little J-3 and made another circle. This time I hit it on the nose—the landing was smooth as silk.

That night, back at the barracks, I went through the rites for those who make their first solo. Out of respect for my readers, I will not go into detail, but will say that it involved red paint. Though I never became an Air Force pilot, I treasure my memories of those few weeks of flight training at JBU.

The flight line consisted of four Piper J-3 Cubs. The little underpowered aircraft was fondly referred to as the Yellow Peril. Two of the planes were older or cheaper models powered by Franklin 40 hp engines. The later planes had 65 hp Lycoming engines. The Franklin-powered Cubs were tricky to taxi as they had no wheel brakes. They also had other problems, such as the engine stopping dead still on approach if you let the rpm drop below 1200. We also found that the Franklins were reluctant to spin. Instead of a spin the plane tended to fall into a tight spiral. The Lycoming-powered craft were much easier to fly, and for that reason there was always some complaining if you drew a Franklin for your solo time.

There were sixteen cadets in our program. They were a cross-section of America. One cadet, Ed Bethel, was a law professor at the University of Arkansas. Another was a bank vice-president. Most of us were simply young kids who wanted to fly. Cadet Stinson was a freshman at the University of Arkansas when he came into the program. A few of the cadets were natural flyers—Stinson was not one of them. After nine hours of dual the instructor decided to let Stinson solo.

We had a north wind that day. As Stinson took off he apparently noticed the KUOA tower on his right, just where it should be. So far, so good. Somehow he misjudged the distance to his first 90-degree turn. Looking around, the town appeared to be too far away. He made a 90-degree turn to the right to get a better look at the town. As he expected the town was there but the airport to the west of town seemed to be missing. He decided to make a full 360 circle of the town and when the airport came into view he would attempt a landing; the trouble was, the airport was not where it should be. As a matter of fact there was no airport.

Meanwhile on the ground, his instructor, T.K. Moose, a young man long on ability and short on patience was straining his eyes trying to see the airplane, which was now just a speck in the sky. Moose was at a disadvantage—he never used swear words. "That bloomin' idiot is lost, he is over Gentry." Gentry, was ten miles north of Siloam Springs and had no airport. We watched as the speck in the sky kept going in circles. Moose was stomping the ground. His face was livid and big veins stood out on his forehead—veins as large as spaghetti.

We had no radio contact with the training planes. Moose jumped in a plane, I spun the prop, and he immediately took off crosswind. Fifteen minutes later the two planes returned. Moose had to fly to Gentry, pull up alongside Stinson, and motion for him to follow while he led him home. To the best of my knowledge, Stinson broke some kind of record. I believe he is the first cadet ever to become lost on his solo flight.

All cadets knew that after eight hours of dual you might be required to solo. Some cadets required more than eight hours to become competent enough to go it alone. If, after twelve hours you had not soloed, you were out of the program. It was very rare for the instructor to solo anyone with less than eight hours.

I remember the first time I went up solo to do practice spins was in one of the Franklins. I knew the instructor would be watching from the ground. However, I doubted that his eyeballs could detect the difference between 3500 and 4500 feet. To be on the safe side I climbed to 4500 feet instead of 3500 as instructed. To start my spin I backed the throttle off to about 1400 rpm, and then pulled the Cub up steeply until it stalled. With the stick in my gut I kicked the right rudder. As expected I did more of a tight spiral than a spin. I was disappointed. The instructor on the ground would be looking for a spin. I tried again—same result. I decided to try a little idea of my own and see what happened. The third time I stalled the plane, kicked the rudder, and opened the throttle. That did it, and of course once in the spin I backed the throttle off. Cubs were not meant for a lot of abuse. When the plane was pulled up into a stall, and the rudder and throttle were hit at the same instant, the tail flipped straight up and it spun like a top. I knew T.K. Moose would raise a ruckus if I told him exactly what I did to get such a pretty spin. I suspect he knew and decided to keep quiet. Moose was a deeply religious young man, and did not believe in using swear words. His comment meant to really hurt was, "That is the worse bloomin' spin I ever saw."

At this point in our training we were taught to do stall or three point landings. The three points refer to the two wheels and the tail skid or wheel. Such landings were soon to become a thing of the past when planes became faster and more powerful, and nose wheels replaced the tail wheel. Three-point landings were hot stuff back in the period between the two World Wars. Such landings were featured in hundreds of B-grade movies.

The victim of too many James Cagney movies, I liked to come in a bit high and fast, then near the end of the runway, cross control a bit and fishtail the plane to a landing. Older and wiser pilots frowned on such antics but it was fun. Such tactics are OK for pilots with a lot of experience but not so good for beginners. Two things happen when you deliberately turn the plane to an angle from forward motion: the plane loses both airspeed and lift.

There was a story about the cadet that crashed on landing. When his instructor asked what happened, the cadet replied, "I ran out of altitude, airspeed, and experience—all at the same time." That will do it every time.

Most of our class graduated with high hopes. According to the rumor mill, secondary flight training at Miami, Oklahoma was due to start within days. We were all expecting a three-day pass with orders to report to Miami. Those hopes were raised even higher one morning when three BT-14 trainers, better known as the Vultee Vibrator, landed the day after our graduation. Yes, the officers flying the planes were from the Miami Air Force Base. We went to lunch, and the three visiting pilots from Miami sat with our flight instructors and a JBU official.

As usual, our plates were face down on the table. The JBU official spoke first. "Before you eat, please turn your plates over and read the paper underneath. It is important you check one of the three options offered. One of the officers from Miami will collect the papers before we eat."

Our program had been discontinued without any warning at all. We were offered three choices: 1. a discharge from the air corps; 2. a transfer into any other branch of service; 3. immediate active duty as an enlisted man in the air corps. In blissful ignorance, I assumed I would be assigned to radio school, becoming either a radio operator or a radio mechanic. After all, on my qualification exam I scored 98% on the radio exam and 136 on my IQ exam.

Months later we gradually learned what brought our program to an end. By the summer of '43, the Pentagon was relatively sure the war would be won by 1945. They had enough pilots on active duty or in advanced training to finish the job. The same was true with training technicians. What was needed was personnel to fill out the TO (Table of Organization) of groups ready to go overseas and prepare for D-Day. Any training that would take a year or so to complete was cut to the bone. Little did we realize that day that we cadets were headed for some very rough duty. Orders came within days. We were given almost six weeks to report for duty. When you are twenty years old, a lot can happen in six weeks.

A friend, Charles Hallock, was completing his advanced flight training at Spartan School of Aeronautics in Tulsa. One weekend he came home on a two-day pass. As old friends we double-dated Saturday night. Charles had to return to Tulsa by 11:00 P.M. Sunday night. We went to a movie and afterward stopped at the Red Pig for hamburgers and Cokes.

"Why don't you go back to Tulsa with me," asked Charles. "We can get there about six o'clock tomorrow evening and see some of Tulsa before I check in. There is always someone on furlough. You can

Bruce Jr. with a Piper Cub airplane.

wear his uniform and identification badge. I am through with ground school, and when not scheduled to fly, we can go to town. We wear our ID badges on our belts and they are normally crooked. If you put the badge upside down, the mess hall boys will never notice you don't look like the picture. They don't check it all that close. We will come back to Springdale next Saturday. It's like a week's free vacation." With an offer like that, how could I refuse?

It seemed like a great idea at the time. "Sure I'll go. I would like to put one over on Uncle Sam," I replied. The idea was foolproof—well, almost foolproof. "Drop by when you are ready to leave for Tulsa tomorrow afternoon. I'll be ready."

All worked well until Friday. I had no problems in the mess hall, and during the day I sat in the barracks reading. After all, the man whose uniform I was wearing was on furlough, so I was immune from anyone placing me on duty. Our little prank was working perfectly. Absolutely nothing could go wrong, or so we thought.

Friday morning we were sleeping soundly when some sergeant came through the barracks blowing his brains out on a whistle. When he had everyone awake, he spoke. "Everyone hear this. This barracks is under quarantine for two weeks. There is a guard on each door. No one—I repeat, NO ONE will leave this barracks. Food will be brought to you. If you become sick and need to go on sick call, let one of the guards know." The sergeant left the barracks.

It seems that some inconsiderate soldier had gone on sick call and turned out to have the mumps. I had multiple problems. I did not want to spend two weeks shut up in a barracks when my time at home was running out, the soldier I was impersonating would be returning from furlough and my ploy uncovered, and I had never had the mumps.

Well, I managed to put on my civilian clothes, sneak past the guard one morning about 2:00 A.M., slip past MPs on the gate, walk several miles to town, and catch a bus to Springdale. I shudder to think what might have happened had I been caught.

I reported to the induction center at Camp Joe T. Robinson in North Little Rock at 7:00 A.M. one bright August morning. By 3:00 P.M. we were on base. By 3:30 we were assigned to winterized six-man tents.

Bruce Jr. and 1937 Chevrolet.

June, 1943. I had just graduated from primary flight school and was proudly wearing the wings issued to us. I remember my happy life was about to hit a rough spot—I was in basic training a few days later. Note the slender build—129 pounds, 6 feet tall. By Christmas of 1943 the Army had my weight up to 165 pounds.

The so-called winterized tents had wood floors and screens and shutters on the sides. The tent was stretched over a wooden framework.

Our first assignment was to scrub down the tent and get it ready for inspection by 5:00 P.M. One of the fellows in our tent had attended a well-known military school. "If you want to get along in the army, do exactly as you are told, and do it the very best you can," he told us. We all pitched in and really gave the barracks a scrubbing like it had never had before. Proudly we waited for inspection. We were sure to be complimented on how great the barracks looked.

"Atten-shut," yelled our military school expert when a young second lieutenant came through the door. Everyone in the barracks snapped to attention looking like the proverbial row of statues.

The lieutenant strutted about while pulling on a pair of white gloves. He looked around the barracks with contempt on his face, and then he climbed up on the wall studding until he reached a two by four supporting the canvas top. He lifted the canvas from the two by four and ran a finger along the top of the support. Naturally there was some dust on the white glove when he got down from the roof.

"Do it all again," he yelled, "There will be no chow or rest until this place is clean, and I MEAN CLEAN."

This was one of the most impressive and valuable lessons I learned in the military—no matter how hard you try, you cannot please someone that doesn't intend to be pleased. I learned that shave-tail officers are always going to use their rank. There is little to be gained from putting out extra effort.

In late August I was sent to Keesler Field in Biloxi, Mississippi, for basic training. The base commander was a bird colonel who shared a lot of credit for the massacre at Pearl Harbor. His punishment was assignment to a basic training unit rather than a combat command position. This was the story that was told at the base. I found the story easy to believe—whether it is true or not I do not know.

The colonel's wife made many decisions about how to run the base. As usual it was the non-coms who actually ran the field; the colonel signed papers and instituted policies. After six months at Biloxi, all recruits better understood why we were caught completely by surprise at Pearl Harbor.

One recruit who came into the base for basic training was a baritone with the Metropolitan Opera in New York City. He was promptly removed from basic training and installed in more comfortable quarters near the colonel's home. His sole duty and contribution to the war effort was singing at social affairs arranged by the colonel's wife.

A group of Navy aviation cadets, completing their training in fighters, were stationed at Keesler at the time. Occasionally one would end up in the Gulf of Mexico. The base had a crash boat, staffed with trained personnel, that was always ready to fish a Navy pilot out of the water. The colonel's wife decided it was a shame to see such a pretty boat unused most of the time; it should be used as a yacht for her personal use. It was just the thing to impress her lady friends.

Everyone in basic training was required to do two hours of calisthenics every afternoon. One hot day in August, the colonel's wife was showing a group of her friends around the base. They drove by

Bruce emptying a "honey bucket."

For a few months preceding D-Day, the 440th TCC (Troop Carrier Command) shared a base with the RAF (Royal Air Force) at Exeter, Great Britain. Some toilets were not connected to a sewer or septic system. The relief stations were somewhat primitive—a board seat with a round hole, and one of these "honey buckets" beneath the hole. Those assigned the job of emptying the contents at least once a day were known to be on the "S--t List." The term was so perfectly descriptive, it became common usage for any unpleasant job assignment.

the exercise field to watch the proceedings. Horror of horrors! There were hundreds of virile young men stripped down to their shorts.

From that time forward we had to do calisthenics in full fatigue uniform. With the temperature around 100 degrees and with a humidity to match, heat stroke became commonplace, but the delicate colonel's wife could show her friends around the base without embarrassment.

~

Keesler Field was home for approximately 40,000 basic trainees, 5,000 more in the airplane and engine school, 8,000 MPs in training, and a cadre of around 6,000. Eleven mess halls fed approximately 6,000 people each. Sixty-five years later, I still have nightmares about KP at Keesler. KPs were required to fall out at 2:30 A.M. You were allowed thirty minutes to dress, make your bed, and shave. Then we fell in and a high-ranking corporal marched us to the assigned mess hall. All mess halls were hell to work in but the MP mess was absolutely the worst. Upon arriving at the mess hall a non-com assigned you to a specific duty. The most dreaded duty of all was pots and pans. Following at a close second place was duty on the China Clipper.

The China Clipper was a large commercial machine designed to clean, sterilize, and dry those stainless steel mess trays used by the armed forces in World War II. The unit was not unlike some automatic car washes today, just on a smaller scale. The entire unit was built into a stainless steel rectangular box about three and one-half feet square and six feet long. Openings on both ends were large enough to accommodate the mess trays. Even with the highly efficient Clipper, a crew of eight KPs was required in large mess halls to handle the dishwashing. The dishwashing room was small—about twelve feet square, with a four by eight foot window facing the mess hall proper. The window had a shelf eighteen inches wide that made the Clipper room resemble a fast food operation.

As each soldier finished his meal he walked by the Clipper room on his way out, knocked excess food from his tray into one of the three garbage cans available outside the Clipper room, and then set his tray on the counter. Inside the washroom was a large sink, perhaps six feet in length, full of hot soapy water. One of the three KPs grabbed the tray and with a large brush washed the tray clean, then placed it on an endless conveyor leading into the Clipper. Inside the machine the tray was hit with high pressure and hot, soapy water to remove any food the KP might have overlooked. Next came the rinse with boiling water, after that the tray went through a drying area and then out the back end of the Clipper.

All this sounds rather easy, but when you do 5,000 or more, three times a day, it runs into work. One man was busy just carrying the hot trays back up to the serving line, stacking them several feet high to await the next meal.

After the chow line closed and every one but the kitchen crew was out of the mess hall, every table was turned upside down and scrubbed with hot soapy water, then returned to right-side up and scrubbed. After this the tables were pushed to one end of the large hall and the wood floors scrubbed with G.I. soap and G.I. brushes. Then all tables were put back in place. Now we had to carry boiling water and thoroughly rinse down the tables and floors. Excess water was swept into drains and the floors mopped dry.

You finished just in time for the next meal. One day I was on KP in the MP mess. My job that day was peeling potatoes. For that one day alone I peeled one ton of potatoes. Not such a big job in itself, it was tolerating the abuse from the cooks. After peeling one big bunch of potatoes I was washing down the electric potato peeler and a large wood table nearby. I had a large brush in my hands scrubbing the tabletop. A cook came by with a large pan of scalding hot water. I had no idea he was coming to my table, and that is the way he wanted it. He threw the entire pan of water on my arms and hands, blistering them. I think such inconsiderate, sadistic acts are a way people of low IQ try to show their superiority.

After the evening meal, the mess halls closed and were once again cleaned from top to bottom. If some cook did not get upset at something, you could expect to get to your barracks about 8:00 P.M. You just completed an eighteen-hour day doing the hardest work you could imagine. When you fell into bed you could take some comfort in the knowledge that you could sleep until 4:30 A.M. tomorrow.

Please let me say that such action was not the norm. Most cooks work hard, are reasonable to work for, treat KPs with respect, and prepare tasty meals for hundreds. The problem lies with what is known as cook's helpers. This is where all the chronic troublemakers, illiterates, and very low IQ men are sent. The classification is 521, or at least it was years ago. That is the absolute lowest classification in the U.S. military.

Was all this scrubbing and cleaning necessary? You bet your life it was. Still, at least once every four or five months you and everyone you knew, would come down with what we politely called the G.I.s. When you are living in highly crowded conditions and you have hundreds with a serious stomach problem, things get messy in a hurry.

I recall one incident at Keesler, traumatic at the time, but now remains a pleasant memory of basic training. Keesler Field had several service clubs on the base to handle the 60,000 soldiers. The largest and best of the clubs was located about three blocks from my area. Here I could buy, for very low prices, anything you might find in a large soda fountain: Cokes, banana splits, ice cream sundaes, and sodas. And if the food at the mess hall did not seem good that evening you could get any number of sandwiches. If you wanted to remain inside there was a large ballroom with a jukebox.

The service club building was of frame construction, about 200 feet long across the front and perhaps 75 feet deep. A front porch ran the entire length of the building with at least thirty wood rocking chairs on the porch. The lawn in front of the porch was beautifully landscaped and immaculately groomed. This was, for most soldiers, the favorite place to spend time after a hard day in the field. The club was affectionately known as The Old Soldiers Home. Having a distinctive name eliminated confusion when asking some friend to meet you at a service club. There might be other service clubs, but there was only one Old Soldiers Home.

After supper, the chairs on the porch filled quickly. It was a pleasant place to observe the base activities. The corner in front of the service club was the only bus stop on the base. In mornings and late afternoons buses to Biloxi stopped here every fifteen minutes. We longed for the time when we new basic trainees would be eligible for a pass and could ride one of those buses into town. Passes were not issued until you had completed eight weeks of training, and then they were issued with great reluctance. Eventually thirty men from our barracks were allowed passes. With about sixty men to a barracks, that meant we might expect a pass every two weeks or so. Finally, that eagerly anticipated day arrived. A friend and I got a pass good until 10:00 P.M.

We eagerly waited for the bus to stop in front of the service club. We were in town before six o'clock that evening. What to do? Biloxi was like a lot of small towns near army and air force bases—long on bars and short on entertainment. Of course they had movie houses but we had better ones on the base. We wanted something different. Feeling grown up and worldly we headed for a bar and ordered beer—the same as they had at the service club but three times the price. We finished the beer and walked the main street of Biloxi. Some retail stores were open and we looked at things we neither needed nor wanted, and some things we wanted and could not afford. We stopped in another bar and had one more beer. Then we looked at our watch and noted it was 9:30; time for us to get to the bus stop if we were to get to the base by 10:00 P.M.

The city bus pulled up and we asked if this was the bus to the Old Soldiers Home and he replied in the affirmative. We boarded the bus and relaxed for our ten-minute ride to the base. We were engaged in conversation about the sights of Biloxi when it dawned on us at the same time that the ride to base was taking longer than it should. I looked at my wrist watch. It was 9:55 P.M. We were going to be late on our first pass, meaning in all likelihood that it would be our last pass while at Keesler. In a panic I ran forward and asked the driver, "How much farther to the Old Soldiers Home?"

"We're here," he said as he turned off the highway and pulled up in front of the real Old Soldiers Home between Gulfport and Biloxi. We panicked, but there was little we could do except wait for him to make the return trip to Biloxi and then get on the right bus to Keesler Field.

We explained our predicament to the driver. He found a lot more humor in the situation than we did. "This bus will return to Biloxi in fifteen minutes but the last bus to the base is at 10:00, so you will have to walk from the bus stop to the base," the driver told us while laughing.

I still find it difficult to believe we were able to walk to the base, sneak through the fence, and make our way to the barracks without being caught. The entire perimeter of the base was guarded twenty-four hours a day I know, as I pulled thirty-two days of guard duty while at Keesler and much of it was on the fence. I suppose it shows what one is capable of when driven by sheer terror.

I watched as my entire group was shipped out to various assignments. I was the only one left behind. I should have suspected that all was not well but I assumed it was another case of Air Force foul ups. I was moved into a barracks with a bunch of lawyers awaiting assignments to the Adjutant General School. Meanwhile, I was assigned as a permanent guard.

On December 20, 1943, I was handed a large sealed envelope and put on a train to Sedalia Air Force Base at Warrensburg, Missouri. I was to hand over the sealed orders upon arrival. As Warrensburg is less than 200 miles from my home I thought I might get a pass home for Christmas.

My memories of Warrensburg are vivid: tar paper shacks, mud, coal smoke, cold misty rain, and homesickness. I arrived about 9:00 P.M. on December 21. A temperature inversion held the thick coal smoke close to the ground, which covered the all but deserted air base in a black shroud. I stumbled through the darkness along the duckboard sidewalks until I finally found the orderly room. A buck sergeant, obviously teed off because he was stuck in this godforsaken place while almost everyone was home on Christmas Eve, glared at me from behind a beat-up office desk. He took a long drag on his cigarette, ground the butt in an overfilled ash tray, looked up and said, "What the hell do you want?"

I handed the sergeant my envelope. He opened it up, glanced at the contents, and said, "Put your gear in Barracks Six, grab some sleep, and report to Classification at 8:00 A.M. tomorrow."

"How about some chow?" I asked.

"You're shit out of luck," he replied. "The mess hall is closed."

Reaching in his desk he pulled out a K ration. "Here, this will have to do you tonight."

The following morning I reported to a small tar paper building marked "Classification." Two young lieutenants were sitting behind a desk and two privates were sitting on a bench in front of them. I paid little attention to what was going on. They apparently finished with the two privates and called my name.

As I stood before them, one of the officers opened the envelope, read for a few minutes, and then turned to the other officer and said, "I don't believe this. What do you think?"

His fellow officer read my papers, shook his head from side to side, and returned the papers to the lieutenant, who sealed them and mumbled an apology which I did not understand. "Gather up your gear and report to Operations on the flight line. They will issue you a parachute. A plane will be leaving for Alliance Air Force Base at 2:00 P.M. Be on it."

"Yes, sir," I replied. "One question, what was all the serious discussion about when you were reading my records?"

"You'll find out soon enough," he said. "I am not at liberty to discuss your service records with you."

Two pilots and a couple of buck sergeants came out of operations and headed for the only C-47 on the flight line. "Are you going to Alliance Air Base?" I asked.

"No, but we have orders to drop a private off there while en route," one of the pilots said." Are you the lucky one?"

I could tell I was not the only person on board who was homesick. A day before Christmas and here we were, stuck with duty while most of the personnel were home on leave. A few minutes after takeoff we were over the heart of Kansas City.

The pilot dropped down to about 500 feet and did a slow 360 over the downtown area. We could see shoppers, warmly clothed against the December weather, loaded with brightly wrapped Christmas packages. The scene was very depressing to everyone onboard the cold, unheated C-47.

Some two hours plus later we made our final approach for a

deserted runway at Alliance Air Force Base. I noticed a complete lack of activity. I also noted the absence of coal smoke in the air.

As we rolled to a stop, the crew chief opened the door and said to me, "This is where you get off. Merry Christmas."

I threw my gear out the door and, not bothering to attach the aluminum steps, jumped to the tarmac.

The pilot immediately hit the throttle and took off; there was enough runway left so there was no need to return to the runway end.

I looked around. Not one person or vehicle was in sight. I walked to the only hangar that looked like I could get in. The huge door was open about two feet. I walked inside to see if anyone was there. In a rear corner was a well-worn Cessna twin with one engine removed—nothing else. I put my parachute in a corner, picked up my gear and started walking toward the deserted barracks area.

CHAPTER 14

The Troop Carrier Command

I hold that a little rebellion, now and then, is a good thing, and as necessary in the political world as storms are in the physical.

—THOMAS JEFFERSON (1743–1826)

I walked up the deserted streets, past a mess hall, towards the barracks area. Shortly I came to what appeared to be a main thoroughfare. Placing my heavy barracks bag on the ground, I stood looking and hoping for some sign of life. Across the asphalt street the Post Exchange, normally a beehive of activity, stood lonely and quiet. Gusts of cold wind, rolling across the northern prairie of Nebraska, rattled a loose shutter on a front window. I wondered if any of the buildings were open. If I was on a deserted air base I did not intend to freeze to death even if I had to break a window to get out of the cold. Few places on this earth are as lonely as an uninhabited Air Force base.

I glanced at my watch—not many hours of daylight left. I picked up my bag and started walking towards the barracks area. I knew there should an orderly room somewhere near the center of the complex. I walked about three more blocks then, to my relief, spotted a jeep parked in front of what might be an orderly room.

I tried the door and found it was open. I stepped inside the warm room. A pleasant looking staff sergeant was sitting beside a coal stove, drinking a cup of coffee. "Where in the hell did you come from?" he asked.

I lowered my heavy load to the floor. "I just got off a plane with sealed orders. Is this where I turn them in?"

"Yes, I was expecting a few new men today but when that C-47 touched down and took off immediately, I thought he was just shooting landings," replied the sergeant. "How about a hot cup of coffee?"

"That sounds great to me," I answered. "I'm just about frozen stiff. The cargo bay in a C-47 is no place to be in mid-winter over Nebraska. The walk from the flight line almost finished me off. I was bucking a cold, strong, headwind."

"You better get used to it," said the sergeant. "Out here there's nothing between us and the North Pole but a barbed wire fence, and it's down."

For the first time in months I felt like a member of the human race again. The sergeant was not only civil; he had a sense of humor as well. It's amazing what a hot cup of coffee and a few kind words can do for one's morale.

"How far is it to your hometown?" asked the sergeant as he sipped his steaming hot coffee.

"I'm not sure," I answered. "I live in northwest Arkansas. I'd guess it is at least 800 miles."

"Well, I have authority to write three-day passes, but there is no way you could get to Arkansas and back in three days," he said. "I'm going to go ahead and write the pass anyway. There are still MPs on the main gate, so if you decide to go to town to take in a movie this will get you through the gate. I'm going to write myself one and head for Omaha. I think I can get one day at home for Christmas."

"Okay," I replied. "I'll get by just fine. I'll spend the time reading and catching up on some rest. What barracks do you want me to bunk in?"

"Take your choice—they are all empty," he said. "I'm sure there will be others dropping in during the next three days. If I were you I'd pick one right away and carry in several buckets of coal. It gets pretty darn cold here at night. By the way, everything is unlocked and the freezers are full. Cook yourself a steak or a big platter of ham and eggs. The supply room is unlocked. Help yourself to blankets or anything else you need. For the next few hours a private may be the highest ranking man on base."

The sergeant took a final sip of coffee and said, "I hate to leave you here alone, but if I'm going to catch the bus to Omaha I have to get going, and a Merry Christmas to you—such as it is."

"One question before you go, Sergeant," I said. "If I am the highest rank on this base, do you think that makes me base commander?"

"Don't push your luck," he replied. "Just eat well, rest a lot, and enjoy the break. It will end all too soon."

"Have a great Christmas, Sergeant," I yelled as the jeep disappeared around a corner.

I got busy, moved into a barracks, built a fire, made my bed, and found some K-rations in the supply room, and brought them back to the barracks. I did not feel like firing up a stove in the mess hall to cook. K-rations would be my supper tonight.

I went up to the orderly room, got the coffeepot the sergeant had been using, and brewed a fresh pot of coffee. So here I was, nice and warm, a good fire, a nice clean bed, a fresh pot of coffee, and no one to ride my butt or put me on detail. Christmas Eve, all alone on a big air base. For the first time in my life I truly felt lonesome.

I selected a barracks next to the mess hall. All bunks were in place with a mattress and pillow on each bed. All the blankets were neatly stacked in one corner. The barracks I chose did not have a coal bucket, so I liberated one from the barracks next door.

It was still good daylight outside and I had nothing to do. I returned to the mess hall, where I found some eggs and a lot of ham. I cut two big slices so I'd have one for breakfast. My search of the kitchen for a small frying pan was disappointing, and then it dawned on me—use my mess kit. Of course I would need a bit of butter, some salt and pepper, and a plate to eat in. I gathered up my loot and returned to the barracks where I cooked up a good supper. I'd keep the K-rations until another day.

The loneliness of the base began to close in on me. I decided the sergeant was right. I'd use my pass and go into Alliance to take in a movie. Alliance was much like Springdale, with one main street about three blocks long and one movie theater. As everyone knows the '20s through the '40s was the golden era of movie palaces. If ever excess was displayed in America it was in our great movie houses. But the theater in Alliance was not one of them. It was more like our local theaters—bare bones instead of opulence. The movie showing was Bing Crosby in *Holiday Inn*. I had seen it months before, but I watched it again and got even more homesick.

I returned to the base. The large uninsulated barracks was cold when I stepped inside; the fire had almost burned itself out. The sergeant had been right when he advised me to carry in several buckets of coal. Within minutes the fire going again. The iron stove glowed a nice cherry-red by the time I went to bed. I began to like this idea of being alone. I could sleep as late as I wanted in the morning and was assured a good breakfast.

I slept well. It was near 8:00 A.M. when the sound of a C-47 floated across the cold, deserted base, waking me up. I quickly dressed and went into the latrine to shave. There would be some G.I.-type officers arriving sometime, maybe today. It is best to try and look like a soldier even when you don't feel like one.

I had just finished shaving when eleven men came noisily into the barracks. It seemed that all were talking at once. I welcomed the shattered silence.

"Where is everyone?" one of the fellows asked. "We noticed smoke coming from the chimney on this barracks, but the rest of the base seems deserted."

"I came in late yesterday," I explained. "Last night I had the entire base all to myself. I'm glad to have some company, The Troop Carrier Group has moved to Fort Bragg, North Carolina. Before the CQ (charge of quarters) left on Christmas leave, he told me that stragglers would be dropping in for the next few days. We will just have to wait and see what's going on."

"What do we do for chow if the mess hall is closed?" one PFC asked.

"No problem," I said, "just follow me."

I led the way to the mess hall and showed them the well-stocked refrigerators. The place was literally bulging with food. One of the older men, about thirty-five years old I would presume, was wearing a buck sergeant's stripes. The dark-complexioned sergeant seemed especially interested in the freezer contents.

"Fellows," said the newly arrived buck sergeant, "if you will all pitch in and help me we are going to have a Christmas dinner like the Air Force has never had before."

Though short in stature the sergeant had a look that demanded respect. We were not to learn until much later that he was a chef in one of New York City's best restaurants before enlisting in the Air Force.

"Do I have the help and cooperation of everyone here?" he asked.

It was about four o'clock that afternoon when we finally sat down to eat. Never before had I tasted such food. I am sure that no general grade officer, including Ike, ate as well as we did that day on the deserted air base.

We had a great turkey, a big ham, several vegetables, the best hot rolls I ever tasted, three big pies, cake, and coffee and iced tea to drink. The cook was simply amazing. I often wonder where he spent the rest of the war. One thing I am positive of: he darn sure was *not* cooking for the 98th Squadron.

After eating, we all chipped in and did an hour's KP. The kitchen looked just as we found it: immaculate. One of the group said, "Fellows, I'll bet the service club is open. Bruce said everything on the base was unlocked. We could build a fire, warm up the place, and shoot some pool."

Our sergeant (and gourmet chef) took command. "Two of you fellows start carrying in coal and build a fire. I'm going to see if I can get the jukebox working."

We spent the next two days eating, sleeping, shooting pool, playing darts, writing letters, and reading. In the background, big band music from the Wurlitzer never ceased. I must have heard Artie Shaw's "Summit Ridge Drive" at least fifty times.

Our Christmas of 1943 was so good we were starting to feel a bit guilty. That feeling was to disappear all too soon. Three days after Christmas most of the officers returned from their Christmas leave. Personnel to fill out the TO of the 440th continued to drop in from various places until we had over 150 troops ready to join the main group.

Much of our time before leaving Alliance was spent freezing our rear ends off on the firing range. We were issued the small .30 caliber carbine the Army was so fond of. Mine never shot accurately; therefore I never qualified with it. I could shoot qualification with the .45 automatic pistol, the old 1903 Springfield, and the Thompson, but our outfit only issued medals for the carbine.

Between trips to the rifle range, we pulled the usual shit details: KP, guard duty, latrine orderly, and lots of scrubbing and polishing. Two hours each day we listened to lectures: what the Troop Carrier Command was, its mission in the war, the importance of that mission, and the equipment we would be expected to use to accomplish our mission.

It was almost mid-January before we left by troop train—Pullman cars, no less—for Pope Field, near Fayetteville, North Carolina. During the three-day trip I made friends with a couple of radio operators who were also hams. I assumed I would be assigned to some sort of radio training.

The troop train arrived at Pope Field in a blinding snowstorm about 10:00 A.M. We had been traveling through a heavy snow and blizzard-like conditions since early morning. Several inches of snow covered the base.

We were ordered to fall out and form groups according to our classification: glider mechanics, A & E (airplane and engine mechanics), radio, wire (telephone), cooks, motor pool, etc. This became a sort of caste system, even though I am sure it was never intended that way. For example, A & E mechanics were considered by most to be superior in skill and ratings to glider mechanics. The radar group felt superior to those in radio, etc. This sort of unspoken attitude was seldom discussed, but nevertheless it existed. A & E mechanics normally did not associate with glider mechanics. Practically no one associated with kitchen personnel.

That snowy morning when T/Sgt. Trzeciak, duty non-com of the 98th Squadron yelled, "All radio fall out here," in blissful ignorance I took my place with that group. The sergeant then marched us to our assigned tar paper-covered barracks.

We were in the process of making our bunks and unpacking our duffel bag when the duty sergeant returned. "As of this minute," he said, "the entire group is on twenty-four-hour alert. Everyone below the rank of staff sergeant will walk a post. Staff sergeants will pull sergeant of the guard duty. I am posting the guard schedule in every barracks. If your name is on the list, fall out in front of the orderly room twenty minutes before the times indicated on the list. Do you understand?" Receiving no questions he walked to the bulletin board by our front door and attached the guard list.

After the sergeant left we all ran to the bulletin board to see what time each of us pulled guard. Times listed were the standard G.I. schedule of two on four off duty. I was surprised and deeply puzzled as to why my name was not on the list. I learned the first week I was in the Air Force to avoid the orderly room like the plague. I knew better than to ask why I was not listed. I will admit I felt a bit guilty sitting by the fire while my buddies were freezing their butts off walking a guard post in ten inches of snow. Two hours on and four off is a killer schedule. It really boils down to very little sleep, as it takes twenty minutes to get posted, and at least twenty minutes more to get to the barracks after you are relieved. Take time out for shaving, eating, dressing and undressing, etc., and you are lucky to get three hours sleep a day.

On the third day after our arrival, about 9:00 A.M., Sgt. Trzeciak came in the barracks blowing that infernal referee's whistle. "Is there a Private Vaughan in this barracks?" he asked.

I jumped down from my upper bunk and said, "I'm Private Vaughan."

"I've got you listed as AWOL," he shouted. "What in the hell are you doing in this barracks? You are classified as a 521. Now, get your gear together and get your ass over to the cooks' barracks immediately or I'll have your ass thrown in the guard house. Do I make myself clear?"

I was stunned—a 521 classification is reserved for illiterates, chronic goof-ups, and those with the IQ of a turnip.

"What do you mean, move into the cooks' barracks? I'm not a cook," I said.

"You sure as shit are not a cook," replied the sergeant. "You are a permanent KP."

Now I knew why all the head-shaking and apologies were about when I went through classification at Sedalia AFB.

"Sorry, Sergeant," I replied. "I refuse to move to the cooks' barracks. There is no way in this world that I will become a permanent KP."

"Soldier, do you understand what it means to refuse to obey a direct order in time of war?" asked Trzeciak.

"Yes, Sergeant, I fully understand," I replied.

"Then you have exactly ten minutes to get clean shaven, in your Class A uniform, and report to the commanding officer. I'll notify him that you are coming." Red faced with anger, Trzeciak stormed out of the barracks.

I moved faster than ever before and made it to the CO's office with seconds to spare. The first sergeant was sitting behind is desk, a very serious expression on his weathered face. Detail Sergeant Trzeciak was standing beside the desk. He spoke for the first sergeant. "Do you know how to report to a commanding officer?" he asked me.

I was beyond caring what happened to me. At no time did I think I would actually face a firing squad. However, I was pretty sure I would soon be busting rocks in Leavenworth Prison. But I also realized they could, according to the Articles of War, shoot me and be done with it.

"Hell, yes, I know how to report to the CO, but I did not learn it in this outfit. I learned it during two years of ROTC." I was starting to enjoy this. If there is anything that the old-line, non-commissioned officers truly hate it is someone with ROTC training. It is like waving a red flag in front of a charging bull.

The first sergeant got up from his desk and walked to the door of Major Neal's office. He knocked two times, and I heard the major say "Enter."

He was in the office for less than a minute. He came out of the major's office, then looking at me he said, "Major Neal will see you now." As I walked by him he said in a very low voice, "Your ass is mud, soldier."

I walked as proudly as I could, under the circumstances, and stepped in front of the major's beat-up old desk, threw him the best salute I knew how, stood at stiff attention, and said, "Major Neal, sir, Private Vaughan has orders from the first sergeant to report to the commanding officer, sir."

I held the salute for some seconds before the major returned it and then said, "Stand at ease, private."

This is the first time I had seen the major. He was in his late thirties or early forties, I would guess. Broad-shouldered, heavy set, and with the look of an ex-football star, he seemed like a fair and reasonable man. His black hair was beginning to get a bit gray here and there. Above his left pocket were two rows of ribbons. Above the ribbons were the brightly polished command pilot wings.

While standing at parade rest I waited for the major to speak. "Private Vaughan, when was the last time the Articles of War were read to you?"

I replied, "Sir, the Articles of War were read to me before I shipped out of Keesler about three weeks ago, sir."

"And what exactly do the Articles of War have to say about refusing a direct order in time of war?" he asked.

"Sir, the Articles of War state that refusal to obey a direct order in time of war is punishable by death before a firing squad, or such other punishment as the court martial may direct, sir."

"Stand at rest, soldier. Then you fully understand that it is within my right to sentence you to be tried by a court martial, and that the court martial has the power to stand you before a firing squad where you will be shot to death. Tell me, why you are being so unreasonable?"

"Sir, I am neither an idiot nor an illiterate, and I deeply resent being classified as a 521. I know I have something to offer this group in other classifications. And one more thing, sir. There is no need of a court martial. Before I move in the cooks' barracks I will take my .45 and blow my brains out on the barracks floor. This is not a threat sir, just the plain truth. I am very sorry that I have put you in such a position, sir."

The Major read and re-read my service record. At last he said, "Wait in the outer office."

I snapped to attention, gave the officer a salute, and left his office. I took a seat in the small orderly room and pondered my fate as I waited for the MPs to arrive. What exactly had I done to bring about such hatred and need of revenge? I decided that somewhere, probably back at Keesler Field, I had made it onto an officer's shit list but I had no idea when or how.

I saw a young, studious-appearing captain approaching the orderly room. There was no black MP band on his arm so he must have been from the adjutant general's office. He said to the first sergeant, "The major is expecting me."

"Yes, Captain Quigley, I'll go in with you."

It was a few minutes before the first sergeant returned. He looked at me and said, "The major wants you back in the office. Go in, come to attention, and salute, but please don't waste his time with all that reporting crap."

I did exactly as directed. Major Neal returned my salute, and said, "At ease, Vaughan. This is Captain Quigley. Quigley is our communications officer. You will go with him now. You will obey every command he gives you; heaven help you if you screw up one more time. DISMISSED!"

"Thank you, sir," I replied, coming to attention. The captain and I both saluted the major and left the building. We walked along the board sidewalk, past the barracks, toward the communications building. I noticed someone had shoveled snow off all the walkways.

"Tell me Vaughan, can you do radio repair?" asked the captain.

"I have two years experience working part-time in a radio repair shop," I replied. "I was working to pay college expenses."

"I see on your record where you are a ham radio operator. What is your code speed?"

"I'm fairly comfortable at speeds up to twenty wpm. Twenty-five wpm makes me work, and thirty wpm makes me sweat. Above that, it is just a word here and there."

I could tell that the captain thought I was either lying or bragging.

We stepped inside the warm radio room. It was mostly bare of everything but a few pieces of strange-looking radio gear and what I assumed was a code practice machine. The captain walked directly to the machine. Turning to me he said, "I'm going to check your code speed. All our operators are just out of radio school and we don't have anyone who can copy fifteen wpm. Most do well to copy ten wpm. I am going to start this at ten wpm," said Captain Quigley.

The code was a breeze but I preferred it a bit faster. "How about moving that up to twenty wpm, Captain," I requested. "That's a lot better," I told him. "I run into a little trouble at very slow speeds." The captain looked pleased.

"How much do you know about radio repair," asked Captain Quigley.

"I am certainly no hot-shot repairman," I replied. "I don't know many repairmen who are perfect, but I know enough to keep most radios working. Sometimes it takes me a while to find the problem."

"How would you feel about repairing regular broadcast radios?" asked the captain. "The officers are always at me to get someone in the radio gang to repair their home and car radios. I don't have anyone that knows beans about home radio repair. If you can do the job, go through our equipment and pick out what you need. If you need tubes or parts you don't have, make a list and I'll go into Fayetteville this afternoon and buy what I can."

By late afternoon I had a service bench set up with an RCA Senior voltohmist, a Supreme signal generator, and a modest supply of parts. My first customer was a pilot—a second lieutenant driving a well beat up '38 Pontiac convertible, as I remember.

"What is your radio doing?" I asked the lieutenant.

"The doggone thing surges, is the best way I can describe it. It will come on loud, fade out, and come right back loud again. It is a constant up and down. Does that make any sense?"

"Yes, it makes perfect sense, Lieutenant," I replied. "Your car radio uses a cold cathode rectifier called an OZ4. If you can run into Fayetteville and pick up one at the Radio Wholesale Supply, I think I can cure your problem."

Captain Quigley was listening to the verbal exchange. After the lieutenant left, the captain said, "You seem pretty sure of yourself. We are both going to look bad if your diagnosis is wrong."

About ninety minutes later, the pilot came back to the radio shack with a brand new RCA OZ4. I grabbed a nut driver and ran out to the car. I swung my legs over the back of the seat and crawled under the dashboard (oops, instrument panel, the pilot would call it). It took all of five minutes to remove the back panel, plug in the rectifier, and button the set up. I turned it on, and it came in loud and clear.

"You are all set to go, Lieutenant. I hope the radio store did not charge you retail for the tube. It should have cost you about two bucks," I said.

"You are right on the button as far as costs go. Thanks a lot for getting my radio going," said the smiling lieutenant.

Captain Quigley was impressed, I could tell. My next repair job

My radio repair workbench in Orleans, France. The visitor sitting on the bench is lost to my memory.

was almost as easy—an open filter capacitor in a small All American Five radio.

Our stay at Pope Field was short; the powers that be seemed in a rush to get us overseas. Though I don't remember why, everyone in the outfit seemed to know we were headed for Great Britain. I was not to lay hands on another radio for almost a month—when we finally arrived in Merrie Olde England.

Back in the good graces of the Air Force I decided to push my luck. I went to the orderly room and asked the clerk for a pass into Fayetteville. "I'm Private Vaughan, Corporal. I would like a pass into town. I have not had a pass since I arrived here."

The corporal looked at me like I was some kind of idiot. "What the hell do you want with a pass?" he asked. "You've been on furlough since yesterday. I wondered why you never picked up your papers."

Then I remembered—some time before all men were handed a stack of papers to fill out: G.I. insurance, a will, and application for furlough. I assumed that with my luck in the Air Force a furlough was out of the question and thought no more about it.

THE TROOP CARRIER COMMAND

The past two months I had been ahead of my pay and my shot records. The Air Force handled my shots with dispatch and precision. I had three rounds of shots but they were not so interested in my pay. Here I was, over 1,000 miles from home, a bit over twenty-five dollars in my pocket, twenty-four hours into my furlough, and headed overseas. I did what any red-blooded American boy would do—I called home and asked my parents to wire me fifty bucks.

I returned to the barracks and packed my gear. I decided there was no way I was going to wait another day for money to arrive—I was going home now.

At the Southern Railway depot the ticket agent said I could get to Little Rock for about twenty-three dollars. I bought the ticket. Now my problem was what to eat for the next two days. Remember this was the Southern Railway—not exactly an express train. I went across the street to a grocery store and bought thirty-five cents worth of apples. That would keep me from starving. Once in Little Rock, I'd hitchhike my way home. I could get maybe three days at home out of my ten-day furlough. Ha. I'd never ridden on the Southern Railway. I would be lucky if I got one day home. I looked at my watch. It was now almost 8:00 P.M., four hours until my train left at midnight.

I had not eaten since noon and was beginning to feel a bit hungry. I looked in my Musette bag and counted apples. I decided I better wait until tomorrow to eat. I went outside and took a seat on one of those Railway Express carts on the depot platform, and prepared to spend four hours watching the traffic in downtown Fayetteville, North Carolina.

"Hi, you waitin' for a train, too? Where you going?" a voice asked. I looked to see who was talking to me. A PFC about my age had approached so quietly that I was unaware of his presence until he spoke. I noticed he was wearing Airborne insignia. He climbed up on the cart and took a seat beside me.

"I'm waiting for the Little Rock train," I said. "I live in Springdale, it's up in the northwest corner of the state. I figure to hitch hike from Little Rock on home. My name is Bruce."

"Call me Cliff. I'm headin' for Little Rock too. I live in Brinkley. If I can't catch a bus without waitin' several hours, I'll use my thumb to get home."

Across the busy street was one of those modernistic pre-fab diners. You could look through the large windows and see the coffee cups and glasses carefully arranged on either side of the large chrome coffee maker. Three or four diners were sitting at the counter. Only two of the dozen or so booths were occupied. In one window was a neon sign blinking on and off that said simply "Beer/Coffee."

In the other window the message was different—"16 Oz Sirloin, 1.50" was the message. Due to some sort of electrical problem, the "Oz" part of the sign had a bad flicker, like there was a poor electrical connection.

I resumed reading a paper someone had left on a bench in the depot. Cliff fell silent, watching the activity in the bustling city. Occasionally a serviceman and young lady would enter or leave the café. Apparently it was a popular place. When a well-stacked girl would pass, Cliff would punch me in the side and say, "Hey, Bruce, get a load of that one." No news in the paper was so interesting that I could not stop and look.

"Hey Bruce, we've got hours to kill. Let's go across the street and try one of those steaks," said Cliff. "I'm so hungry I could eat the south end out of a northbound jackass."

I stammered a refusal. "You go ahead Cliff; I'm not all that hungry right now."

"Did you have time to eat at the mess hall before coming into town?" asked Cliff.

"Well, no," I replied. "It's just that I am not very hungry. You go ahead. I'll still be here when you come back."

Cliff paused, then looked directly at me and asked, "Bruce, are you broke?"

"Flatter than hell," I told him. There was no need to lie about it.

"Hey, I'm loaded," Cliff said. "Now cut the bullshit. I've got almost a hundred bucks. The steaks are on me. Get off your rear and let's get one of those steaks. After that we will cruise down the street and check out the girls. It doesn't cost a thing to look."

Maybe it was the hunger pains or maybe it was realizing that I would hurt Cliff's feelings if I declined. Whatever the reason, I decided to take him up on the offer of buying me a steak.

I believe it was one of the best steaks I ever ate. Cliff and I enjoyed three cups of black coffee and stuffed ourselves with dinner. We left the diner and started walking down Main Street. We had not gone a block when we passed a Western Union office. I was surprised to see it brightly lit and open for business. This was wartime and I knew some offices were on twenty-four-hour days. I worked for Western Union for some time after I graduated from high school. I was a trainee, janitor, message boy, and sometimes clerk, but never allowed to hold down a wire (act as main operator).

Expecting nothing, I decided to go in and ask if there was any way I could receive a money order in town if it was addressed to the WUTEL office on base.

"Sure thing," said the Western Union operator, "the WU office at Pope Field is a branch of this office. I'll just go through the Pope Field messages and see if there is anything for you. Yeah, sure enough, here is a money order for Private Bruce Vaughan. If you have any positive identification on you I'll just count out the cash."

"Would my dog tags be enough?" I asked.

"I can't think of any better identification," he said, looking at the dog tags I was holding in front of him.

"Now, I can pay you back for that steak, Cliff," I said holding out a five-dollar bill.

"No way, Bruce. That steak was my treat. We've got to stick together in this man's Army. Tell you what—if that darn train has a diner or snack car, buy me breakfast in the morning."

As it turned out the apples were a good idea. The train had neither diner nor snack car. Before we got to Little Rock, we would not have been surprised if we had been asked to get out and push.

It took two days travel time to get to Little Rock. I figured it out: we averaged around 20 mph on that trip. The only slower way to travel would have been by stagecoach.

Somewhere east of Huntsville, Alabama, the train came to a dead stop in the middle of a cotton field. The conductor, when asked, told us we had a hot box that had to be repaired before we continued. He said it would be at least two hours before help could come and repair the box. What is a hot box? Most trains before World War II had wheels and axles that turned inside a sleeve. The axle ends were enclosed in a box that was packed with heavy grease. If the grease disappeared, the axle became hot, expanded, and thus increased heat-generating friction. Repairs only took an hour or so once the repair crew arrived.

The breakdown occurred about midday. Two hours to sit still, with nothing to eat. Cliff and I noticed that there was a highway about a quarter of a mile off to the north. We could see a country store and filling station that looked to be busy. They just might have some food. I would estimate that we had around twenty-five people in our car.

"I've got an idea, Bruce," said Cliff. "Let's walk over to that store and buy some food."

"That's a great idea, but what about the others in our car?" I asked.

Cliff stood up and yelled, "Attention please. Let me have your attention. I don't know about you folks, but Bruce and I are hungry. We are going to walk over to that store and get some food. If anyone else is hungry, drop some money in my hat as I pass it around. We'll make a fast trip over there and bring something back."

The other passengers were glad to chip in. We left with enough money to load us down for our return trip across the cotton field. We returned to the train with all the food we could carry. I remember we had two loaves of bread, sliced lunch meat, sliced cheese, a small jar of mustard, canned Vienna sausage, a head of lettuce, potato chips, some plastic forks, a small bag of ice, paper cups, and a case of Cokes. For dessert we had Moon Pies and assorted candy bars. While not exactly a gourmet meal it was welcomed by those on that stranded railway coach.

When we arrived in Little Rock, I walked a couple of blocks to the bus station and bought a ticket to Fort Smith. The bus schedule was to leave at 11:00 P.M. and arrive in Fort Smith at 7:00 A.M. How it can take eight hours to drive 125 miles, I'll never figure out. I suppose that the 35 mph speed limit we had during the war applied to buses as well as passenger cars. Before leaving I called home and asked my parents to pick me up in Fort Smith. They were on time. We had a nice breakfast and were home by 10:00 A.M.

I called Pope Field as soon as I got home and asked for a twenty-

In 1943, my longtime friend Jim Ritter and I drove to Camp Chaffee together to take our Army physicals. A few months later, in January of 1944, we met back home in Springdale while on furlough before going overseas. The weather was nice so we decided to take a spin on my motorcycle.

four hour extension, and it was granted. All told, I had about one week at home before returning to Pope Field.

From Pope Field we went by train to Baer Field, Indiana, for more processing before proceeding to the port of embarkation at Camp Shanks, New York—better known as "Chancroid on the Hudson."

At Baer Field we received the extremely rough overseas physical. The squadron was marched to a gymnasium where we were ordered to strip completely. The temperature inside the gym was slightly below that outside where the sun was shining on a ten-inch snow covered base. While standing in side by side lines the length of the gym the medical personnel passed in front of each man. If, at the end of thirty minutes, you were still breathing, you passed. I am happy to say that 100 percent of our squadron passed with flying colors, mostly blue from the cold. We were now qualified for combat duty—all of us, and that included one poor fellow who could walk, but with difficulty.

Only one incident at Baer Field is worthy of mention here. Tech

Sergeant Bishop, Wire Chief, had served for a few weeks at Baer Field when the group was being organized. During that time he made friends with a most cooperative young lady from Fort Wayne. The problem now arose as to how he could visit with this young lady as we were on full alert and confined to the 440th area—even the PX and Service Club were off limits. All movement was confined to a one-block area. Trips to the mess hall had to be in formation with close supervision of both commissioned and non-commissioned officers. An impossible situation, you say. Well, perhaps not totally impossible. Where there is enough desire a good soldier can overcome impossible odds.

Bishop found out that a friend, Corporal Adler, had undergone an emergency appendectomy two days ago. Adler was not a member of the Ninety-eighth Squadron, but was one of the permanent personnel of Baer Field.

Bishop requested permission to visit his friend in the base hospital. Of course, permission was granted. Bishop made a fast trip to the hospital and explained his plans to Adler, who though still somewhat groggy, and in considerable pain, agreed to go along with the complicated plan.

Bishop returned to the barracks area and called his girlfriend. She was instructed to tell the MPs on the main gate that her cousin was in the base hospital, and that she would like to visit him. The girlfriend was receptive to the idea but there was one small problem. Her friend, a seventeen-year-old girl from the country, was visiting her and she did not want to leave the girl alone. She asked if she might bring her friend. Bishop told her that he would call her back.

This was where I entered the complicated scheme. "Bruce, you just have to help me out here," said Bishop. "You go request permission to visit Corporal Adler tonight at 7:00 P.M. The four of us will meet in Adler's room. He's in on all of this. Adler is in a double room. There is an extra bed in there with a privacy curtain. After we visit for minute or so, you take the friend outside the room and sit on that bench in the hallway. If you see someone coming down the hall, open the door and cough real loud. You will help me out, won't you?"

"Sure, it sounds like you have it all under control," I replied.

Poor Corporal Adler was having a lot of gas pains, and though anxious to help his friend, he was really too sick to savor the planning that had gone into this escapade. While Peggy and I sat in the hallway, we entertained ourselves by trying to guess which bed in Adler's room the loudest moans were coming from.

Camp Shanks, our final destination in this country, was our port of embarkation. A dreary camp near New York City, our short stay there was far too long. I believe the camp was designed in such a way that no matter where you were going or what dangers you might face, you would be glad you left Shanks. Hours of lifeboat drills gave us some idea that we might board a boat soon.

On Sunday before we shipped out, two friends and I got a pass and went into the city. Like most soldiers we headed straight to Times Square. Sometime around 11:00 A.M. we decided to eat in a restaurant. We found a modest looking place near Jack Dempsey's that looked affordable. The three of us took a table near the back of the restaurant. Most tables were empty.

The waiter, perhaps the head waiter, approached our table. He was a slender man nearing middle age. "I'll have to ask you boys to leave the restaurant," he said. One of my friends was a hot-headed young man from Kentucky. I saw Bill's face turn red. I was afraid we might be in for trouble. "Why in hell are you kicking us out? We just now came in and all we want to do is eat," said Bill.

"This table is worth twenty bucks an hour in tips," said the waiter. "Soldiers can't afford to tip that much."

We were really surprised at the patriotism and support of the Big Apple. It is a sad thing that one selfish man can create such a bad impression in the minds of three soldiers. I'm sure this treatment was not typical of most residents of the city.

※

The 440th TCC fell out about 6:00 P.M. in a cold, drizzly rain. The date was March 14, 1943. We marched over two miles to our troop train, carrying everything we owned. Many of the less athletic in the group ended up dragging their barracks bag; they simply could not carry one hundred pounds for two miles. Unfortunately, I was one of the draggers.

The ride on the troop train was short—very short. Then we

boarded a ferry across the Hudson to a large barn-like building. Though it was long since dark, I figured that we would board a boat here. By this time we would have been glad to board a sinking rowboat. All we wanted was a place to drop our gear and take a breather. I did not realize we were already onboard the *Louis Pasteur.*

We looked around at the room full of hammocks. There were a few mattresses on the floor. I was a bit skeptical when assigned to a hammock; it did not look especially inviting. I was wrong. With the swaying and pitching of the *Louis Pasteur,* a hammock was a better place to sleep.

Someone, I have no idea who, woke us up about 6:00 A.M. "If you want a last look at the Statue of Liberty, you better get up on deck in a hurry."

I believe all of us were unaware the ship was moving. Quickly we dressed and hurried up on deck where we lined the rails as the big ship glided smoothly past the monument. The smoothness of the boat ride gradually gave way to constant pitching and rolling as we crossed the cold North Atlantic.

CHAPTER 15

Merrie Olde England

*Soldiers who wish to be a Hero
are practically zero,
but those who wish to be civilians,
Jesus, they run into the Millions.*

—Graffito, collected by Norman Rosten

From the day I was shipped into the Troop Carrier Command, it was common knowledge we were headed for Europe. Somehow, the thought of the Pacific theater of operations seemed like another war, a remote part of the world involving unfamiliar fighting groups.

So, as we glided past the Statue of Liberty that cold winter morning in 1944, our main concern was surviving the journey to Great Britain—a trip that would take five long days of travel through the cold rough waters of the North Atlantic. A surging vibration, slight though it was, gave us an indication of the power being generated in the engine rooms below.

As troopships go, we were fortunate to be crossing on the *Louis Pasteur*. First launched in the 1930s, the French luxury liner was designed to compete with Great Britain's ships for the lucrative transatlantic passenger service. A magnificent liner, *Pasteur* made only a few crossings before France surrendered to Germany in 1939. The French crew had no intention of letting the vessel fall into Nazi hands; instead, they sailed it to Canada and turned the ship over to Her Majesty's Royal Navy. Slightly smaller than the *Queen Mary*, the *Pasteur* was more of the *Normandy* class. Very fast, the turbine-driven ship broke several speed records for ships of its size. For this reason, the Royal Navy chose to run the German U-boat blockade rather than crossing

Once a unit arrived overseas, most COs (commanding officers) relaxed many rules of dress. You could let your hair grow and even sport a mustache if your body cooperated. My hair grew fine; the mustache was a bad idea from the start.

with a safer, but much slower, convoy. Still vivid in our minds was the sinking of a troopship less than one month before our departure. The ship, a U. S. vessel similar in size and speed to the *Pasteur,* was torpedoed and sunk off the coast of Greenland. Some 6,000 troops and most of the crew were lost. Today, as I write this chapter, the *Pasteur* rests on the ocean floor somewhere in the South Pacific.

Totally ignorant about ships at sea, for the first few hours I thought we were going to have a smooth crossing. If I had applied Newton's laws of motion I would have realized that it takes time to set a mass the size and weight of our troopship in motion. By nightfall of the first day, the sea had become rougher and rolling and pitching of the large vessel gradually increased. Seasickness started at the same time. Those not affected by the ship's movement became sick listening to the gagging, and by the terrible odor of vomit—soured, partially-digested food. It was no longer necessary to walk anywhere. You just stood still until the ship's deck tilted in the direction you wanted to go, and then slid to your destination. I am not attempting humor—the decks were covered with vomit. I found a spot on the top deck, near a heat exhaust, where I could breathe clean air and stay relatively warm. More importantly, it was a place where I did not have to listen to the constant gagging, moaning, and vomiting of hundreds of men crammed into an impossibly small space.

My relief was not to last. The supply officer came by, noticed me sitting with my back to the warm exhaust, and asked, "Are you seasick, soldier?"

"No sir, I feel just fine," I replied.

"Good, follow me," said the officer. "As you are one of the few not sick, it's up to you to scrub the latrine in your squadron's area."

Before I was through cleaning up after sixty seasick men, I no longer felt so well myself.

Our menu for the entire crossing never varied. Two times each day we had a mixture of stale bread and canned tomatoes. They would come into our area, put a five-gallon G.I. can of tomatoes on the floor, open it, throw in a few loaves of bread, and stir the mess with a wood stick similar to the one my grandmother used to punch clothes with as she boiled them in an old iron wash kettle. This slop was served two times each day to those brave enough to eat it. I never got hungry enough to try it. A few soldiers had enough foresight to stow away a few candy bars before leaving Camp Shanks. When the little PX on board ran out of candy our third day at sea, those soldiers became rich overnight. The going price for a Hershey bar was five bucks.

Lifeboat drill was a daily occurrence. It did not take a genius to see the logic behind these useless formations. The *Pasteur* carried twelve lifeboats. Each lifeboat would hold, at most, 100 men. We had enough men on board to fill all lifeboats several times. The water of the North Atlantic in early March is below the freezing point. We were told that no one could expect to survive more than three minutes or so in such conditions.

Lifeboat drill was for one reason only—to keep down a mad scramble for lifeboats while the chosen few were lowered to safety.

It was more than obvious that enlisted men were disposable. To hell with it! If we were hit by a torpedo I assumed I was dead, but darned if I would be told to die in an orderly fashion. If I had to die at sea, I wanted to be comfortable when it happened. I found a stack of barracks bags in one corner of the room. By burrowing down in the bags, I could be invisible and warm at the same time, maybe even catch up on sleep. I let the officers play their little games and never showed up for lifeboat drill again. Through a small opening between barracks bags I could see the squadron returning from the cold deck. They were tired, often wet, and always cold. I was very snug in my hiding place.

On rare occasions I ventured up on deck. I found it comforting to see the radar antennas perched high atop the ship's masts, making their 360-degree rotations as they searched the ocean for U-boats. Looking aft, the wake of the boat was a long zigzag pattern made visible by the trail of roiled water. As a defensive measure against submarine attack, the captain changed course every seven minutes. Youthful optimism, plus confidence in our British crew, contributed to my sense of security—a feeling I would not enjoy today under similar circumstances.

Late in the afternoon of our fourth day at sea, those of us below deck heard a lot of cheering and shouting on deck. We rushed topside. Long range British patrol aircraft appeared overhead. Apparently they were there to escort us into port by keeping a sharp lookout for the dreaded "wolf pack" of German submarines. The following morning we were buzzed several times by British Spitfires, one of the most beautiful sounds in the world. Unfortunately this is a sound most people today will never enjoy; very few flyable "Spits" survive.

The *Louis Pasteur* docked at Liverpool—not exactly the garden spot of the universe. There was a very remote danger of being strafed by German fighters during daylight hours, and no danger at all at night. A decision was made to keep the group on board for several hours; debarking near midnight. Why so late? The British had what they called "British Double Summer Time," which meant that it was not full dark until sometime after 10:00 P.M.

We fell out in formation about 11:00 P.M. The country, especially ports like Liverpool, was under very strict blackout rules. We could hear catcalls and obscene remarks coming from the shadows—the port was a well known hangout for prostitutes. Several men from our squadron carried on a verbal exchange with the unseen ladies of the evening, much to the annoyance of good Captain Jansen. Jansen was a real—well, I simply cannot think of a word that describes him. If you remember the opening scene of the movie *Patton* when George C. Scott appeared in front of a huge American flag wearing his chrome-plated .45s, helmet, and a battle jacket full of ribbons and medals, you have some idea of what Jansen looked like.

"Men, this is it," said Jansen. "We are now in a combat zone."

There was a lot of suppressed laughter and unkindly sounds from both the squadron and prostitutes. The captain was furious. He could not see where the comments were coming from.

Jansen was the squadron misfit. He had an ego as large as a B-29, a brain the size of an APC pill, and the I.Q. of a turnip. He was a constant embarrassment to both the squadron and the Air Force. Contempt for the officer was universal. While he liked to dress and act like General Patton, he wanted to avoid any possibility of being shot at. Still in formation, we waited for Jansen to do something—anything.

"As I was saying, we are in a combat zone. If the troop train comes under fire from enemy planes, the train will come to a stop. Deploy to each side of the train, take cover, and return fire with your weapon."

Someone piped up in the ranks, "What will we use for ammunition, sir? We have never been issued any ammo for our carbines."

Embarrassed, Captain Jansen stuttered and stammered, then finally said, "I'll look into it as soon as we are on board."

"Sir, I never heard of a train being strafed by the Luftwaffe after dark," said the supply sergeant.

"Don't get smart with me, soldier," yelled the frustrated captain. "I'll have your stripes if you make one more smart-assed remark."

In a last ditch effort so save face, Captain Jansen faced the assembled group of tired, hungry, and generally pissed-off members of our squadron. "For the next two weeks every man in this squadron will wear full field equipment at all times. That means a *full* canteen of water, helmet, and shined—*I repeat*—shined combat boots. IS THAT CLEAR? You will have your weapon with you at all times, and heaven help you if it is not clean."

After some time on the train we arrived at our "combat zone,"

Nottingham. It now became clear—Jansen was expecting an attack by Robin Hood. One thing for sure, if Robin Hood showed up he would be up against a well-dressed enemy, even though we still had no ammunition. The only combat we would see on the British Isles was a fight between some airborne infantry troops and a few British sailors in a local pub.

Immediately upon arrival at our base, Sergeant Trzeciak assigned me the duties of a permanent latrine orderly. I did not really mind and it gave Trzeciak a lot of personal satisfaction knowing he had assigned me to what some considered the "shittiest" job on the air base.

In reality, the job was not all that bad. The latrine was in a building about twenty-four feet wide and perhaps 80 feet long. In one end of the long building were two small storage rooms, each about eight by twelve feet. In the latrine proper, mirrors and sinks lined each long wall. Down the center of the building were two rows of commodes, back to back. I decided to move closer to my work by moving into one of the storerooms. Again, I proved that American soldiers will provide a way to live well, given the slightest chance.

My first item to liberate was a cot and mattress. British mattresses are composed of three equal-size "biscuits." They are not bad when you put a couple of folded blankets on top of them. My next need was something to knock off the winter chill. A G.I. tent stove was ideal. The stovepipe had to go through a window and it took a bit of doing to fill in the air gaps around the pipe, but I did it. I needed a bookcase. Concrete blocks and a couple of two-by-ten boards worked out very well. My coffee was made the old fashioned way—I boiled it. Not bad in what Jansen called a "combat zone." By the end of my first week I had a very comfortable corner room. In reality, I was better off than most of the 440th.

The next week was spent in comfort. I was through cleaning the latrines by noon. Afternoons were spent in my room with a warm fire to knock off the chill of the damp island. There, I read books liberated from the Red Cross Club, drank hot coffee on demand, and wrote letters home.

I was on my way to the mess hall for my noonday meal when I saw Captain Quigley walking rapidly in my direction. I froze, and threw him my very best ROTC-style hand salute.

"Vaughan," said Quigley, "where in the hell have you been? Do you realize we have been here two whole weeks and you have not reported for duty? We need you on the flight line."

"I know, Captain, and I am really sorry about that," I replied. "You see, the day we arrived I was made permanent latrine orderly."

"We'll see about that," said the red-faced captain. He was normally very even-tempered, but I could tell he was very upset. "Trzeciak has no authority to assign one of my men to permanent duty, or even temporary detail, without first checking with me. I want you on the flight line this afternoon. Report to me at 1400 hours. I'll take care of Trzeciak and the rest of the crew in the orderly room." I could tell the captain was in a very, very, bad mood. He continued, "I doubt that you will hear any more from Trzeciak."

I reported to the captain as ordered. I knew when I entered his office that there was a big problem. His desk was cluttered with papers and he looked as though he was carrying the entire war effort all by himself.

"Vaughan, I have a real big problem," said Captain Quigley. "What do you know about the SCR-522 transceiver?"

"Absolutely nothing," I replied. "I never heard of it until this very moment. You know that I never attended any Air Force technical school so I am totally unfamiliar with Air Force equipment and nomenclature."

The captain looked even more despondent. "Have you noticed that the crew chiefs are busy right now painting big white stripes around the wings and fuselage of all our ships?"

"Yes, I noticed that early this morning when on my way to the mess hall for breakfast. It sure doesn't do anything to help the appearance of the C-47. They were painting with what looked like a broom or scrub brush."

"They are painting all planes that belong to the U.S. and Britain. Our group is taking part in a D-Day practice mission tomorrow morning. As you probably know there have been reports of friendly fire bringing down several of our planes. The High Command hopes that the wide stripes, on both wings and the fuselage, will be highly visible from the ground and stop this friendly fire thing." The captain continued talking. I listened.

"Now back to the SCR-522. I will tell you what I know. It is rumored that it is a British invention, and that we traded our Norden Bombsight for it. You know, a lend-lease type thing. Our 522s are supposed to be manufactured by Bendix, but that it unimportant. The 522 is a VHF four-channel transceiver. It is located on a small shelf behind the crapper in the C-47, and remotely controlled by a small box behind the pilot's right ear. One channel is for the control tower, one for direction-finding, one for air-sea rescue, and one for ship-to-ship. They say it really proved itself in the Battle of Britain."

He then explained his big problem. "Vaughan, I have six radio mechanics. All six have been through Air Force technical school. The unit is brand new to the AF, and they have decided to use this radio almost exclusively. Not a one of my mechanics knows anything at all about this radio. I can tell you this—each channel is crystal-controlled and is remotely tuned by a series of cams in the 522 proper. The units in the planes are untuned—maybe even missing crystals. I have a box of several hundred crystals here by my desk. My mechanics have been messing with the units for a week and not a single one is working. Take-off is scheduled for tomorrow morning at 5:00 A.M. If my planes are grounded due to inoperative radios, my ass is mud. The colonel will come down hard on me. Is there a way in the world you could help me out of this mess?"

"Do you have any tech manuals on this 522 transceiver?" I asked.

"Sure, right here on the desk. Take a look and tell me what you think," said Quigley.

I studied the book for some time. It seemed like a relatively simple crystal-controlled unit. The electrical circuits were not all that strange, but the mechanical construction was a Rube Goldberg mechanical nightmare. But I figured if they had been used for some time in the Spitfires and Hurricanes that they did what they were designed for.

"Sir, this is really a two-man job. I need someone to work from a fixed 522 while I check out each plane," I said.

"Fine," replied the Captain. "Just tell me which radio mechanic you want to help you."

"With all due respect, sir, I would feel a lot better if you would let me pick another man from the squadron."

"Who exactly do you have in mind?" asked Quigley.

"I have an acquaintance that has a lot of ability. I have not known him for all that long, but I can think of no one better qualified to help me. His name is Ralph Hils. Ralph is a corporal and I am unsure of his classification, but I know he's on the base. If you could get on the Tannoy* and ask him to report here, I'll bet he'd show up within minutes."

"You've got it," said the captain. "I'll have him paged. What else do you need?"

"Does the radio department have a spare 522? If I had one to go through as I read the manual it would sure help. In addition, out of the twenty-five planes in our squadron, the odds are pretty good that at least one will have a serious problem," I said.

"We don't have a spare, but I'll get you one within minutes," said the captain.

Quigley wasted no time. He got on the phone and started making calls. Soon Ralph came rushing through the radio shack door. "Hi Bruce, what's going on? Am I in some kind of trouble?" asked Hils.

"Maybe more trouble than you want," I said, laughing. "Let's go in the captain's office and we will all go over this together."

About this time a corporal from the signal depot came through the front door carrying a new 522. "Here is the 522 Captain Quigley wanted. Where do I put it?"

I told him to set it on the table where I had all the service manuals spread out, thanked him for the speedy service, and, with Ralph at my side, walked into the captain's office.

We dispensed with formalities. "Captain, this is Ralph Hils. Do you want to explain our problem or do you want me to bring him up to date?"

After explaining the problem to Ralph I showed him the tech manuals and the spare 522 that had just been delivered. The captain stood by looking anxious, and worried.

"What do you think, Ralph?" I asked. "Can we pull it off by the 5:00 A.M. take-off?"

"Let's go to work," said Ralph. "There are twenty-five planes in the

---

*British term for PA system

squadron and we only have about twelve hours to do the job. Thirty minutes per plane. We will have to keep moving to get it done."

I turned to the captain. "Sir, I will need a list of frequencies for each channel. I need the ship numbers of our planes—I don't want to screw up another squadron's plane. I will also need a jeep or other transportation, and most importantly, I need you to tell the officer of the guard that we will be working all night. I don't want some trigger-happy guard ruining my day."

"Hold on one minute, fellows," said the Captain. "I don't have to tell you that if you can pull this off, I will be very grateful. Vaughan, if all the ships are ready for takeoff tomorrow morning, I will make you my radio repair chief, and that calls for a staff sergeant rating."

"Ralph," said Quigley, "what job would you like in communications? Or perhaps you are happy where you are?"

"Captain, I would really like to be in charge of the DF (direction-finding) station. That is a job I would really like."

"I have no problem with that," said Quigley. "I need a good man to handle that station, and it also calls for a staff sergeant rating."

Quigley continued, "In addition to the ratings, I will see that you both get a three day pass, *and* I will give you each two pounds to spend in the pubs of your choice. But remember, these promises are only good if you deliver the goods."

Hils and I worked all night. One thing that speeded our work up was discovered by accident. We found that if you pulled the jeep close to the plane, the 522 receiver could be tuned up roughly by tuning in ignition noise. Lifting the hood on the jeep delivered a louder signal. Not perfect, but much faster than using a signal generator in the dark.

As each plane was tuned up, we gave it a check on all four channels with our control plane which we had tuned up carefully using the signal generator.

The sky was not yet light in the east when we checked out the last plane on our list. We signed the last log certifying the radios were all working, then returned to the radio shack. We decided to brew up a pot of coffee and wait to see the takeoff at 5:00 A.M. Already there was a lot of activity on the flight line.

The captain left us about 9:00 P.M. the previous evening when he saw that we were making good headway. I suppose he slept a little better than he did the night before. About 4:30 A.M. he came into the shack. "Tell me," he said. "Is the news good or bad?"

"Sir," I said, "Every ship is ready for the mission. We want to stick around and listen to the base station as they take off. Only after they are all in the air can I rest easy."

The smile on Quigley's face grew bigger as each plane made contact with the tower on take-off. After the mission was completed, the captain received a letter of commendation from Colonel Krebs, the commanding officer of the 440th TCC Group. The Ninety-eighth Squadron was the only squadron in the group in which every channel on every ship worked perfectly.

Captain Quigley called Ralph and me into his office. "I want to congratulate you fellows. I am very proud of you." With that comment he handed us each three-day passes and two pounds.

I put two more pounds with my money and bought a used British bike. I had never ridden anything but the large, heavy, American bikes with balloon tires. I was amazed at how much faster and easier it was to ride the British bike. During my time left in England it would serve me well, as I used it for sightseeing and trips to and from the flight line.

The Nottingham Air Base was actually located outside the city, near a small typical English village. The stone cottages with thatched roofs, large stone barns, and stone church with a towering steeple looked like an eighteenth century painting; what travel agents refer to as "picturesque." To the men of the 440th it had less charm. To most of us it was cold, damp, dull, and too far from home. Nottingham was seventeen miles away and visiting the city involved a long walk to the railroad station to board a train. We had no bus service into town. Even our dreary Quonset hut barracks were widely deployed around the base— a necessary arrangement dictated by the frequent German bombing raids during the Battle of Britain.

At the end of April our group was moved to a Spitfire base near Exeter, on the so-called "Riviera of the British Isles." The day of our move, I had the pleasure of being in the same plane with Captain

Jansen. Almost immediately after take-off we encountered very rough air.

Sergeant Sinclair, the crew chief, pulled a footlocker to the rear of the overcrowded plane. "Take this seat here, Captain," said Sinclair. "It will be a lot smoother near the rear of the ship."

The rest of us in the ship cast knowing glances at each other. The chief had placed Jansen in the roughest part of the cabin. Soon the prayers of everyone on board were answered. Off came the captain's helmet and, while holding it under his nose, his face green and his pride wounded, Jansen heaved up his insides. From that moment on, Crew Chief Sinclair was a hero in the Ninety-eighth Squadron.

I hesitate to mention names in this book that might offend someone, but I must tell you about Suzette, as I am sure she saved my life. Perhaps I should start at the beginning.

A friend, Andy Bourke, and I went into Exeter with girl-hunting as our primary goal. The logical place to start was the nearest pub. Near the downtown area of Exeter was a nice pub known as the Coach Makers Arms. Stepping inside we noticed two girls in ATS (Auxiliary Territorial Service) uniforms. I was quick to notice that one was a real beauty— tall, black hair, built like a movie queen. The girl with her is best described as "pleasant."

Andy and I approached their table. "May we sit down and buy you a drink?" I asked.

The girls glanced at each other with amusement. Suzette, looked directly at me and said, "I'll have a gin and orange."

During the coming weeks I would see Suzette often. Her craving for gin and orange knew no limits. I had been outrunning my pay for several months. It caught up with me in Exeter and I was in the money for a few weeks. At twenty-four years of age, Suzette was well on her way to becoming an alcoholic. She went through most of my back pay in record time. On the small pay which girls received in the British Army, there was no way Suzette could keep herself in gin. Her choices were to give up drinking or find an American who could afford a bit of gin.

Then there was the American citizenship thing. Suzette was a very sweet girl, cosmopolitan in nature. Her mother was French, her father was British, and she ended up married to an American serviceman. She was very frank: "I decided that I wanted to go to America after the war. The best way to do that was to marry the first American that asked me." One of Patton's tank commanders wanted Suzette, and Suzette wanted a ticket to America. You might say that the marriage was one of supply and demand. I would say that in Suzette's case, she and her husband were both winners.

The British had a rough time during the war. Suzette joined the ATS in 1939. She told me of her first day in service. A sergeant marched the girls out into a hayfield and handed each girl two sacks—one large and one small. "Fill those sacks with hay," they were told. "The large one is your mattress, the small one is your pillow." For several weeks they did not even have tents—they slept on the ground. Food was always in short supply, and sweets and fruits were practically non-existent. ATS uniforms were made for durability, especially their undergarments, which were both rough and coarse. I could fully understand why she needed a lot of gin to keep going.

~

In order to tell this story properly it is necessary to give you a bit of background. One of our C-47s suffered engine failure on take-off. It crashed in a field but no one was seriously injured, just badly shaken up. The plane was declared a total loss. With Quigley's permission, I stripped all the radios from the wreck.

I checked the gear, made what repairs were needed, and mounted the radios in an Air Force packing crate. To put an emergency control tower on the air, I could set the packing crate on a table, hook up an emergency antenna, run a cable outside to a small generator, and be on the air in minutes. I had no idea if the emergency control tower could be of any value to the group, but it would cost us nothing. If I had not removed the command sets from the wrecked plane, they would have been destroyed or ruined by the elements. I might mention that this was a project underway and never was fully completed. Nevertheless, the captain was impressed and pushed me to get the thing operational.

By the way, Hils was now a buck sergeant comfortably settled in the direction-finding station. I was still a private, trying to keep all the radios going in about twenty-five aircraft. Each plane, if my memory is correct, carried the following radio equipment:

One SCR-522 four-channel VHF transceiver
One BC-375 HF transmitter
One BC-348 HF radio receiver
Three SCR-274N command radio receivers
Two command transmitters
One radio compass
One trailing wire antenna
Intercom system
Antennas for all of the above

I devised a plan to keep up with the maintenance work. On a large sheet of plywood I listed all the plane numbers across the top of the board. Down the right side I listed all the radio gear by its designation. The board was marked off in vertical and horizontal lines. In each square I placed a small finish nail. A box attached to the bottom of the board held a supply of red and green poker chips. I drilled a small hole in the perimeter of each chip.

All operators had to check in when a flight was completed, so my board was not any extra work for the operators. If plane number 926 had a problem with their BC-348, all they had to do was pick out a red chip and hang it in the appropriate square. When I was sure the radio was working okay, I removed the red chip and replaced it with a green one. Before any flight, the operator could look at the board and know if his problem had been resolved.

Shortly after I got my status board up and running the captain came in one morning, looked it over carefully, and said, "I see you have room for one more ship on your board."

"Are we getting another ship for the Ninety-eighth?" I asked.

"Well, not exactly," answered Quigley. "Colonel Krebs has requested that you do all the maintenance of radios in his ship. He is not satisfied with the way his radios have been working."

"I thought his ship was under Headquarters Squadron," I said.

"When Colonel Krebs speaks, we listen. Add his plane number to the board. One more won't break our back," said the captain.

"Personally, Captain, I consider it an honor," I replied. "I think I can keep the colonel's radios going well enough to please him."

"I think so too," said Quigley. "It seems that there have been a few too many problems with his radio maintenance. I have a suspicion that some heads are going to roll. Do you know where he parks his ship?"

"Yeah, I believe he parks his plane over in front of the control tower. I know his radio op and his crew chief. I'll add his ship number to the board and give his plane a weekly check, even if there are no complaints. It would help if his crew was notified that the Ninety-eighth might be snooping around the radios."

Our T.O. called for six radio mechanics. My problem was that I had only one man who could be trusted to not foul up something instead of fixing it. A plane can fly okay most of the time with no radio. However, they may not fly so well if there is a problem in the wiring—like a fire, for example.

It is very easy to understand that a newcomer to the squadron, a private, would have a problem ordering a corporal or buck sergeant around. The end result was that Corporal Miller and I did all the repairing. Miller was a very fine mechanic and a great fellow, but we could only do so much. I was getting rather discouraged with my lack of promotion.

One morning in early May I was in the radio shack when the captain came in with an armful of mail. I continued working on a stack of tech manuals I was trying to organize, while the captain went through his mail.

"Listen to this, Vaughan," said the captain. "They are calling for volunteers to attend a special radio school in London. It is a three-week course that starts next Monday. Some new sort of thing they call 'Pathfinder.' It sounds like it might be a feather in your cap if you want to attend. Besides, you sure deserve some time in London. Shall I put your name down?"

"Sure, I'll go," I answered. "Can you tell me anything at all about the equipment?"

"Nope, I don't have any idea what it is. Look at this letter," he said, holding up the envelope.

I left the radio shack and walked up to the repair building. I had a date with Suzette that evening. I had forgotten all about her when I was so quick to give a "yes" to leave for three weeks. After all, what kind of an idiot would leave a nice job here in Exeter with a beauty like Suzette waiting for him in town? I turned and RAN back to the radio shack.

"Captain, I've changed my mind. I don't want to go to that school. If it's okay with you I would like to leave things just as they are," I said.

Quigley smiled, "I saw you and that good looking girl at the Odeon last night. Your decision would not have anything to do with her, would it? I don't blame you for staying here. I think you just made a wise decision."

As it turned out it was the best decision of my entire life. The Pathfinders were jumped into France well ahead of any other troops. Their job, provided they survived the jump into the middle of the German army, was to scout around until they found a suitable field for our gliders to land in. After the found such a field, they set up a portable homing radio so that the incoming airborne infantry and gliders could "home in."

Casualties among the Pathfinders we dropped the night before D-Day was 100 percent—no one survived. Thus, I credit Suzette with saving my life.

∼

There is a strong feeling of purpose and comradeship in combat units. No longer individuals with no idea of why we were in the Air Corps, or what exactly was expected of us, we developed a feeling of family. I had been assigned to the Ninety-eighth Squadron, 440th Troop Carrier Group, Ninth Air Force.

I believe this is a good place to clarify (or further muddle) the difference between the Air Corps and the Air Force. In the early years, actually up until World War II, the Air Corps was considered a part of the Army. The primary purpose of the Air Corps was in support of ground forces in the Army. This began to change long before the name "Air Corps" was officially changed. I can remember as a primary school student many of the boys talking of becoming an Air Corps pilot. By the time of the Pearl Harbor attack, most young men, when talking about the Air Corps, called it the "Air Force." The Air Corps did not officially become known as Air Force until September 18, 1947.

Even though the above is true, I was officially in the Ninth Air Force during World War II. In my short time of three years in the service I never heard anyone in my outfit use the term "Air Corps." The Eighth Air Force bombed heck out of Hitler—not the Eighth Air Corps.

So, as George C. Scott said in the movie *Patton* when he put on a second star before it was approved, "Congress has their timetable, and I have mine." Apparently the Air Force had their own timetable, and the U.S. government was a bit slow in catching up.

Now for a bit of the 440th TCC history. The 440th Troop Carrier Command was formed on June 7, 1943. After two months training at Sedalia AFB, the group, growing in strength and combat readiness, moved to Alliance, Nebraska. With the facilities at Alliance they were able to do practice missions involving both single- and double-glider tows, paradrops, and supply missions. The entire Troop Carrier was under pressure to achieve combat readiness. The High Command understood that there would be heavy casualties on the beaches when we invaded the coast of France, as everyone expected us to do. They hoped to alleviate this to some extent by dropping parachute troops behind the German lines, and using both airborne and glider-borne infantry.

The duties of the Troop Carrier Command were changed to meet battle conditions. We did air evacuation of wounded, and supplied ground forces with everything from toilet paper (I'm deadly serious) to hundreds of thousands of gallons of gasoline to General Patton's army. Near the end of the war Patton constantly outran his supply. Our group flew as many as three missions a day to supply fuel to the rapidly advancing army. I might mention that our planes had neither armor nor armament and were constantly in danger from small arms fire as we went in slow and low. Our first planes flew without self-sealing gas tanks. Some of our planes were fitted with fold-down litters. A company of registered nurses were assigned to the 440th and on air-evac runs, one or more were always on board.

The idea of airlifting the wounded from a battlefield then flying to a good hospital well behind the lines had one serious flaw—you needed a large and smooth field to land your C-47s near the battlefield. This created a lot of danger for all involved. After arriving in Exeter, some of the ships were modified to allow them to snatch a CG-4A off the ground without landing.

The theory was that a C-47 would tow a CG-4A to a suitable landing place near the front lines. The glider would cut loose, land, be loaded with wounded, then snatched off the ground by a low flying C-47. The field did not need to be more than one-fourth the size needed for a C-47 to land and take off.

Ideally the CG-4A, once cut loose from the tow ship, circled and made a landing almost anywhere. While medics were loading the injured, a ground crew went to the edge of the field and installed two twenty-foot-high collapsible poles about twenty-five feet apart. The poles were held erect by very lightweight nylon cord. On top of each pole was a hook. A heavy-duty nylon rope was formed into a loop some forty feet in diameter and attached to the glider's tow rope. The loop was draped over the hooks. A C-47 with a hook attached to the belly of the ship would make a pass at the field and snatch the loop from the poles. This would jerk the glider off the field, and all would be fine ever after. Well, maybe.

There were problems aplenty. Even though nylon tow ropes do stretch a bit, to go from 0 to 125 mph almost instantly was inviting disaster—like the glider parting company with its wings. What was needed was a way to bring the glider up to flying speed a bit slower. To do this, the mother ship needed to be highly modified.

Inside the C-47 cabin, a Rube Goldberg machine was bolted to the floor. This machine had a BIG reel of tow cable on it. The cable went from the machine to a long hollow metal tube on the side of the ship. The cable ran through the metal tube and ended up with a massive hook tied to the cable end. This tube could be cranked up parallel with the fuselage when flying, or cranked down at a 45 degree angle for snatching the glider. There was a large hand brake to apply pressure on the reel. The brake was operated by the crew chief.

Now, when the C-47 snatched the glider rope, the reel started spinning and the crew chief slowly applied pressure. This eases the sudden 0 to 125 mph in one second thing.

They said it worked pretty well. It was never used much by our group. By actual measurement, pulling gliders actually stretched a C-47 an inch or more in length.

Of course during the early months of 1943, I knew absolutely nothing of this. I only knew that I was in the Air Force, a buck private with no Army specialized training at all. I had no idea at all what duties I would be assigned to but was ninety-nine percent sure it would have something to do with radio as I had scored exceptionally high on that classification examination.

On a mission while still at Exeter, the colonel had a bit of a problem on one operation and was three days late in returning. I don't remember the full details. Jansen, as our squadron executive officer, immediately assumed command. His first order, issued almost immediately after the colonel did not return, was that no flying clothes would be worn outside the airplane. This meant that crews had to get up in damp, unheated barracks, often at 4:00 A.M., dress in fatigues, then go eat breakfast. After eating, they rode in an open jeep to their respective ships. When they got to the plane they had to undress in a frigid airship and put on their flying gear. Smart. Only an idiot, or a non-flying officer, could come up with something like that. Jansen qualified on both counts.

A week or so after this insane order was issued a badly shot up B-17 made an emergency landing at our base. I was on the flight line installing a dorsal antenna and saw the B-17 approaching. A red flare was fired from the ship indicating that wounded were on board. An ambulance was on the field before the B-17 slid to a stop—it was a belly landing as his hydraulics were out. I stood frozen in fear expecting the darn thing to explode at any minute. The ball turret gunner was dead. One waist gunner was missing, and the other waist gunner was wounded. Both pilots and the bombardier were okay, but badly shook up.

The pilot was a young kid, perhaps twenty-one years old. He got out of the heavy flying gear and put on his A-2 jacket. (One of a pilot's most prized possessions is his A-2 jacket. Warm, lightweight, comfortable, it was easy to slip off before putting on one of those heavy sheepskin flying jackets. It was more than a garment—it was a badge second only to pilot wings.) He was trying to light a cigarette but shaking so badly he could not hold his lighter near the end of his cigarette. One of our 440th boys lit a cigarette and handed it to the second lieutenant. He returned to the ship and got his 50 mission hat he had lost in the confusion. I noticed the gold bars on his jacket were in need of polishing. It was plain to see the air crew had been going through hell for weeks past.

"Lieutenant, why don't you get in this weapons carrier and let me drive you and your crew up to the mess hall," I asked. "Even if you don't feel like eating, a cup of coffee might help. It's not the best coffee in the world, but it's hot."

"Thanks," answered the bomber pilot, then he turned and spoke to his crew. "Come on fellows. Grab a seat, and after we eat, I'll get us some transportation back to our base. They will pick us up today or tomorrow, but frankly, I'm in no hurry."

Though we had both officers and enlisted men's mess at Exeter, due to some repairs on the officers mess we all ate in the same mess hall for a time. It was segregated to the extent that the officers ate on the west side of the long, narrow room, while the enlisted men ate on the east side of the room—one big happy family, you might say.

The young lieutenant and his crew took seats with other officers. As far as those of us who witnessed the B-17 landing and aftermath, every crew member was a hero, and we were honored to have them with us. The crew had just gotten comfortably seated when Captain Jensen stepped into the mess hall. Slowly he walked down the aisle between the officers and men, plainly looking for something to raise hell about.

Then, horror of horrors, there was a lieutenant with an A-2 jacket on. Worse still, he was eating beside a tech sergeant. The captain strode firmly and grimly toward the offenders. He stood behind the lieutenant for several seconds, then he tapped him on the shoulder, and said in his loudest voice, "Lieutenant, where in the hell have you been with that A-2 jacket on?"

The young lieutenant stopped eating. Very slowly and deliberately, he stood, faced the captain, and in an aggressive voice said, "We've been over Berlin all morning, Captain. Where in hell have you been?'

The entire mess erupted in loud applause from both sides of the aisle. How can a captain put the entire squadron on report? Red-faced, the captain made a fast exit.

After that day, the captain was too embarrassed to enforce his orders. As far as I know they were never rescinded but were universally ignored.

Oh yes, it would happen again during Operation Market Garden.

Our base commander's plane was hit in mid-air by another plane approaching him from below. There was no way the colonel could see the plane that caused his crash. Even with the aid of sympathetic people in Holland, it took some weeks for he and his copilot to work their way back.

Everyone on base was overjoyed when the colonel, and common sense, returned to our base. Captain Jensen spent the rest of the war trying to imitate Glenn Miller. He led the squadron's dance orchestra. Not a very important job, but at least he could do no damage.

After June 6, 1944 (D-Day), our group was very active. By the time V–E Day rolled around, we had seven battle stars. The 440th participated in the following campaigns: Normandy, Southern France, Northern France, Rome-Arno, Rhineland, Ardennes, and Central Europe.

My work was sporadic during the months of June, July and August. All the planes might be on base for a week during which time we repaired or replaced radios in many of them. Much of our work involved replacing or repairing wiring which had been damaged by either ground fire or antiaircraft fire. There is not much you can do if a radio is hit by a piece of shrapnel from antiaircraft fire, or by a .50 caliber slug. Those radios were replaced with new units. Twenty-hour work days were not uncommon.

This frantic activity would be followed by days with little to do when the planes were away on temporary duty at another air base. Ground personnel, and the six or eight air crews left behind, welcomed these days of rest. Time was spent playing ball or sunbathing during the all-too-rare warm summer days. It was during such time that I had my most frightening wartime experience.

How will we react if and when we face sudden death is a question pondered by most of us. I was fortunate enough to find out, and to live through it. The date was September 9, 1944. I was out on the flight line draining some 100 octane out of the sumps on one of our C-47s. With no dry-cleaning service for eighteen months it became quite a problem as to how to keep our class A uniforms clean. We found that a good rinsing in 100 octane gasoline, then hanging the uniforms out to dry in the sun was almost as good as dry cleaning. The gasoline fumes would evaporate within hours.

I was thinking to myself that afternoon, "I hope all the fumes are gone by tonight. I have a big date with Suzette." We were going out to eat at six o'clock, then take in a movie at the Odeon.

Captain Quigley stepped outside the radio room door. "Hey Vaughan," he yelled. "Get over here immediately—double time—this is important."

I ran the block back to the radio shack. I knew it must be important for the captain to be outside yelling like a fishwife.

"Get that radio you salvaged ready to move out immediately. Pack all our spare gear and test equipment. We are shipping out to France in one hour."

"You mean we are going to move to another base in France and only have one hour until takeoff?"

"That's it," he said. "Takeoff in one hour. You are in 726(?). We will be flying in a seven-ship formation to our new base in Rheims, France. Pack the radio stuff first. If any time is left over, take care of personal gear. We may have to set up some sort of control tower in Rheims. Patton liberated it just minutes ago."

I could not figure what the panic was. Most of our outfit was still up in northern England busy with Market Garden. I would figure out the goof-up later on but it was never mentioned by the brass.

I did not even have time to give my bike away, and the class A uniform, doused good with gasoline, was left hanging on a fence in Exeter. However, I did get all the radio gear on board along with enough clothes to get by.

In 726 we made a pile of boxes, barracks bags, bedding, etc., down the middle of the cabin. Ropes tied at front and back anchor points were laced over the top of the big pile of gear and pulled taut. This, in effect, divided the plane's cabin into two walkways, one on each side of the cargo.

There were six passengers and a crew of five. Normally our planes carried a navigator only on lead ships, but today it was a case of moving everything and everybody.

Immediately after takeoff, a poker game started up in the floor of the ship directly in front of the forward tie point. I was sitting on the right side of the cargo. Corporal Urban, a radio operator, was sitting on the left side of the cabin. We could not see each other but could be heard if we yelled at each other.

The plane climbed to about 8,000 feet and leveled off. I was looking at all the boats in the channel. I could imagine the problems of keeping our armies in France supplied. Looking ahead a few miles, I saw some islands. I walked up to the navigator's position and asked him what the islands were called. He stood, looked over the copilot's shoulder, and said, "Oh, those are the Channel Islands."

I returned to my seat along the west side of the cabin. Just seconds later, I heard this very loud explosion. Corporal Urban yelled, "My God, we broke a spar. The left wing's gone."

At the time he was talking, the plane did a half roll and headed straight for the channel. Cards, money, and the poker players themselves were floating in the air. I grabbed a tie point alongside the cabin. We were all weightless—only my grip on the tie bar kept me from banging my head against the aircraft skin. The engine speed was increasing—I could tell the pilot, if in control, was running the engines at full rpm. I thought to myself, "So this is what it feels like to die." I remember my one thought was that I hoped my parents found out how I died. I'd hate for them not to know the details.

I watched as the channel water drew nearer and nearer. I could make out each wave now. From the corner of my eye I saw a boat, much too clearly. I thought any time now we are going in. Then, the most comforting feeling I ever had—gravity was pulling down on me. I was confused; we must be leveling out, otherwise I would not feel that pressure on my rear end. Only feet above the waves, I would estimate less than 100 feet, we were actually flying. I looked over the cargo and the left wing was in place. I have no idea what Urban saw or thought. I went forward. "What happened?" I asked the navigator.

"Those islands were simply bypassed on D-Day. They are still in German hands. We knew that, but we didn't think of it until they opened up with their 88s."

The pilot had done what any good pilot would do under the circumstances. He put the plane in a vertical dive to throw off the antiaircraft aim. Then he got down on the deck where the gunners cannot see you.

I returned to my seat. I still could not believe we were alive—I was so sure we were dead. Some time later we circled the Eiffel Tower before proceeding to Rheims. It was a beautiful sight. I began to feel alive again.

~

> *And I saw, and behold, a pale Horse:*
> *and he that sat upon him,*
> *And his name was Death.*
>
> —JOHN THE DIVINE (first century A.D.), Apostle of Jesus

Less than one hour later we landed on a grass airstrip at Rheims. Planes and hangars were still burning from the heated battle which raged just hours ago. To the north the sky was alive with flashes of light from artillery shells as Patton pushed further into Germany.

Oh yes, I was still a private.

CHAPTER 16

Heroes are Made, Not Born
or
How I Won the Air Medal

In the spring of 1945, the 440th Troop Carrier Group was flying three supply missions a day, trying to keep Patton's army supplied with gasoline. During the last months of the war, his fast-moving Armored Division was consistently several miles ahead of Allied motorized supply columns. Now, with the German army in full retreat, old "Blood and Guts" Patton had no intention of lessening the pressure. To diminish his attack would give the Germans a chance to reorganize. Patton had no intention of letting this happen. He intended to keep his tanks and half-tracks rolling. He could not afford to lose the momentum of his offensive.

Air crews arose well before daylight and were lucky to see their bunks again before 8:00 P.M. Fatigue was a constant companion.

As I watched the planes taking off on another supply mission I felt a twinge of envy. I was missing out on some interesting adventures and the war would soon be over. I realized this was a very unique period in history. I would never again have the opportunity to experience combat flying; I also needed to log a few hours each month to keep drawing my flying pay. With our planes in the air so many hours each day, we had little time for test flights to check radio operation. Our repair and maintenance was restricted to a fast exchange of various radios while the planes were on the ground being loaded for the next mission.

It was not unusual for the same plane to fly three trips to Germany every day with a different radio operator on at least one flight. I found it easy to talk one of the operators into trading places with me for a flight. Normally, our radio operators had strict orders to maintain radio silence. Their main duty was to help load and unload the five-gallon jerry cans of gasoline. I knew absolutely nothing about operating frequencies, or procedures, even though I was officially classified as a 756 Air Crew Operator.

We took off at 1:30 P.M. The sky was partially overcast. As usual we carried the maximum load of gasoline. Our destination was a grass airstrip near the recently liberated city of Worms, a few miles behind Patton's advancing army. Almost immediately I began to regret my passion for combat flying. The weather closed in; our plane entered black clouds. Rain was coming down so hard it seemed like we were flying underwater. I stuck my head up in the astrodome to get a better look. Lightning was streaking through the sky on all sides of the bouncing C-47. I walked forward. Standing between the pilot and co-pilot, I found it necessary to grasp the backs of their seats to keep from being tossed all over the ship. The pilots were fighting the controls in an effort to keep the plane on course and on a more or less even keel. I could tell they were as terrified as I was. This gave me no comfort at all. Anyone as terrified as I was had no business flying an airplane. I returned to the radio compartment, took a seat and fastened my seat belt. I put the "cans" on my head so I could hear the pilot. I heard him almost immediately: "Pilot to radio. Pilot to radio."

Picking up the mike, I answered, "This is radio, go ahead, sir."

"I need a Queen, Dog, Mary, and make it fast. To hell with radio silence, do it now!"

My blood turned to ice. A QDM is a fix to establish your exact location. I knew the theory well enough and I was certainly competent with the code, but I had no idea what frequency to use. To find our location I would need to contact two widely separated stations and request each station to give me a compass reading. I believe one station was in Great Britain and the other station in Spain, but I am not positive of that. Plainly, I was worthless as a radio operator.

I stalled for time, tuning the knobs on the BC-348 receiver trying to think my way out of this mess.

"Pilot to radio—pilot to radio, what the hell is taking so long back there?"

"Sorry, sir," I answered. "This electric storm has me blacked out. Both stations are unreadable. I'll keep trying."

I could see us landing behind the German lines, crashing into a mountain, or even worse—returning to base where I would receive a general court-martial.

"Pilot to crew, pilot to crew, this could be serious, fellows. Get your chutes and sidearms on. We may be over Germany."

The crew chief and I wasted no time in getting our sidearms on. I had fired a .45 a few times on the rifle range but certainly did not feel comfortable with it. We went forward to the cockpit.

"Here we go, fellows. Let's hope we don't hit rock on the way down." He cut both throttles and we started a slow descent through the overcast sky. I was watching the altimeter as we lost altitude. At 1,500 feet, we saw an opening in the clouds. As we dropped through that hole, the most beautiful sight in the world lay below us—a grass field with a few P-51s parked here and there.

Our plane touched down. Sheets of muddy water splashed up under our wings as the pilot fought the gusty wind. It was like landing on ice. We started skidding sideways into a runway marker. The marker knocked a hole in the left elevator. We suffered only minor damage. We were lucky, considering the circumstances.

Within hours the P-51 mechanics had our elevator patched and ready for our uneventful trip back to A-50 at Orleans. For the next few days I slept poorly. I expected at any moment to be called on the carpet, maybe even drawn and quartered. With the passage of time I started breathing easier. I had all but forgotten the incident until the day I received my discharge.

A young lady officer, a first lieutenant, was typing up my discharge. "I see you got the Air Medal," she said.

"No, I was not awarded an Air Medal," I told her. "There is a mistake somewhere."

"No mistake," she answered. "It's right here on your record."

"I am sorry to say that there just has to be an error," I argued.

"No mistake," she said. "Did you not fly combat missions? Is your serial number 18113200?"

"That's my serial number, but I still say there is an error somewhere.

You see, I flew a bit here and there but I have no idea how they could possibly put me down for an Air Medal. Well, I did fly a little as a relief radio operator, but I'd rather not go into detail—it is something best forgotten—one mission in particular."

"I understand," she nodded.

"Oh, no, you don't," I thought, "and thank God for that."

CHAPTER 17

The War Ends

There was never a good war, or a bad peace.
—BENJAMIN FRANKLIN (1706–1790)

Our flight of five C-47s circled in the warm summer sky above Rheims Air Base, formerly one of the finest air bases in France and home of the French Air Academy. We were astonished at the scene of destruction below. Two times our formation made low passes over the field looking for a section of runway unmarked by shell holes. After one narrow escape today we did not want to lose a plane on landing. Dropping a wheel in a shell hole can ruin your entire day.

Our planes finally found a stretch of undamaged runway and made a smooth landing. Unloading of our cargo began immediately. We were constantly interrupted by French civilians handing us flowers, shaking hands, and yelling, "Viva la Françoise." Many of the Frenchmen brought buckets, and after a brief greeting—which they felt gave them unlimited access to the base—ran to damaged German planes, some of which still had gasoline dripping from their bullet-riddled tanks. Our personnel stood around watching the fun. As the Frenchmen got a bucket of gas, they ran to the road and poured it into their ancient Renaults, Citroens, and Fiats. The engines in their small cars roared to life with the extra power of 100 octane aviation fuel. I suspect some of the engines blew soon afterward.

We found planes and hangars still smoldering. A few of Patton's halftracks remained behind on the base. After unloading I went over to talk to one of the halftrack commanders. He was a young second lieutenant hardly old enough to shave. He was trying to light his cigarette and had the shakes really bad.

> **To** Mrs. Bruce C. Vaughan
> Box 335
> Springdale, Ark.
> U.S.A.
>
> **From** Cpl. Bruce C. Vaughan
> 18132200
> 440 TC Gp 98 Sq
> APO 133 %PM, NYC
> Aug 24, 1944

THINKING of YOU!

I think of you OFTEN
   And want you to know it
So this friendly Greeting
   Is simply to SHOW it —
To tell you I'm fine
   And that everything's swell
In this job that I'm hoping
   To really do well!

Love,
Bruce

Long before e-mail came into use we had V-mail. During World War II, a soldier's mail was sent free of charge. This resulted in a very heavy load of mail to be transported daily, so the government came up with V-mail. Letters written by servicemen were first censored, then passed to a unit that photographed the letters on microfilm. The film was then sent to the U. S. where it was printed on lightweight paper designed to be folded into a small lightweight envelope suitable for mailing. The savings in space and weight meant a lot during the war. It took a lot of shipping to keep the Army and Air Force supplied. Saving hundreds of pounds of freight on a daily basis was a great help.

Notice the V-mail letter here. It was one of the many "special occasion messages" that were available to soldiers.

"That son of a bitch," he said, referring to General Patton. "He ordered us halftracks to knock out pillboxes. There is no way in God's world that a halftrack can go up against a pillbox and win."

The thought crossed my mind that German stragglers, or perhaps even snipers, might still be on the base. We had never been this close to the line of battle before.

The 440th Group's official publication, *DZ Europe*, had this to say:

> Closer examination of the base showed the almost unbelievable destruction done by Allied bombing and strafing attacks. Hangars were nothing but twisted steel and shattered concrete while fragments of German aircraft littered the entire area. Few of the engineering, administrative, or living quarters had escaped and few unbroken panes of glass remained on the entire base.

As it turned out, I did not have to haywire a temporary control tower—someone already had one up and working. I assumed it was the P-47 group's radio men that moved in shortly before the P-47 group arrived. The control tower may very well have been a parked P-47 near the grass runway.

We had been on the base perhaps one hour when our attention was drawn to the sky east of the airbase. A group of P-47s was returning from a mission. As they passed over the field in formation they started peeling off and buzzed the field, literally clipping daisies, then they pulled up, did a slow roll, and entered the landing pattern. The experienced combat pilots set those heavy fighters down as gently as if it were a PT-19.

Captain Jansen, our hero, was in charge and the temporary C.O. of our group. He watched the P-47s as they taxied to a stop in a perfect line down on the south end of the runway. "I'll go down there and have a talk with someone," said the captain. "It's plain to see that they cannot operate here—this is a troop carrier base."

He picked on the wrong airplane to approach. It was piloted by a light colonel, commander of the fighter group. I will never know the verbal exchange that followed, but our fearless captain returned very angry at everyone, his face a vivid red. One of the fighter mechanics heard the short conversation. He said it went like this:

"Colonel, you are on the wrong air base. This is the 440th TCC base. I want these fighters out of here immediately," said our temporary leader.

Because of our more sensitive readers I will not repeat the colonel's reply word for word, but the Biblical translation would go something like this: "Captain, you can go forth and multiply, all by yourself." The colonel was flying constant combat missions. When he was ordered to the base at Rheims, his group made a flyover of the base before landing. All they saw on the base were five old C-47s, two of which were pretty well shot up and in need of repair.

Here is my take of what actually happened, though it was never made public. Patton's army ran through Rheims like water through a tin horn. One of the most valuable assets to an advancing army is close support of fighter bombers. That is why fighter bases are located as near the advancing line as possible. The boys in the P-47 group were flying four sorties per day—they had to be right on Patton's rear end.

I believe that back in Exeter some private first class or corporal was manning the intelligence office when the radio printer came alive. He read a message that probably went something like this: "The 440th P-47 group is to move immediately to Rheims."

Being overeager, the corporal thought to himself, "They mean C-47, not P-47. The 440th part was correct."

The corporal corrected the error without asking for a confirmation, and handed the communiqué to someone acting as commanding officer—quite possibly our beloved Captain Jansen. If the corporal had checked, if Colonel Krebs had been on base, if anyone had used common sense, then no way would anyone have ordered the 440th to make a move like this with only one hour's notice.

In retrospect, things begin to make sense. I thought it strange that we should move out while over seventy-five percent of our group was up in Northern England supporting Montgomery's folly, strange that we should be expected to move within one hour, and even more puzzling that our type of ships should be placed so close to the line of combat.

Well, as expected, you know what hit the fan. Plans were started immediately to get us out of the way of the P-47s who were busy fighting a war. Meanwhile, things in the 440th, under the command of Jansen, sort of went to hell.

The P-47's day started at dawn. When fighters take off, the gun holes in the leading edges of the wings are covered with masking tape, so as to present a smooth surface. When they returned from a mission it was easy to know if they had fired their guns (they always did) because there is a peculiar sound, sort of a shrill whistle, caused by the gun openings after the masking tape is shot away. It made perfect sense for the P-47 group to be operating on this base. It made absolutely no sense for a troop carrier group to be located here.

We had a few low-ranking officers and practically no equipment at Rheims. Equipment and supplies were what we could load on seven C-47s. I would estimate we had about five percent of the equipment, and even less supplies, needed to operate a TCC group. The only food we had for the first few days was emergency K rations carried in each plane. It was late summer; tomatoes in France were good and ripe. We looted many a French farmer's tomato patch. The usual method of liberation was to brazenly walk into a tomato patch, grab only what we could eat, yell "C'est la guerre" ("such is war") and run as fast as we could.

One thing we had in abundance was champagne. Rheims is the champagne capital of the world. The German army had looted the champagne cellars of Rheims and stored hundreds of cases in one of the hangars. For eight days we existed on expensive champagne and tomatoes. It kept us from starving but the tomatoes gave us terrible headaches.

Fiction writers and movie producers have long been fond of stories about soldiers in the military digging latrines as punishment for some minor offense. I dug my first, and only, latrine at Rheims. It happened this way:

There was really no habitable shelter in Rheims. Between our air force and Patton's armored division, every pane of glass on the base was broken. There were not many places you could stay out of the rain. Our squadron moved into an old French barracks, obviously built many years before. Windows on the second floor were large with oval tops. I would estimate that they were five feet wide and eight feet high. The second story had a wide hallway down the center with rooms off of each side. Every room was large, and had one of the big arched windows.

Corporal Lecher, Corporal Urban, and I, Private Vaughan, picked a room on the north side of the building and started making it comfortable. With only three men, there was plenty of room. Our room had three good sides and a roof. We did not expect to be here long enough to be concerned about the opening where a window once had been. We would be long gone before cool weather. Our quarters were not ideal but much better than a tent.

Early in the morning of our seventh day at Rheims, our acting C.O., Captain Jansen, ordered all men to report to the flight line. Our ships were due to return from their detached duty associated with the Market Garden disaster. If we had been blessed with a few more officers like Montgomery and Jansen, we would all be speaking German today.

The day was heavily overcast and cool, with a very light drizzle—not enough to wet you through and through unless you were exposed for an hour or more. There was no shelter on the flight line so by 10:00 A.M. we were pretty well soaked. Noon came and went; no lunch was mentioned by Jansen. No one really minded as the K rations and tomatoes were beginning to dull our appetite. By 3:00 P.M., we had been standing in the rain for seven hours. The ridiculous part of the captain's orders was that there was shelter less than 400 feet from where we were standing. It takes a few minutes for a plane to land. We could have been warm and dry, listened for the sound of returning planes, slowly walked to the flight line, and waited five more minutes for them to taxi in position for unloading. Such was the intelligence of Jansen. I suppose it added to his fantasy of being a heroic combat leader.

About 3:30 that afternoon, it became obvious to many of the wet and hungry gang that our planes were not coming. Our bombed-out stone building, uninviting as it was, was better than this. Members of our group started disappearing. We watched as many made their escape while the captain stood with his back to us, his eyes on the overcast sky. If one wanted to live dangerously, there was a good chance you could sneak off and not be seen. I got with my roommates and discussed our chances of slipping away. They seemed to be better than fifty percent so we made a dash for it. We made it.

Two things contributed to our downfall: 1. the darn planes finally did arrive, and 2. when the captain turned to his unloading detail, half of them had disappeared.

When we got to our room, we stripped down to our shorts which were still dry, crawled into our sleeping bags, and fully enjoyed warmth and dryness for the first time that day.

Suddenly, there was the sound of someone running down the hall. As he passed our door he said, "Captain Jansen is coming, and he's mad as hell."

All three of us jumped out of bed. Lecher, near the window, stood up on the windowsill and prepared to jump. It was a twenty-five foot drop to the ground, Lecher was barefooted, and the ground was covered with broken glass. I suppose that is why he hesitated. Suddenly the door burst open. Captain Jensen stood there looking like he could eat us alive. I yelled "Attention!" and all three of us stood rigid and straight. All of us were in shorts. Lecher was standing on the windowsill, facing outside. I could not keep a straight face and started laughing. I suppose that contributed to our latrine-digging detail.

We dug latrines—BIG latrines—laughing all the while at the thought of Lecher, standing at rigid attention, with nothing on but his shorts, his backside facing the captain, his slender figure perfectly framed by the arched window.

We moved. Our next base was a temporary one at Le Mans. The landing strip, such as it was, was located in the center of the famed 24 Heures du Mans racetrack, home of the oldest and most prestigious sports car race in the world. No barracks, no plumbing to speak of, no hangars, with a grass (read: mud) runway. It rained and rained, and everything was wet and soggy. We slept in tents, ate in tents, and did repairs in the open.

Major Neal called the squadron out in formation. He explained that he fully realized how screwed up things were, and that he, with Colonel Krebs, was working tirelessly in an effort to make things better. "One thing I am doing immediately," he said. "I am ordering the mess tent to stay open twenty-four hours a day, and I promise you that there will always be hot coffee, any time day or night, for anyone who comes in." He kept his word. Now, sixty-six years later, I still prefer coffee to plain water. Yes, I suppose I am a caffeine junkie.

After two weeks of this they moved us into an apartment building in town. Our stay there was a very short. During the previous two weeks, engineers had been busy laying one of those erector set runways: sheets of steel with a lot of three-inch holes in them, all hooked together, covering the entire runway to keep planes from disappearing in the deep mud.

It was raining when we were ordered to fall out in formation. A general from Wing Headquarters, name unknown to me, was to visit our base. We waited and waited, in formation, wet through and through, for the general's plane to appear. At last the C-47 came into view. What a beauty. It was not painted olive drab green like our C-47s, it was highly polished aluminum—just like the old DC-3s that American Airlines used to fly. The pilot made a perfect approach and touched down gently. As the plane slowed, the temporary sheet metal runway slabs lifted off the mud and formed a moving wave, like a wave on water, right behind the landing gear, and did not return to flat until the tail wheel passed. It was beautiful. All antennas and what ever else that protruded from the ship's belly were wiped off clean. The highly polished aluminum skin of the ship's underside was a mess. I knew then we would be moving within days—and we did.

The 440th moved to a large base near Orleans and the small village of Bricy on November 4, 1944. Airbase A-50 would be our last home. We remained there until well after V-E Day. A-50 had one of the longest runways in Europe. It was long enough to get 90 planes and 180 gliders lined up on one end of the runway and still have room enough for the C-47s to take off, each pulling two CG-4A gliders.

A-50 resembled a zero with a slant through it—the zero being a taxi strip, and the slant, the runway. Along side the taxi strip was a number of revetments, built by the base's former tenants, the German Luftwaffe. Scattered at random on the base were a few usable frame buildings, though most were badly shot up. One such building became the Ninety-eighth Squadron's communications shack.

THE WAR ENDS

The nearby village of Bricy looked like a picture postcard. The town was small—about a dozen houses, a café and bar, and a church. The café and bar was about as bare bones as you are likely to see. A room about sixteen-by-forty feet in size housed the entire operation. The kitchen consisted of a wood-burning cookstove and a crude wooden table at one end of the room. Shelves in the kitchen held the food and spirits. Tables and seating consisted of four homemade picnic-style tables. Eight people could be seated comfortably at each table. Prices were reasonable—about half of what we paid in Orleans. You would think the café would be very busy with over 1,000 men on the nearby airbase. It was not busy at all. Apparently it was a bit too primitive to appeal to the servicemen.

All 440th personnel were housed in barracks in Orleans. Enlisted men's barracks were old French cavalry barracks. Stables for horses, on the backside of the fenced compound, were now converted into a PX, post office, archery range, supply depot, motor pool, etc. It was approximately ten miles from our barracks to the flight line. Transportation to and from the air base was in the old Army standby, the six by six.

Our noonday meal was delivered in the same trucks. The 440th was now beginning our most active period of the war. Air crews, now more than ever, earned their flying pay.

From *DZ Europe, the Official History of the 440th TCC*:

> It was a long flight from the A-50 Airfield at Bricy, near Orleans, France, to the German lines. Hardly a sortie was flown that did not consume six or seven hours in the air, going and returning. Often too, the group's allotment of tonnage to be delivered was so great that it could not be borne in a single trip, so the returning planes were reloaded on their return to the base airdrome and sent off again toward the Rhine not to return until long after dark.
>
> Flying crews were awakened at dawn. There was little chance for dawdling. Sleepy-eyed, yawning, and still tired from the previous day's flights, the pilots, copilots, navigators, crew chiefs, and radio operators took the rattling ten-mile ride from their quarters to the field and began loading the aircraft to be ready for takeoff as soon as daylight permitted. At night, convoys of

service units brought in the freight for the day's missions, piling up the masses of tonnage in huge piles beside each ships parking stand. When loading, our crews pitched in together, officers and enlisted men alike.

When weather delayed takeoff or the road convoys were late bringing freight in, ground personnel, including everyone available, assisted in stowing cargo. Captains and lieutenants working shoulder to shoulder with privates and sergeants, rushing the gasoline-filled jerry cans from the piles on the ground to the planes and handing them to the air crews, who stowed and distributed them inside the cabin to conform to the weight and balance requirements necessary to sustain level flight and minimize the hazards caused by overloading.

Though I put in long days, seven days a week, I found that with the added workload brought on by our ship spending so many hours in the air, I was no longer able to keep all the radios operating. Also, when the ships landed most were on the ground for only a few hours before takeoff. Maintenance work had to be done quickly while trying to keep out of the way of loading details, and often during darkness.

The Air Force knew what they were doing when they set up a T.O. (table of organization) for every job. It was more than a two-man job keeping all the radios working in a twenty-six-plane squadron. I had the men (though only one was really a good radio mechanic) who could have made the work go smoothly—if only I had the rank to get them off their backside and on the flight line. Inept as they were they could at least take repaired units to the planes, install them, and give the unit a final check.

Captain Quigley was a good friend, and a prince of a person. I simply could not understand why he sat calmly by watching the communications department struggle with such a problem. He certainly had the rank to get my mechanics off their butt, but he was a person who disliked any controversy or contention. I repeatedly asked him to come to my rescue. He would, in a very gentle voice, request that my corporals and sergeants do as Private Vaughan requested. You can guess how that went over.

The next time I ordered one of the mechanics to do a little something I would very likely be told to go to hell, or worse. Without rank, I was helpless.

That is when I decided to go on strike. I'd let the captain find out how the unit worked when I was not there. I'd get his attention one way or the other.

The following two days I did not report to work on the flight line. I slept late each morning, and then lounged around the barracks, reading and writing letters. The morning of my third day my peace and quiet was disrupted by our good T/Sgt Trzeciak.

"Vaughan, Captain Quigley called from the flight line and wants to know why you have not reported for work the past two days. You sick or something?"

I marked my place in the book I was reading, and then looked directly at the fuming sergeant.

"No, I'm not sick. I never felt better, but it's this way, Sergeant. I can't go to work because I'm on strike."

"STRIKE HELL—this is the Army. You can't strike in the Army."

I was enjoying watching Trzeciak's blood pressure rise. "Oh yes, Sergeant, you can strike; I am on strike now as a matter of fact."

"Get in your class A uniform," yelled the sergeant. "Report to the orderly room in ten minutes." He stormed from the room muttering to himself. This was the second time I refused to do as the good sergeant requested.

I walked into the orderly room five minutes late. I knew the sergeant was too upset to notice the time. He was hanging up his phone as I walked in.

I could not believe my eyes—Sergeant Trzeciak was actually smiling.

"Well, you've finally done it," he said. "That was Captain Quigley on the phone. He'll be here shortly, and he is hauling your ass before Colonel Krebs. Boy, I sure wish I could go along to see the fun. They're gonna put you so far back in Leavenworth that they will have to shoot biscuits to you with a shotgun."

∽

Now, dear readers, every word of this is 100 percent true. I realize that most readers will not believe me, but this is an absolutely TRUE story. Did I feel confident? No way. I was literally scared stiff. My gut feeling was that I'd crossed the line. Stripes or no stripes, I was off base from the beginning. In retrospect, my rebellion was born of both youth and ignorance.

Colonel Krebs' office was in a two-story building across the street from our Ninety-eighth orderly room. I went out front to wait for Captain Quigley to drive up. I did not have to wait long. I saw his jeep come through the main gate and come to a stop by the curb. He stepped from the jeep, I gave him the best salute I knew how, and said, "Good afternoon, Captain."

I waited for him to speak. "Vaughan, we are going over and report to the colonel. Conduct yourself like a soldier." I was greatly relieved that he never mentioned my strike. He returned my salute, but he was grim-faced and not inclined to make small talk.

We entered the outer office; Captain Quigley went directly to the sergeant major: "I am Captain Quigley. Colonel Krebs is expecting us," he said.

I was totally unprepared for what was about to happen.

The colonel put Captain Quigley and me at ease, then said, "What's all this about, Captain?"

"Sir," answered Quigley, "I have been putting this man in for a promotion ever since we moved to Exeter. Every month I put him in, and every month you turn him down. I want to tell you his story." The captain went back to the first practice mission for D-Day and reminded the colonel that I was the radio mechanic that checked the colonel's radios. He even went back to the Pope Field incident.

Colonel Krebs shuffled some papers on his desk, looked up, and said, "I had to turn him down because of his classification. He is classified a 726 airborne radio operator. My T.O. is completely filled. If I approve his promotion, Wing Headquarters will raise hell with me. Now, I can make him a staff sergeant but I will have to bust him down to a radio mechanic which is a 754; theoretically, a demotion. To reduce Vaughan in classification I must have just cause, or a written request from both of you."

"Colonel, that's what his classification should be. He is my chief radio mechanic. I gave him the 756 classification back at Pope

Field when I was unsure where I would end up using him," replied Quigley.

"Then I can bust Vaughan to a 754 immediately. Put him in for a promotion every month, Captain. Four months from now he will be a staff sergeant. To partially make up for those many months as a private, I am putting Vaughan on flying status immediately. That means a fifty percent increase in monthly pay. Are you both agreeable to this action?"

"Sir, I am very pleased," I replied.

"By the way, Captain," said Colonel Krebs. "Is this the young man you put in for a Bronze Star?"

"Yes, he's the one. He's also the one who keeps all your radio gear going. He goes down to the flight line after supper and checks your ship."

"I have a very strong feeling that the medal will be approved," said Krebs. Looking in my direction, he said, "You have no objection to flying a few hours each month, do you?"

"No, sir," I answered. "I put in a lot of air time now—checking radios in the air and flying as radio op on occasion—just to get a look at Germany."

"Then start signing the log," said Colonel Krebs. The captain and I saluted the colonel, thanked him, and left his office. My strike was never mentioned by either of us.

∼

Germany was retreating miles each day—Patton was determined to beat Russia to Berlin. Within weeks it appeared that our armies would reach the Rhine, while from the East the Russians were pushing forward like a giant steamroller, crushing the German troops. On a wall in the Enlisted Men's Club a huge map of Europe was updated daily, tracking the Allied advances. A red yarn string, attached to the map with pins, marked the position of Allied troops as they moved closer and closer to the heart of Germany. General Patton was really on a roll.

My stripes started arriving, one every four weeks. I never bothered to sew any on until the S/Sgt rating came through—then I sewed on the stripes. I realized that was as far as I could go. For the first time since I had been in the ETO I was able to keep all radios working perfectly without working nights. All my men but one accepted my promotion. One, an Italian boy from Philly, as he called it, was a corporal. When my name appeared on the bulletin board as being a sergeant he was really upset. He came to me and said, "Youse tinks youse is smart. I gonna tell youse here and now, I never do anyting youse tells me to do. Youse is a hillbilly from da sout. Youse don' know shit."

"That's great with me Marconti. I promise I'll never ask one thing from you," I told him.

I then went to Master Sergeant Charlie Wantshouse. "Sarge, my boys are pretty busy with some important work. However, I have one man you can have for any shit details that come up. All I ask is that you don't bother my good men." I knew Charlie would do as I requested. He was the man who taught me what little I knew about Air Force radios.

"No problem, Bruce, one man out of six is about right for details. I'll keep him busy."

I suppose you know whose name I gave the communications sergeant. Then I called in Marconti. "Marconti, effective immediately, you are relieved of any duties as a radio repairman in this squadron. Do me a big favor and do not clutter up the radio room with your presence."

In Orleans, we burned wood in our stoves and a daily wood detail was deployed to the country to chop and saw firewood. Our one big latrine served the needs of 1,200 men. Our compound was in the heart of the city, and the colonel liked it spotless.

It was not many days before Marconti wanted to come back to work. I did not need him. I had five good men who never drew any kind of detail. "You have finally found your rightful place in our group," I told him.

Many of us thought Christmas of 1944 would be our last Christmas away from home. Then all hell turned loose at Bastogne. Here is what one writer had to say about it in the book *DZ Europe:*

THE WAR ENDS

"Nuts," said the general, and his men pulled their belts tighter. "Our tactical situation?" said the general. "You know what a doughnut looks like? Well, we're the hole . . ." His headquarters was at a town called Bastogne. You may have heard of it. His outfit was the 101st Airborne Division. Perhaps you know of it . . . His enemies were all around him. But in modern war, when you box up a foe, you must put a lid on the box. The Germans had no lid on Bastogne, the city they overran but never conquered in their final Ardennes gamble . . . The cry from Bastogne was answered by the Troop Carrier Command. Over the rim of the doughnut, over the sides of the lidless box, went ammunition, food, medical supplies, and weapons . . . The 440th flew in its share . . . and Bastogne stood.

Our supply missions over Bastogne lasted about a week, but in that time the 440th Troop Carrier Group suffered forty-two percent of all our casualties of World War II.

We members of the 440th are sure that our supply missions to Bastogne were of great help to the 101st Airborne, enabling them to hold off the German army and turn the major offensive of Germany's best infantry and armored units into a disorganized retreat. We carried food, ammunition, medical personnel and supplies, weapons, and gasoline to the surrounded troops.

Our 1944 Christmas party, planned weeks before the German breakthrough at Bastogne, went ahead at full speed.

Christmas of 1944 was to become a Christmas to remember. Victory was not only assured, but the Allies seemed to be moving toward a victory sooner than expected. There was an optimistic expectation that we would all be home by Christmas of '45. The party was for those in radar and radio only. We made a promise that any cakes, cookies, and gifts from home would remain unopened until the big party.

Sergeant Straub, a radar mechanic, was appointed party coordinator. The party was to be in the radar barracks. It was a large room for the six men who graciously offered to find sleeping quarters somewhere else for three days while the room was prepared. Straub appointed me to build tables. He assigned others to jobs such as stealing white sheets from the hospital to use for tablecloths. I might mention that this idea went sour, and we ended up using parachutes as table covers.

Other fellows liberated C rations—peas, corn, etc. One man's job was a dandy—bribe the cooks out of two cooked turkeys. French bread was easy, just walk outside the gate and buy it from a bakery. Portable stoves for heating food were not difficult to find. Ralph Hils, because of his imagination and craftsmanship, was chosen to build a Christmas tree. He made it from scraps of aluminum, highly polished, with ornaments made from brightly painted burned-out bulbs and radio tubes.

The easiest job of all was drink. Two of the radar boys made a trip to Germany in a jeep, pulling a small trailer. They returned with enough booze to open a liquor store. Perhaps the most difficult job was finding real dishes. Finally it was decided to liberate them from the base hospital.

I carried in lumber from a bombed building and made an L-shaped table that would seat about twenty-four people. We intended to keep this party relatively quiet so we would not be bothered by riff-raff, meaning everyone but the radar and radio group and a few select friends.

It was a beautiful party—two turkeys, a ham, canned vegetables, french bread, cakes and cookies from home, champagne, and for those who wanted to live dangerously, 200-proof Calvados.

After eating and opening presents, each of us got up and told about his favorite Christmas at home. I recall a master sergeant from engineering who dropped by uninvited. He was a rough, tough, and mean old-timer of thirty-five years of age, plus or minus a year or so. Master Sergeant Egan was the most feared non-com in the outfit. It was rumored that he was a former oil field machinist. No one, *but no one*, crossed Egan. He could outfight and out swear any man in the outfit.

Full of the Christmas spirit and some other spirits as well, we invited M/Sgt Egan to join our party. He gladly did so. As we each told our story, Egan got more and more homesick. We filled his glass several times as the storytelling worked its way toward him. When Egan

Bruce receiving the Bronze Star

rose to talk, we assumed the air would turn blue. For the next twenty minutes or so, Egan recited many poems, some of his own composition, and all of a highly sentimental content. When Egan finished there was not a dry eye in the room. We rose as a group and gave him a long and loud ovation.

I am pleased to report that M/Sgt Egan's reputation suffered no permanent damage. We all agreed to never speak of the incident outside the room. He resumed his gruff attitude, keeping the men in engineering, and all who came near him, intimidated until the end of the war.

Early in 1945 my Bronze Star citation came through. There were several citations for Air Medals and Purple Hearts to be awarded at the same time. I treasure the memory of Sergeant Trzeciak standing at attention in formation while the major pinned the medal to my chest. The squadron photographer made a picture to release to my hometown paper, the *Springdale News.* The paper chose not to run it. I would have preferred to have a picture of the look on Trzeciak's face. Somehow, after this day he became very cordial, at times even civil toward me. As for me, I never disliked Trzeciak. I was amazed that he never learned to lighten up and not take the Air Force so seriously. After all, ninety-five percent of us were civilians at heart, even though temporarily on duty in the military.

Early March of 1945 was unusually warm and sunny. The mood of the group matched the weather. The war was winding down—there was an optimistic attitude among our men. Ground supply finally caught up with Patton, and we started having some leisure time. Most of our work was accomplished during the morning hours. During the afternoons, we sunbathed and jogged around the perimeter of the base.

This idyllic existence was not to last. About March 10, a detachment of airborne engineers moved onto our base. We knew something big was brewing. Then orders came down for a maximum effort mission, which meant that every plane that was flyable was to go on this mission. Every plane that was not flyable must be made flyable if at all possible. Every plane and glider in our group MUST be airworthy by March 20. Our rest was at end.

By the looks of the map in the Enlisted Men's Club, we could be almost positive that the Allies were getting ready to cross the Rhine. Our troops were stalled there and needed bridges built, and very soon. The longer the delay, the more men we would lose.

Colonel Krebs called a briefing, and revealed the magnitude of the coming mission. He explained that we must be prepared to launch a double glider tow, using as many of our 100 C-47s as possible. Four ships would be kept in reserve on the taxi strip, ready to take the place of any ship that developed trouble before takeoff. This meant that less than 300, but more than 250 planes, including the CG-4A had to be lined up on one end of the runway prior to takeoff. Though we had a very long runway it was plain to see that the first planes would have a very short distance to get airborne. The gliders were loaded with heavy airborne engineer equipment. As the colonel talked, groans from the pilots of both C-47s and gliders were audible.

When he finished the briefing, he turned to the grim looking pilots. "Any questions?" he asked.

Several voices answered at once, "We'll not have enough runway to get our heavily loaded ships, towing two heavily loaded CG-4As, airborne."

"Gentlemen, I have tried a double glider tow from the shortest distance we will be using. On this mission I will be flying the lead ship. Every pilot in this room will have more runway than I have. Every ship that takes off gives the remainder of the group more takeoff room. If I crash on takeoff, you have the option of not trying, but heaven help you if I get airborne and you don't."

I think every man in the outfit turned out for the Operation Varsity takeoff. The road to Orleans passed about fifty feet from our perimeter. There was a wide blacktop area between the perimeter and the highway. On the opposite side of the highway was a barbed wire fence. I was standing by the side of that paved area.

The 190 radial engines coughed to life, and sat idling while the pilots warmed up the engines. After a few minutes I heard the noise rise in loudness. Colonel Krebs had his engines at full throttle. Slowly the plane gained speed. Suddenly both CG-4-As behind the colonel's ship lifted off the runway and leveled off at forty feet or so. We waited. Would the C-47s wheels lift off the runway? As the plane passed me, I saw the colonel's landing gear start to retract. He cleared the barbed wire fence by eight feet.

The number two ship cleared it by a foot or two more. Within minutes our group was in the air with not a single aborted plane or glider. Once in the air our group experienced a bit of trouble. Ship number 642 had one engine cutting out. He ordered the gliders to cut loose, returned to the base and landed. One of the reserve ships moved into place, the glider tow ropes attached, and he was in the air some twenty minutes later.

The group was just dots on the horizon when ship 731 developed a runaway propeller that refused control. A second reserve ship moved into position. Once 731's gliders had safely landed, ground crews attached them to the reserve ship and he was on his way, though about thirty minutes behind the group.

This was one of the largest and most successful missions the 440th made during the war. Losses were low and the effectiveness of the mission was great. This Rhine crossing was the last major obstacle between Patton and Berlin.

We continued to haul gasoline and supplies to Patton after he crossed the Rhine. Now that Patton was near Berlin the gas runs became longer and longer. On April 24, the Air Echelon moved to A-94 at Conflans-Jarny, near the city of Metz. With a much shorter distance to travel we could haul a lot more gasoline in a day. The 440th TCC, during the month of April alone, flew 3,182 sorties, of which 2,508 were classified as combat sorties, for a total of 13,330 flying hours. During this same time our group was down to eighty-two aircraft but they were kept busy. During April they flew more than 2 million air miles, delivered 13,500,000 pounds of freight, and 10,000 evacuees—liberated war prisoners or wounded troops. In addition we hauled over 1,230,000 gallons of gasoline or the equivalent of 150 railroad tank cars.

General Eisenhower had this to say about our group:

> The great job of flying done by your command in moving repatriates out of Germany during April and May is one that has given me personal satisfaction of the highest order. While all air commands participated in this, some seventy percent of Allied repatriates flown from Germany were in aircraft of the IX Troop Carrier Command, and your total lifts in the two months passed the unbelievable figure on a quarter-million passengers. To have done this at all is remarkable, but to have done it without a single casualty is perfect.
>
> You have written a page in Air Force history and in Allied cooperation that will live forever.
>
> Sincerely,
> Dwight D. Eisenhower

On the morning of May 7, 1945 I walked over to the squadron barber shop to get my hair cut. I took a chair and waited as Corporal Montalvo finished trimming the hair of one of our pilots. As usual, a radio in the background was tuned to the AFN—Armed Forces Network. The program was interrupted to announce the surrender of Germany.

THE WAR ENDS

Amazingly, everyone kept their cool. We had been expecting Germany's surrender for some weeks now. Montalvo continued the snip, snip, snip with his scissors. Then the chatter started—would we get to return to the States? Would we stay in Europe to move men and equipment? Was there a possibility we would move immediately to the Pacific theater of operations? I suppose it was because the surrender had been expected for so many weeks now that the announcement was an anti-climax.

The French love parades. We had a dandy in downtown Orleans. French troops showed up by the hundreds wearing old uniforms and driving tanks that had been obsolete for generations.

Perhaps the write up from our group publication tells it best:

> The returning Air Echelon found the city of Orleans a city in jubilation, decked out in flags and banners. The birthplace of the French National Heroine, Joan of Arc, Orleans was the center for an annual deliverance festival week, beginning the 8th of May, paying homage to the martyred Joan, and the liberation of the city. 1945 was the 516th year since her event occurred and it was also the first time during five years of war that the people were permitted to carry out their celebration.
>
> The incidence of Victory Day in Europe on the same date as the beginning of the National holiday made the event overwhelmingly joyous. Orchestras played in the streets for four days and nights while every square and green in the city had a great street dance. Wine flowed like water, fireworks illuminated the night skies and a lot of sun and fine weather beamed upon the many, hour long, parades by day. In two of these parades, elements of the Group, led by the 440th band participated, receiving showers of applause and spilling cordiality from the assembled throngs along the roadway.

In the heart of Orleans is a huge bronze statue of Joan d Arc, in full battle dress, atop a beautiful bronze horse. The horse is prancing proudly; Joan has her sword drawn ready to do battle with the enemies of Orleans. The German troops had defaced the statue and broken off her large bronze sword, probably taking it as a souvenir. Our group, as a gesture of good will, took up a collection and had a new sword cast at a French foundry. When repaired, the statue looked almost new. Inscribed in both French and English on a plaque at the base of the statue the inscription reads:

> Bronze sword presented by
> the 440th Troop Carrier Group,
> 456th Air Service Group
> United States Army Air Forces
> to the City of Orleans.
>
> 6 June, 1945

Long before the war ended the High Command worked out a point system to be used to determine which soldiers would be discharged first once the war ended. I long ago forgot everything that added points but I remember that eighty-five points was the magic number. Those soldiers with eighty-five points or above would get out first. Each month overseas added points, awards counted points, and I do remember that being a volunteer added five points. My points added up to eighty-six—one point over the magic number. I never put a lot of hope or expectations in the system but was glad I was over the line.

After all the celebrations our echelon returned to duty hauling everything from civilians to foodstuffs. Once again our planes left our base at Orleans and moved closer to Germany. Those remaining behind spent the remaining days of May, and the months of June, July and August doing a few details but mostly basking in the knowledge that we would soon be returning to the States.

As ground personnel our work was much lighter, mostly repairing war weary C-47s from other groups. Even after a year of combat the reliable DC-3s, or C-47s, if you prefer, were in fair to good condition.

I remember one ship that was transferred was as full of holes as a colander. Every time this ship became airborne a new short would develop in the wiring which often led to a small fire. (Well, in reality, there are no small fires in airplanes—they are all serious.) At last the problem was located more or less. I replaced the entire radio compass and cured the fire problems. But wait . . . there's more.

One of the engines continued to run forty degrees hotter than normal. I followed the engine work on the old airplane out of curiosity. After trying many different things, the crew chief finally got both engines running the same temperature. He simply removed the glass cover of the temperature indicator gauge, took a pair of needle nose pliers, and bent the needle to the desired temperature. Now both engines read exactly alike.

Then one of the engines started leaking oil badly. Every time the pilot wrote up the problem, the crew chief drained a few gallons of gasoline from a sump and threw the gas on the oil-covered engine. The aviation gasoline cleaned off all the oil and made the engine look like new. The airplane was considered a jinx.

It was a beautiful sunny afternoon near the end of July. Captain Quigley and I put on our track shorts and were jogging around the outer perimeter of the base. Quigley was at least fifteen years older than me and a trifle overweight. I got a bit ahead of him and stopped to wait until he caught up.

"Let's take a break," said the captain. "I have something I need to talk to you about." I thought he wanted a chance to catch his breath and rest a minute. We sat down in a shaded area provided by one of the large C-47 wings.

I was sure I had fouled up something. "Okay, Captain, let me have it. What did I screw up this time?"

"Vaughan, the Air Echelon leaves for the States in the morning at 6:00 A.M. I will be on it. I am allowed to take one man with me. I checked with the orderly room and you are okay point-wise. How would you like to go home?"

"I can't believe it, Captain. Do you mean we could actually be in the States within two weeks?"

"Sooner than that if all goes well," he answered. "I want you to keep this as quiet as you can. When the Ground Echelon finds out we are going home there will be a lot of hard feelings. Go to the barracks tonight and pack a minimum of stuff in one barracks bag. That is all we are allowed on the planes going home. As you know, the range of the C-47 is not great enough to fly direct to the U.S. We will go by the southern route which is darn near half way around the world, but with two 400-gallon ferry tanks in the cabin the range can be stretched considerably. We will make a stop at Marseille before noon, then on to Marrakech for our first night. Then we fly to Dakar the next day. From Dakar we go to Ascension Island. That is a long hop. Then we go thru Fortaleza or Natal Brazil for a night. From there we will go to British Guiana, then Puerto Rico, then Palm Beach.

"We will meet in front of the orderly room at 5:30 A.M. On the orderly room bulletin board will be a list of planes going home, and the names of those assigned to each plane. Tonight, after packing your bag, take everything you don't need to the supply room and turn it in."

"Captain, if my name is on that darn jinx plane I may decide to stay here."

"I couldn't blame you. That is one war-weary crate," said Quigley.

The following morning I was at the orderly room at 5:15 A.M. I was not surprised to find my name on the jinx airplane. I wanted to come home so bad I would have climbed aboard a World War I Jenny.

Our group landed at Marrakech, North Africa, about midafternoon. No sooner had we touched down than MPs swarmed the landing aircraft. We rolled to a stop and found the door blocked by two MPs. No one leaves this ship until it is thoroughly searched, they said. None of us had any idea what the trouble was.

Looking out the side window we saw all the crew members of one ship being loaded into the MP jeeps. It was then that the MP on our ship gave us permission to leave the plane.

We were not long finding out the trouble. It seems that one crew was trying to bring a pet home with them. That seems harmless enough, but in this case the pet was a twenty-year-old French girl. The crew had given her a G.I. haircut, dressed her out in fatigues, and she could have passed for a crew member, but some big mouth ruined a very pleasant trip home for one crew.

We were kept over an extra day in Marrakech while the C.O. tried to fix the problem. It was fixed by keeping the crew in jail and letting the rest of us proceed home. I have always wondered if they were assigned to a co-ed jail.

Our flight from Dakar to Ascension Island was flown at about 8,000 feet, extended formation. "Extended formation" means that you are flying as a group, but widely separated. The prime requisite in such formation is that you maintain visual contact with every ship in the formation.

We were flying along smooth as silk. I was standing between the pilot and copilot watching a few widely scattered cotton-like cumulus clouds drift below us. It was a beautiful day and the air seemed smoother than usual. Suddenly I felt my feet come up off the floor, and for a few seconds I was weightless. My first thought was that we had a mechanical problem. Then we hit bottom. Apparently we had encountered a violent downdraft and lost approximately 1,000 feet of altitude. The rest of the squadron's planes were well above us.

There is one comforting thought when flying in a C-47: should one engine fail, the second engine will take you all the way to the crash site.

The pilot gradually climbed back up to our original altitude and continued the flight to Ascension without difficulty. Once we were on the island, everyone headed for the PX for sandwiches and beer.

Ascension is basically a hunk of volcanic rock sticking up out of the ocean. The island is a British possession approximately halfway between Africa and South America. With a total area of only thirty-four square miles, Green Mountain, the island's tallest peak, has an altitude of 3,000 feet. The United States built an airfield on the island at the start of World War II, and during the war over 26,000 planes made use of the facilities.

The PX at Ascension is built on a volcanic ledge over looking the ocean. The group from my plane gathered around a table near a large window. We were having hamburgers and beer when a crew chief from another plane came over to our table. "What happened to you on the flight from Dakar? You were not far from our ship when you must have lost over 1,000 feet in altitude. I was wondering if you would ever bottom out. I never saw anything like that."

Our crew chief replied, "Oh, it was nothing. Back in Dakar we bought a mascot—a monkey—and I thought I'd take him home with me. I put him back in the tail, and closed him up. I guess he got to swinging on the elevator cables."

A group of officers were sitting at a table near us and overheard the entire exchange between the crew chiefs.

One officer, a major, decided he needed to show some authority. He got up from his table and came over to ours. Standing beside the crew chief's chair, in a loud voice he said, "Just how in hell do you think you can run that monkey through customs, sergeant?"

"Oh, I have that all figured out, sir. I'll just dress him in a major's uniform."

The PX exploded with laughter. The major returned to his table without further questions.

Every night when we landed I was actually amazed that I was still alive. I was not scared on the ship during our flight home, I was terrified.

The 400-gallon ferry tanks were each about the size of a small refrigerator. On top of each tank was a relief valve to allow air to escape when pressure became too high. Our chief topped the tanks off each night after we landed. When I say "topped off," I mean he filled the tanks until he could not get another drop in. As soon as we took off and gained a bit of altitude, gasoline in the tanks started expanding. A continuous stream of gasoline about the size of a soda straw shot upward from each tank. The gasoline fountain continued until the pressure was equalized, or until enough fuel was burned from the cabin tanks.

When we were briefed every morning, we were warned several times not to smoke during our flight. The warnings were ignored by everyone. No sooner were we airborne than out came the cigarettes and trusty Zippo lighters. With rivulets of the explosive 100 octane fuel running down the aluminum floor of the aircraft, crew members and passengers alike casually knocked the ash off their glowing cigarettes onto the floor. It is nothing short of a miracle that we did not explode.

The briefing at Fortaleza, Brazil, was anything but comforting. We were told that if we survived a crash in the jungle, under no conditions should we leave the crash site. Possibility of survival was slim, but if we attempted to make our way through the jungle, death was certain.

About one hour flying time over the jungle, both engines lost power. The airplane started a deep descent, with a spiral to the left. I ran to the cockpit to see what the problem was. It seemed our pilot had spotted a native village and wanted close-up pictures of it. He had the window open and was leaning outward with his Argus camera to his eye, snapping pictures of the village.

I must say that I was terribly relieved three days later to see the coast of Florida on the horizon. Though we were in sunshine, we could see the airstrip ahead was wet. A typical Florida rain shower passed over the base, and by the time we made our rollout the sun was out again.

The old battle scarred C-47 that brought us home was parked on the grass near a bunch of trees on the back side of the West Palm Beach Air Base. It appeared to be some sort of emergency field. I looked back at the plane one time as we left riding in the back of an Army six by six. I don't think a one of us were sad to be leaving the plane that brought us home.

Epilogue

So we approach the end of this bit of Vaughan history, and perhaps the end of the Vaughan bloodline in Northwest Arkansas. To the best of my knowledge, with the passing of Jim Vaughan, descendent of Daniel, and Bruce Vaughan, descendent of Samuel, the two remaining members of the Vaughan clan in this part of the country are gone—the story of the NW Arkansas Vaughan's is very nearly ended.

I do not claim that the data in this book is flawlessly accurate. It is the result of years of study and research—yet there are most certainly some errors. Let's simply say that it is the best I can do with material available. I have attempted to assemble in one short manuscript, an informative history of the Vaughan family, from Welsh immigrant William Vaughan up to the present generation. Dialogue when used is of course a figment of my imagination and used only to improve readability.

In her story of the Vaughan's printed in the *History of Washington County*, Ruby Vaughan, of Hindsville has the Vaughan's arriving in the Van Buren area by raft. I had not thought of this possibility, but if they missed their destination, NW Arkansas, by several miles it might have been easier to build a raft and float down river, than to make their way through the dense underbrush. Most travel in the state was by water in the early 1800s. Long trips on foot were both slow and difficult. Only on the Great Plains was travel by horse drawn wagons practical.

Some historians insist that Fereby Vaughan, wife of William, was white rather than Native American. The friendship that William had with Indian tribes, his constant association with them, seems to tilt the opinion towards her being Indian. I do not consider her bloodline of prime importance. I chose to go with the popular opinion that she was indeed Indian.

One conflict I have not resolved is whether of not Phillip Harp arrived with the Vaughan's. One historian, using courthouse records, says that John Harp, the first Harp in NW Arkansas, did not arrive until 1856. Why do I mistrust courthouse records? The courthouse at Huntsville was burned during the Civil War. The records were moved to Springfield where they were either lost or destroyed. Washington County also had a bit of record problems due to the Civil War.

Another reason to mistrust Court House records as a final word is that many citizens, especially pioneers in the early years, were reluctant to get on the county books and start paying taxes. Then there are other errors. When I first went into business on Emma Street I had a total of $700 with which to buy stock, fixtures, and equipment. I was surprised to find my taxes higher than expected. I went to an accountant and he found that my store was assessed for more money than the Famous Hardware Store, then the largest store in Springdale. My taxes came down substantially. Such errors do occur.

It seems only logical that Phillip Harp came to Arkansas with his family. I again, go along with interviews with descendents stories. Let's keep an open mind—the historian could be correct, our pioneer ancestors did not always act in a logical manner. If they had, this country would still be a wilderness.

Bruce and Zack.

BIBLIOGRAPHY

Devlin , Gerald M. *Silent Wings: The Saga of the U.S. Army and Marine Combat Glider Pilots During World War II.* St. Martin's Press, 1985

Goodspeed Publishing Co. *History of Madison County, Arkansas.* Chicago: Goodspeed Publishing Co., 1889.

Goodspeed Publishing Co. *History of Washington County, Arkansas.* Chicago: Goodspeed Publishing Co., 1889.

Neal, Joseph C. *Washington County History.* Springdale: Shiloh Museum of Ozark History, 1989.

Vaughan family oral history

Drop Zone Europe—the official history of the 440th Troop Carrier Command

Family bibles